# A SHORT HISTORY

OF

# SYRIAC LITERATURE.

# A SHORT HISTORY

OF

# SYRIAC LITERATURE

BY

THE LATE

WILLIAM WRIGHT, LL.D.

PROFESSOR OF ARABIC IN THE UNIVERSITY OF CAMBRIDGE.

WIPF & STOCK · Eugene, Oregon

Wipf and Stock Publishers
199 W 8th Ave, Suite 3
Eugene, OR 97401

A Short History of Syriac Literature
By Wright, William
ISBN 13: 978-1-60608-260-7
Publication date 3/1/2016
Previously published by Adam and Charles Black, 1894

## PREFATORY NOTE.

THIS volume is a reprint of the late Professor W. Wright's article on *Syriac Literature*, which appeared in vol. XXII. of the *Encyclopaedia Britannica* in 1887. A number of brief additions have been made, in order to note publications subsequent to the date of the article: these are enclosed in square brackets. A few of them are derived from notes made by Professor Wright on his own copy, or were suggested in letters written to him by M. Duval and Dr Nestle; and many of the others are due to the late Professor W. Robertson Smith, who was keenly interested in the preparation of this edition. An index has been added which will, it is hoped, increase the usefulness of the work.

N. M.

*September*, 1894.

## ERRATUM.

On p. 185 l. 9 *for* Bar-Sāhdĕ *read* Bar-Sāhdē.

# SYRIAC LITERATURE.

THE literature of Syria, as known to us at the present day, is, with the exception of translations from the Greek and some other languages, a Christian literature. The writings of the Syrian heathens, such as the so-called Ṣābians of Ḥarrān, which were extant, at least in part, even in the 13th century[1], seem to have now wholly disappeared. The beginnings of this literature are lost in the darkness of the earliest ages of Christianity. It was at its best from the 4th to the 8th century, and then gradually died away, though it kept up a flickering existence till the 14th century or even later. We must own—and it is well to make the confession at the outset—that the literature of Syria is, on the whole, not an attractive one. As Renan said long ago[2], the

[1] Bar-Hebræus, *Chron. Syr.*, ed. Bruns and Kirsch, p. 176 [ed. Bedjan, p. 168]; Chwolsohn, *Ssabier und Ssabismus*, i. 177.

[2] *De Philosophia Peripatetica apud Syros*, 1852, p. 3.

characteristic of the Syrians is a certain mediocrity. They shone neither in war, nor in the arts, nor in science. They altogether lacked the poetic fire of the older—we purposely emphasize the word—the older Hebrews and of the Arabs. But they were apt enough as pupils of the Greeks; they assimilated and reproduced, adding little or nothing of their own. There was no Al-Fārābī, no Ibn Sīnā, no Ibn Rushd, in the cloisters of Edessa, Ḳen-neshrē, or Nisībis. Yet to the Syrians belongs the merit of having passed on the lore of ancient Greece to the Arabs, and therefore, as a matter of history, their literature must always possess a certain amount of interest in the eyes of the modern student. The Syrian Church never produced men who rose to the level of a Eusebius, a Gregory Nazianzen, a Basil, and a Chrysostom; but we may still be thankful to the plodding diligence which has preserved for us in fairly good translations many valuable works of Greek fathers which would otherwise have been lost. And even Syria's humble chroniclers, such as John of Ephesus, Dionysius of Tell-Maḥrē, and Bar-Hebræus, deserve their meed of praise, seeing that, without their guidance, we should have known far less than we now know about the history of two important branches of the Eastern Church, besides losing much interesting information as to the political events of the periods with which their annals are occupied.

As Syriac literature commences with the Bible, we first briefly enumerate the different versions of Holy Scripture.

The most important of these is the so-called Pĕshīṭtā (*mappaḳtā pĕshīṭtā*), "the simple" or "plain version," the Syriac vulgate. This name is in use as early as the 9th or 10th century[1]. As to the Old Testament, neither the exact time nor place of its translation is known; indeed, from certain differences of style and manner in its several parts, we may rather suppose it to be the work of different hands, extending over a considerable period of time. It would seem, however, as a whole, to have been a product of the 2nd century, and not improbably a monument of the learning and zeal of the Christians of Edessa. Possibly Jewish converts, or even Jews, took a part in it, for some books (such as the Pentateuch and Job) are very literally rendered, whereas the coincidences with the LXX. (which are particularly numerous in the prophetical books) show the hand of Christian translators or revisers. That Jews should have had at any rate a consultative

[1] See the passage of Moses bar Kēphā, who died in 903, cited by the Abbé Martin in his *Introduction à la Critique Textuelle du Nouveau Testament*, p. 101, note.

share in this work need not surprise us, when we remember that Syrian fathers, such as Aphraates, in the middle of the 4th century, and Jacob of Edessa, in the latter half of the 7th, had frequent recourse, like Jerome, to the scholars of the synagogue. To what extent subsequent revision may have been carried it is not easy to say; but it seems tolerably certain that alterations were made from time to time with a view to harmonizing the Syriac text with that of the LXX. Such an opportunity may, for instance, have been afforded on a considerable scale by the adoption of Lucian's text of the LXX. at Antioch in the beginning of the 4th century. On all these points, however, we know nothing for certain, and may well repeat the words of Theodore of Mopsuestia in his commentary on Zephaniah i. 6[1]: *ἡρμήνευται δὲ ταῦτα εἰς μὲν τὴν Σύρων παρ' ὅτου δή ποτε· οὐδὲ γὰρ ἔγνωσται μέχρι τῆς τήμερον ὅστις ποτὲ οὗτος ἐστίν.*

The canonical books of the Old Testament according to the Pĕshīṭṭā are substantially those of the Hebrew Bible. In the Massoretic MSS. (see below, p. 20 *sq.*), whether Nestorian or Jacobite, the books of Chronicles, Ezra, and Nehemiah are passed over, and in the Nestorian the book of

[1] Mai, *Patrum Nova Bibliotheca*, vol. vii. 252.

Esther also. But, on the other hand, it must be noticed that all these books are cited by Aphraates, and that they all appear in the *Codex Ambrosianus*. Of the Chronicles there is a MS. of the 6th century in the British Museum, Add. 17104. Esther appears in a volume of equal age (Add. 14652) as one of the constituent parts of the "Book of Women," the others being Ruth, Susanna, Judith, and the history of Thecla, the disciple of St Paul, which last is excluded from Biblical MSS. The oldest dated MS. of any portion of the Old Testament at present known to us is Add. 14425 in the British Museum (Gen., Exod., Num., Deut.), transcribed at Āmid by a deacon named John in 464. The deutero-canonical books or apocrypha, translated by different hands from the Greek[1], are nearly the same as in the LXX.[2] The *Codex Ambrosianus*[3], for example, contains Wisdom, the Epistle of Jeremiah, and two Epistles of Baruch; the Song of the Three

[1] Some scholars, such as P. de Lagarde and Bickell, think that Ecclesiasticus was translated from the lost Hebrew text.

[2] See Ceriani, *Monumenta Sacra et Profana*, vol. i. fascc. 1, 2; vol. v. fascc. 1, 2; P. de Lagarde, *Libri Vet. Test. Apocryphi Syriace*.

[3] Splendidly reproduced at Milan by the process of photo-lithography under the direction of the Rev. Dr A. M. Ceriani, 5 parts, 1876 foll.

Children, Bel and the Dragon, and Susanna; Judith, Siracides or Ecclesiasticus; the Apocalypse of Baruch; the fourth book of Esdras; and five books of the Maccabees, the fourth being the history of Samona and her sons, and the fifth *Josephi de Bello Judaico lib. vi.*[1] To these must be added from other MSS. the first or third book of Esdras, the book of Tobit, and the prayer of Manasses. Of the first book of the Maccabees two recensions are extant, as far as chap. xiv. 24. The book of Tobit presents the text of the LXX. as far as chap. vii. 11[2].

The canonical books of the New Testament are the four Gospels, the Acts of the Apostles (to which are annexed the three catholic epistles, viz., James, 1 Peter, and 1 John), and the fourteen epistles of St Paul. The shorter apostolic epistles, viz., 2 and 3 John, 2 Peter, and Jude, and the Apocalypse of St John, were rejected by the early Syrian Church[3].

[1] See *Das 6te Buch d. Bellum Judaicum übersetzt u. kritisch bearbeitet*, by Dr H. Kottek, Berlin, 1886; only capp. 1 and 2.

[2] See the Syriac note on p. xii. of De Lagarde's edition.

[3] The principal editions of the Pĕshîṭtâ are contained in the Paris polyglott of Le Jay and the London polyglott of Walton, to which latter is attached the immortal *Lexicon Heptaglotton* of Edmund Castell. The Old Testament (without the apocrypha) was edited by S. Lee

As to the Pĕshīṭtā version of the Gospels (P), a variety of critical questions arise when we consider it in connexion with two other works, the *Dia-ṭessarōn* of Tatian (T) and the *Curetonian Gospels* (Sc)[1]. Tatian, the friend of Justin Martyr, afterwards counted a heretic, composed out of the four Gospels a work which received the title of Τὸ διὰ τεσσάρων εὐαγγέλιον, in Syriac more briefly *Dia-ṭessarōn* or *Evangelion da-Mĕḥallĕṭē*, "the Gospel of the Mixed." It is a subject of controversy whether Tatian wrote this work in Greek or in Syriac, and whether he compiled it

in 1823 for the Bible Society, and is frequently bound up with the New Testament of 1826. The first edition of the New Testament was that of J. A. Widmanstad, with the help of Moses of Mārdīn (Vienna, 1555). Those of Tremellius (1569), Trost (1621), Gutbir (1664), and Leusden and Schaaf (1708, 1717) are well known. To the last named belongs Schaaf's admirable *Lexicon Syriacum Concordantiale.* The American missionaries at Urūmiyah have published both the Old and New Testaments in ancient and modern Syriac, the former in 1852, the latter in 1846. [A convenient and cheap edition of the N.T., with the Psalter, in Nestorian characters, has been published at New York. An edition of the O.T. printed by the Dominicans of Mosul (2 vols, 1887, 8) follows the order of the Vulgate and claims to be free from Protestant corruptions. A third vol. containing the N.T. is reported as published in 1891.]

[1] *Remains of a very Antient Recension of the Four Gospels in Syriac, hitherto unknown in Europe, discovered, edited, and translated by W. Cureton, D.D., F.R.S.*, 1858.

from the Greek Gospels or from a previous Syriac version. According to Zahn[1] and Baethgen[2], the author's language was Syriac, his sources Greek. They hold that this was the only Gospel in use in the Syrian Church for nearly a century, but that about the year 250, under the influence of Western MSS. of the Greek text (see Westcott and Hort, *The New Testament in the Original Greek*, Introd., §§ 118, 214), a version of "the Separate Gospels," *Evangelion da-Mĕpharrĕshē*, was introduced[3]. The translator, according to Baethgen[4], made use of T as far as he could; and of this text Sc is, in the opinion of these scholars, the solitary survival in our days. The evidence for this view does not, however, appear to be conclusive. It seems that a Syriac version of the four Gospels, as well as of the other parts of the New Testament, must have existed in the 2nd century, perhaps even before the version of the Old Testament. From this Tatian may have compiled his *Dia-ṭessarōn*, or he may have written that work in Greek and others may have done it into Syriac. Be that as it may, T certainly gained great popularity in the early

[1] *Forschungen zur Geschichte des neutestamentlichen Kanons*, &c., 1. *Theil: Tatian's Diatessaron*, pp. 98, 99.

[2] *Evangelienfragmente. Der griechische Text des Cureton'schen Syrers wiederhergestellt*, 1885.

[3] Zahn, *op. cit.*, pp. 104–106.

[4] *Op. cit.*, pp. 59, 60, 72 *sq.*

Syrian Church, and almost superseded the Separate Gospels. Aphraates quoted it[1]; Ephraim wrote a commentary upon it[2]; the *Doctrine of Addai* or Addæus (in its present shape a work of the latter half of the 4th century) transfers it to the apostolic times[3]; Rabbūlā, bishop of Edessa (411–435), promulgated an order that "the priests and deacons should take care that in every church there should be a copy of the Separate Gospels (*Evangelion da-Mĕpharrĕshē*), and that it should be read"[4]; and Theodoret, bishop of Cyrrhus (423–457), swept up more than two hundred copies of it in the churches of his diocese, and introduced the four Gospels in their place: *τὰ τῶν τεττάρων εὐαγγελιστῶν ἀντεισήγαγον εὐαγγέλια*[5]. The result of these and similar well meant efforts is that not a single copy of T has

[1] Wright's edition, p. ܝܛ, l. 10, "as it is written at the head of the Gospel of our Lifegiver, In the beginning was the Word."

[2] Now extant only in the old Armenian version, translated by the Mechitarist Aucher, and revised by G. Mösinger under the title of *Evangelii Concordantis Expositio facta a S. Ephraemo*, Venice, 1876.

[3] Phillips's edition, p. ܠܘ, l. 17.

[4] *S. Ephraemi Syri Rabulæ epi Edesseni Balæi aliorumque opera selecta*, ed. J. J. Overbeck, Oxford, 1865, p. 220, 3.

[5] *Αἱρετικῆς κακομυθίας ἐπιτομή*, i. 20.

come down to our times[1]. Both Aphraates and Ephraim, however, made use of the Separate Gospels. The former seems to have employed a text which Baethgen calls a slightly revised form of Sc (*op. cit.*, p. 95); we would rather speak of it as a revised form of the old Syriac Gospels of the 2nd century. The latter made use of a more thorough Edessene revision, closely approaching in form to, if not identical with, P (Baethgen,

[1] Martin's article "Le Διὰ τεσσάρων de Tatien" (from *Revue des Questions Historiques*, April 1883) contains much curious literary information, particularly regarding similar compilations of later date. See also Ciasca's article "De Tatiani Diatessaron Arabica Versione," in Cardinal Pitra's *Analecta Sacra Spicilegio Solesmensi parata*, iv. 465. [The Vatican MS. of] this Arabic *Diatessaron* begins with Mark i. 1, John i. 1–5, Luke i. 5–80, Matthew i. 1–25a, Luke ii. 1–39. Ciasca's copy is now (1887) in the hands of De Lagarde, who has published a few pages of it in *Nachrichten von der königl. Gesellschaft der Wissenschaften*, 1886, No. 4, pp. 150–158. According to De Lagarde, the text is that of the ordinary Pĕshīṭtā. [In 1886 the Museum Borgianum acquired a better MS. of the Arabic Tatian from Egypt, and from it, and the Vatican MS. described in his earlier essay, Ciasca published *Tatiani evangeliorum harmoniæ Arabice*, with a Latin transl., Rome, 1888. According to a note in the Cod. Borg. this Arabic version was made by the Nestorian Abulfaraj 'Abdallāh b. aṭ-Ṭīb († A.D. 1043) from a Syriac copy written by a disciple of the famous Ḥonain b. Isḥāḳ. Thus, *at best*, the Arabic version gives only the form that the Syriac Tatian had assumed in the middle of the ninth century. The Borgian MS. begins with Joh. i. 1.]

p. 95; Zahn, p. 63)[1]. Our oldest MSS. of P are, however, more than a hundred years later than Ephraim's time. We cannot, therefore, expect very important textual results from the collation of even such MSS. as Add. 14470, 14453, 14459, ff. 1–66, and 17117, in the British Museum, all of which may be safely ascribed to the latter part of the 5th or the beginning of the 6th century[2]. Early in the 5th century Rabbūlā, bishop of Edessa, the friend and correspondent of Cyril of Alexandria, occupied himself with "translating the New Testament out of the Greek into the Syriac, because of its variations, exactly as it was[3]." This probably means, as has been suggested by Nestle, that Rabbūlā undertook a revision of the Syriac text according to a Greek MS. or MSS. in his possession, that is to say, still further assimilated P of that day to a Greek (possibly, from his connexion with Cyril, Alexandrian) text. We do not as yet know, however, whether this revision was merely a private effort, or what influence, if any, it exercised on the history of P; more likely it was a first step in the direction of the Philoxenian version (see below).

[1] [See also an essay by Rev. F. H. Woods in *Studia Biblica*, iii. 105 *sq.* (Oxford, 1891).]

[2] [Cf. Rev. G. H. Gwilliam's essay "Materials for the criticism of the Peshitto N.T. etc." in *Studia Biblica*, iii. 47 *sq.*]

[3] Overbeck, *op. cit.*, p. 172, 18–20.

The result of these successive revisions as regards Sc has been that it survives in but one mutilated codex, and that written at comparatively so late a date as 450–470[1],—a phenomenon which has its parallel in the case of the Itala codex *c* of the Gospels, copied in the 11th century. The greater part of this volume is in the British Museum (Add. 14451)[2]; but there are three leaves of it in the royal library at Berlin, forming the fly-leaves of the MS. marked Orient. Quart. 528[3]. Crowfoot's attempt to retranslate Sc into Greek is a

[1] The whole of the Abbé Martin's elaborate argumentation (*Introd. à la Critique Textuelle du N.T.*, pp. 163–236) is of no avail against this palæographic fact. No one who is conversant with Syriac MSS. can for a moment doubt that our codex of Sc was written within a few years of the time indicated above. The handwritings of Jacob of Edessa's time (the latter half of the 7th century) are altogether different. Possessors of the abbé's work should cancel pp. 234–236. The "Postscriptum," as the author himself has explained, is only an elaborate *joke*. There is no MS. Add. 70125 in the British Museum, no catalogue of the Greek MSS. in twenty-five volumes, and of course no such photograph exists as he has described. As for the "special telegram" from "Révérend Crowfoot" through the "agence Fri-Frou-Fro and Co.," dated 25th December, 1882, it is enough to say that Mr Crowfoot died on 18th March 1875.

[2] See Wright, *Catalogue*, p. 73, No. cxix.

[3] See Rödiger in the *Monatsberichte* of the Berlin Academy for July 1872, p. 557; Wright, *Fragments of the Curetonian Gospels* (privately printed).

failure (*Fragmenta Evangelica,* 1870–72); Baethgen's work (*Evangelienfragmente,* &c.) will perhaps be found more satisfactory.

[At the present moment all critical questions connected with the history of the Old Syriac Gospels stand suspended, till the publication of the Sinai Palimpsest, which was unearthed and photographed by Mrs Lewis in 1892; identified from her photographs by the late Prof. Bensly and Mr Burkitt as containing a text closely allied to the Curetonian; and copied by these gentlemen and Mr Rendel Harris at Sinai in the spring of 1893. The publication has been undertaken by the Cambridge University Press.]

The scholars of the Monophysite branch of the Syrian Church were, however, by no means satisfied even with the revised text of P, and demanded a yet more accurate reproduction of the Greek text in use among them. Accordingly Aksĕnāyā or Philoxenus, bishop of Mabbōgh (485–519), undertook to satisfy this want, and with the assistance of his chorepiscopus, Polycarp, produced a literal translation of the whole Bible in the year 508[1]. This seems at first to have met with considerable approval; Moses of Aggēl, for

[1] Assemani, *Bibliotheca Orientalis,* ii. 23. [The *B.O.* is one of those works which may be justly styled κειμήλιον ἐς ἀεί.]

example, who flourished from 550 to 570[1], refers to the version of the New Testament and of the Psalms evidently as the standard work of the day[2]. But it was in its turn superseded by two later revisions, and MSS. of it are now very rare. Portions of Isaiah survive in the British Museum, Add. 17106, ff. 74–87[3], and the text of the Gospels in the codex A. 2, 18 of the Biblioteca Angelica at Rome, of the 11th or 12th century[4], and perhaps also in the Beirūt (Beyrout) MS. described by Isaac H. Hall[5]. At the beginning of the 7th century the work of retranslation and revision was again taken in hand by the Monophysites, the scene of their labours being the different convents in the neighbourhood of Alexandria. There, in the years 616–617[6], Paul, bishop of Tellā dhĕ-Mauzĕlath or Constantina,

[1] *B.O.*, ii. 82.

[2] *Ibid.*, ii. 83; Guidi, *Rendiconti della R. Accademia dei Lincei*, May and June 1886, p. 404.

[3] Edited by Ceriani in *Monumenta Sacra et Profana*, vol. v. fasc. 1, pp. 1–40.

[4] See Bernstein, *Das heilige Evangelium des Johannes*, Leipsic, 1853, *krit. Anmerkungen*, pp. 3, 29; Martin, *Introd. à la Crit. Text. du N.T.*, pp. 160–161.

[5] *Syriac Manuscript, Gospels of a pre-Harklensian Version, Acts and Epistles of the Peshitto Version, written (probably) between* 700 *and* 900 *A.D.*, January, 1884.

[6] See Ceriani, *Monumenta*, vol. i. fasc. 1: *Prolegomena in Edit. Vers. Syr. ex Textu LXX.*, p. iii.; Martin, *Introd.*, p. 139, note.

undertook a version of the hexaplar text of the LXX. at the request of the patriarch Athanasius I.[1] Of parts of this many MSS. are extant in the British Museum and the Bibliothèque Nationale at Paris, and the Biblioteca Ambrosiana at Milan possesses the second volume of a codex of the entire work, which has been reproduced by photo-lithography under the direction of Ceriani[2]. This version not only exhibits the asterisks and obeli of Origen's text of the LXX., but the marginal notes contain many readings of the other

[1] *B.O.*, ii. 333–334.

[2] *Monumenta*, vol. vii. : *Codex Syro-hexaplaris Ambrosianus*, 1874. The first volume of this codex was in the possession of Andreas Masius, but has disappeared since his death in 1573. It contained part of Deuteronomy, Joshua, Judges, (four books of) Kings, Chronicles, Ezra (and Nehemiah), Judith, and part of Tobit. See Middeldorpf, *Codex Syriaco-hexaplaris*, Berlin, 1835, who enumerates in his preface the labours of previous editors. Since his time the books of Judges and Ruth have been published by T. Skat Rördam (*Libri Judicum et Ruth secundum Vers. Syriaco-hexaplarem*, Copenhagen, 1859–61), and Exodus, Numbers, Joshua, 1 and 2 Kings, by P. de Lagarde (*Vet. Test. ab Origene recensiti Fragmenta apud Syros servata quinque*, Göttingen, 1880, printed with Hebrew letters). Ceriani has commenced a critical edition in the *Monumenta*, vol. i. fasc. 1; vol. ii. fascc. 1–4; vol. v. fascc. 1, 2. [Finally, De Lagarde's posthumous volume, *Bibliothecæ Syriacæ* (Göttingen, 1892), contains a fresh edition of Genesis, Exodus, Numbers, Joshua, Judges and Ruth, 1 and 2 Kings.]

Greek translators, which have been largely utilized by Field in his noble work *Origenis Hexaplorum quæ supersunt* (2 vols., Oxford, 1875). At the same time and place the New Testament of Philoxenus was thoroughly revised by Thomas of Ḥarḳel or Heraclea[1], bishop of Mabbōgh[2], who, being driven from his diocese, betook himself to Alexandria and worked there in the convent of St Antony at the Enaton (or Nine-mile-village)[3]. This version comprises not only all the books contained in the Pĕshīṭtā but also the four shorter epistles[4]. The lapse of another century brings us

[1] See *B.O.*, ii. 90, 334; Bernstein, *De Hharklensi N.T. Translatione Syriaca Commentatio*, p. 4.

[2] Or Manbij; according to others, of Germanicia, or Mar'ash. He must not be confounded with an older Thomas of Germanicia, a Monophysite of the earlier part of the 6th century; see *B.O.*, ii. 92, 326; Kleyn, *Jacobus Baradaeüs*, p. 43, note 1.

[3] See Wright, *Catal.*, p. 34, note.

[4] It has been edited by White at Oxford—the Gospels in 1778, the Acts and Apostolic epistles in 1799, the Pauline epistles in 1803. The epistle to the Hebrews is defective, ending in the middle of chap. xi. 27[, but this lacuna has been supplied, from the Cambridge MS., by Bensly's *The Ḥarḳlean Version of the Epistle to the Hebrews, Chap.* xi. 28–xiii. 25, Cambridge, 1889]. The text of the shorter epistles, 2 Peter, 2 and 3 John, and Jude, has been recently reproduced by phototype from a manuscript dated 1471—*Williams Manuscript. The Syrian Antilegomena Epistles . . . edited by Isaac H. Hall*, 1886. Consult also *Transactions of the Royal Irish Academy*, vol. xxvii. No.

to the last attempt at a revision of the Old Testament in the Monophysite Church. Jacob, bishop of Edessa, undertook, when living in retirement in the convent of Tell-ʿAddā or Teleda[1], in 704–705, to revise the text of the Pĕshīṭtā with the help of the Greek versions at his disposal[2], thus producing a curious eclectic or patchwork text. Of this work there are but five volumes extant in Europe, four of which came from the Nitrian Desert and form parts of a set which was written in the years 719–720. It would seem, therefore, never to have attained popularity[3].

One other version remains to be noticed, namely, that used by the Christian population of the Malkite (Greek) Church in Palestine, written in an Aramaic dialect more akin to the language

viii., "On a Syrian MS. belonging to the Collection of Archbishop Ussher," by the Rev. J. Gwynn, D.D. [On a possible revision by Barsalībī, see *Hermathena* vi. 417.] There is a fine MS. of this version, dated 1170, in the university library, Cambridge, Add. MS. 1700. Its peculiar feature is that it has the two epistles of Clement inserted between the catholic epistles and those of St Paul.

[1] Probably the modern Tellʿādi or Tellʿāde; see Socin, *Paläst. u. Syrien*, p. 480; Sachau, *Reise in Syrien u. Mesopotamien*, p. 459.

[2] Wright, *Catal.*, p. 38, col. 1.

[3] See Ceriani, *Le Edizioni e i Manoscritti delle Versioni Siriache del Vecchio Test.*, 1869, p. 27, and *Monumenta*, vol. ii. fasc. 1, pp. xi., xii., vol. v. fasc. 1, pp. 1–40; Martin, *Introd.*, pp. 230–232, 296 *sq.*

of the Jewish Targūms than to that of the Pĕshīṭtā[1]. A lectionary containing large portions of the Gospels in this dialect was described by Assemani in the catalogue of the Vatican library[2], studied by Adler[3], and edited by Count Fr. Miniscalchi Erizzo under the title of *Evangeliarium Hierosolymitanum* (2 vols., Verona, 1861–64) [and again by De Lagarde in his posthumous work *Bibliothecæ Syriacæ* (Göttingen, 1892)]. It was written in a convent at a place called Ābūd[4], not very far from Jerusalem, in the year 1030, and the scribe claims to have copied sundry other service-books for the use of his church (see Assemani, *op. cit.*, p. 102). Fragments of other evangeliaria have been published by Land, from MSS. at London and St Petersburg, in his *Anecd. Syr.*, iv. pp. 114–162, 213–222; of the Acts of the Apostles, p. 168; and of the Old Testament (translated from the Greek), pp. 103–110, 165–167, 222–223. According to the same authority (p. 231), the calendar in the Vatican MS. must

[1] See Nöldeke, in *Z.D.M.G.*, xxii. (1868), p. 443 *sq.*

[2] *MSS. Codd. Bibl. Apost. Vatic. Catalogus*, ii. No. xix. p. 70 *sq.*

[3] *N. Test. Verss. Syriacæ Simplex, Philoxeniana, et Hierosolymitana*, Copenhagen, 1789; see also Martin, *Introd.*, p. 237 *sq.*

[4] See Nöldeke, *loc. cit.*, pp. 521, 527; Land, *Anecd. Syr.*, iv. pp. 227–229.

have been drawn up about the middle of the 9th century. Few, if any, of the extant fragments appear to be of older date. Nöldeke places the origin of the version in the 4th or 5th century, certainly not later than 600 (*loc. cit.*, p. 525)[1].

All the above revisions of the text of the Syriac Bible according to the Greek are, as we have seen, the work of Monophysites, with the single exception of the last, which proceeded from the Malkites. The Nestorian community obstinately adhered to the old Pĕshīṭtā, and the solitary attempt made to introduce a revised text among them seems to have been an utter failure. Mār-abhā I.[2], a convert from Zoroastrianism, who was catholicus from 536 to 552, went to Edessa, studied Greek there under a teacher named Thomas[3], and with his help translated the whole of the Old Testament into Syriac, and perhaps also the New. This statement rests on the authority of the author of the *Kitāb al-Majdal*

[1] The remaining literature in this dialect (all of it published by Land) consists of a few hymns (pp. 111–113), lives of saints (pp. 169, 170), and theological fragments (pp. 171–210). One fragment (p. 177) contains the title of a homily of John Chrysostom. [Several additions to this list are promised from Sinai MSS.]

[2] Properly Mār(ī)-abhā.

[3] *B.O.*, iii. 1, 86; compare ii. 411.

(Mārī ibn Sulaimān[1], about the middle of the 12th century, supplemented and abridged by ʿAmr ibn Mattā of Ṭīrhān, who lived towards the middle of the 14th century)[2], of ʿAbhd-īshōʿ, bishop of Nisībis (died 1318), and of Bar-Hebræus (died 1286); and there appears to be no reason to doubt their word[3].

Before quitting the subject of the versions of Holy Scripture we must devote a few words to the Massoretic MSS. of the Nestorians and Jacobites[4]. In the year 1721 Assemani made mention in the *Bibliotheca Orientalis* (ii. 283), on the authority of Bar-Hebræus in the *Auṣar Rāzē*, of a "versio *Karkaphensis*, hoc est *Montana*, qua videlicet incolæ montium utuntur[5]." About the meaning of these words scholars disputed, and some searched for MSS. of the alleged version,

[1] See p. 255, note.

[2] See Hoffmann, *Auszüge aus syrischen Akten persischer Märtyrer*, pp. 6, 7 [in *Abhandlungen für d. Kunde d. Morgenlandes* vii. (Leipzig, 1880)].

[3] See *B.O.*, ii. 411–412, iii. 1, 75; Bar-Hebræus, *Chron. Eccles.*, ed. Abbeloos and Lamy, ii. 89; Martin, *Introd.*, pp. 292–294.

[4] See Martin, *Tradition Karkaphienne ou la Massore chez les Syriens*, Paris, 1870 (from *Journ. Asiat.*), and *Introd.*, pp. 276–291.

[5] In the Vatican *Catalogue* (vol. iii. 287, No. clii.) he translates the words *akh mashlĕmānūthā ḳarḳĕphāitā* by "juxta traditionem verticalem (!): hoc est, Montanorum in Phœnice et Mesopotamia degentium."

but in vain. At last, N. Wiseman (afterwards cardinal), guided by the light of another passage in the *Bibliotheca Orientalis* (ii. 499, 500, No. xxii.), recognized in Cod. Vat. cliii. a copy of what he believed to be the Karkaphensian version[1]. Later researches, more especially those of the Abbé Martin, have corrected these errors. The MSS. of the Karkaphensian tradition, of which there are ten in our European libraries, are now known to contain a philological and grammatical tradition of the pronunciation and punctuation of Holy Writ and sometimes of other writings[2]. Syria was rich in schools and colleges; most of its towns possessed institutions where instruction was given, more especially to students of theology, in the reading and exposition of the Greek and Syriac Scriptures and their commentators. Such were the great "Persian school" of Edessa, which was destroyed, on account of its Nestorian tendencies, in 489; the school of

[1] See his *Horæ Syriacæ*, Rome, 1828, p. 78: II. *Symbolæ Philologicæ ad Hist. Versionum Syriac. vet. fœderis. Particula prima; de versionibus generatim, deinde de Peschito*, p. 147; III. *Particula secunda; recensionem Karkaphensem nunc primum describens.* We need not here indicate Wiseman's mistakes, but it is a pity to see them all reproduced even in the third edition of Scrivener's *Plain Introduction*, 1883.

[2] See Hoffmann, *Opuscula Nestoriana*, 1880, p. v. *sq.*

Nisībis; of Māḥōzē near Seleucia; of the monastery of Dōr-Ḳōnī or Dair-Ḳunnā; of the monastery of Ḳen-neshrē or the Eagles' Nest, on the left bank of the Euphrates, opposite Jerābīs; of the Dairā 'Ellāitā, or monastery of St Gabriel and St Abraham, at Mosul; and many others[1]. Every such school or college had its teachers of reading and elocution, *mahgĕyānē* and *maḳrĕyānē* (or *maḳeryānē*), who taught their pupils to pronounce, add the vowel-points, and interpunctuate correctly[2], before they were passed on to the higher classes of the *eskōlāyē*, *bādhōḳē* or *mallĕphānē*, that is, the professors of exegesis and doctors of theology[3]. The more difficult words and phrases of Scripture were gradually collected and written down so as to form "collectanea," *luḳḳāṭē dha-shĕmāhē*, or "fasciculi," *kurrāsē dha-shĕmāhē*, and the union of these composed a *kĕthābhā dha-ḳĕrāyāthā*, or "book of readings," in which it was

[1] See, for example, *B.O.*, iii. 1, 341, col. 2 at the foot, and iii. 2, cmxxiv. *sq.*

[2] Hoffmann, *Opusc. Nestor.*, p. vii.; Martin, *Introd.*, p. 289.

[3] Hoffmann, *op. cit.*, pp. xx., xxi. What the whole curriculum of such a student should be, according to the mind of Bar-Hebræus in the 13th century, may be seen from the *B.O.*, iii. 2, 937–938 (*Nomocanon*, translated by J. A. Assemani, in Mai, *Scriptt. Vett. Nova Coll.*, x. cap. vii. § 9, pp. 54–56). [See also Merx, *Historia artis grammaticæ apud Syros* (in *Abhandlungen für die Kunde des Morgenlandes*, vol. ix.).]

shown by means of vowel-points and other signs how each word was to be pronounced and accentuated[1]. One such volume in the British Museum (Add. 12138, dated 899) represents the work of a Nestorian student in the convent of Mār Gabriel at Ḥarrān[2]; but the other MSS. extant in the different libraries of Europe[3] are of Jacobite origin and have a common source, the scholastic tradition of the convent of Ḳarḳaphĕthā, or "the Skull," at the village of Maghdal or Mijdal near Rēsh-'ainā or Rās-'ain[4]. Such are, for example, Cod. Vat., No. clii., now cliii., described by Assemani (*Catal.*, iii. 287) and Wiseman (*Horæ Syr.*, p. 151); Cod. Paris, Ancien fonds 142, described by Zotenberg (*Catal.*, p. 30, No. 64) and Martin (*Tradition Karkaphienne*, p. 36); Cod. Brit. Mus. Add. 7183, described by Rosen (*Catal.*, p. 64, No. xlii.)[5] and 12178, described by Wright (*Catal.*, p. 108). From these and similar MSS., as well as from the words of Bar-Hebræus[6], it appears that the Ḳarḳĕphāyē

1 Hoffmann, *op. cit.*, pp. vi., vii.

2 See Wright, *Catal.*, p. 101, [Merx, *op. cit.* p. 30 *sq.*, and a specimen in *Studia Biblica*, iii. 93–95].

3 Martin, *Introd.*, p. 291.

4 Hoffmann, in *Z.D.M.G.*, xxxii. (1878), p. 745; and in Stade's *Zeitschrift für d. Alttest. Wissenschaft*, 1881, p. 159.

5 [A specimen in *Studia Biblica*, iii. 96.]

6 Martin, *op. cit.*, pp. 122, 129.

were the monks of the convent of Ḳarḳaphĕthā; that they were Westerns or Occidentals, therefore Jacobites; and that one of their chief authorities, if not the actual originator of the compilation, was Jacob bishop of Edessa. Accordingly, the marginal notes indicate various readings from Syriac MSS., from the LXX., and from the Ḥarḳlensian version, as well as from different fathers and teachers[1]. To the collection of words and phrases from the Pĕshīṭtā version is added in several of these MSS. a similar, though shorter, collection from the Ḥarḳlensian version and from the principal works of the Greek fathers which were read in translations in the schools[2], followed

[1] See Wiseman, *op. cit.*, p. 178; Martin, *op. cit.*, pp. 76, 77, 133; Rosen, *Catal.*, pp. 65, 66; Wright, *Catal.*, p. 109. Among these occur ܛܘ and ܣܒܐ. The investigations of Hoffmann (in Stade's *Zeitschrift*, 1881, p. 159) and Duval (*Journ. Asiat.*, 1884, p. 560) have made it certain that ܛܘ designates not the Pĕshīṭtā, nor Jacob of Edessa, but one Ṭūbhānā (perhaps surnamed "the Beardless"), an eminent teacher at Rēsh-'ainā. His colleague Sābhā was probably the famous scribe Sābhā, who wrote Brit. Mus. Add. 14428, 14430 (724), and 12135, ff. 1–43 (726).

[2] Namely, (Pseudo-)Dionysius Areopagita, Gregory Nazianzen (2 vols.), the works of Basil, the epistles of Gregory and Basil, John Philoponus (the Διαιτητής), and Severus of Antioch (*Homiliæ Cathedrales* and certain synodical letters relating to the council of Antioch). A fuller list is given by Assemani, *B.O.*, iii. 2, cmxxxvii. *sq.*

by tracts on different points of orthography, grammar and punctuation[1].

We have spoken above (p. 5 *sq.*) of the deutero-canonical books of the Old Testament. Other apocrypha may now be noticed more briefly; *e.g.*, Ps. cli. (in the hexaplar version of Paul of Tellā); the *Parva Genesis*, or *Liber Jubilæorum*, a fragment of which has been edited by Ceriani (*Monumenta*, vol. ii. fasc. 1, p. ix.); the Testament of Adam[2]; the History of Joseph and Āsyath (Asenath), translated by Moses of Aggēl[3]; the History of Sanḥērīb, his Vizīr Aḥīḳār or Ḥīḳār, and his Disciple Nādhān[4]. Many similar books

[1] See Phillips, *A Letter of Mār Jacob, Bishop of Edessa, on Syriac Orthography*, &c., 1869 (Appendix iii. p. 85–96, issued separately in 1870); Martin, *Jacobi epi Edesseni Epistola ad Georgium epum Sarugensem de Orthographia Syriaca*, &c., 1869. [Compare also Merx, *op. cit.* chap. iii.]

[2] Wright, *Catal.*, p. 1242; see Renan, in the *Journ. Asiat.*, November and December 1853, p. 427, and Wright, *Contributions to the Apocryphal Literature of the New Testament*, 1865, p. 61. [It is not given in the *Syriac* text of the *Mĕ'ārath Gazzē*, but in the *Arabic* version, whence it has passed into the *Ethiopic* Clementines.]

[3] Wright, *Catal.*, p. 1047; Land, *Anecd. Syr.*, iii. 15–46.

[4] Wright, *Catal.*, p. 1207, col. 1; Hoffmann, *Auszüge aus syrischen Akten persischer Märtyrer*, p. 182; see for the Syriac text Brit. Mus. Orient. 2313, and a MS. in the collection of the S.P.C.K. (now presented by the Society to the university of Cambridge). [An addition to the above list is furnished by some apocryphal psalms,

exist in Arabic, some of them probably translated from lost Syriac originals. The names of Daniel and Ezra "the scribe" are prefixed to late apocalyptic works[1], and even to almanacs containing prognostications of the weather, &c.[2] The list of apocrypha of the New Testament is also tolerably extensive. We may mention the *Protevangelium Jacobi*; the Gospel of Thomas the Israelite, or of the Infancy of our Lord; the Letters of Abgar and our Lord; the Letters of Herod and Pilate; prayers ascribed to St John the Baptist; the *Transitus, Assumptio,* or *Κοίμησις Beatæ Virginis,* extant in four or five redactions[3]; Acts of the Apostles, such as St John, St Philip, St Matthew and St Andrew, St Paul and Thecla, and St Thomas[4]; the Doctrine of St Peter[5]; and the Apocalypse of St

published by Wright in Proc. Soc. Bibl. Arch. ix. 257–266.]

[1] Wright, *Catal.*, pp. 9, 1065.

[2] Wright, *Catal.*, p. 352, col. 2; Brit. Mus. Orient. 2084, f. 1, *Kĕthābhā dhĕ-Shūdhā'ē dhĕ-zabhnē dhĕ-Dhānī'ēl nĕbhīyā.*

[3] Most of these are published in Wright's *Contributions*; see also the *Journal of Sacred Literature*, 1865, vol. vi. 417, vol. vii. 129; and B. H. Cowper, *The Apocryphal Gospels*, &c., 1867.

[4] See Wright, *Apocryphal Acts of the Apostles*, 2 vols., 1871; [(Bedjan), *Acta Martyrum et Sanctorum*, Paris, 1890–94].

[5] Cureton, *Ancient Syriac Documents*, pp. 35–41.

Paul[1]. Others of these apocrypha are extant in Arabic, but the Syriac originals have not yet been recovered. To these may be added such works as the *Didascalia Apostolorum*, edited (anonymously) by P. de Lagarde in 1854; extracts from the *Constitutiones Apostolorum*, ascribed to Clement, in the same editor's *Reliquiæ Juris Eccles. Antiq.*, pp. 2–32, 44–60; and the *Doctrina Apostolorum*, in Cureton's *Ancient Syriac Documents*, pp. 24–35, and in *Reliquiæ Juris Eccles. Antiq.* (under the title of *Doctrina Addæi*), pp. 32–44.

Into a description of the service-books of the Syrian Church in its different sects—Nestorians, Jacobites, Maronites, and Malkites—we cannot here enter[2]. The bare enumeration of the various psalters, lectionaries, missals, &c., would far exceed

[1] Translated by Zingerle in Heidenheim's *Vierteljahrsschrift*, iv. p. 139 *sq.*, and by Perkins, *Journal of the American Oriental Society*, viii. p. 182 *sq.*; reprinted in the *Journal of Sacred Literature*, January 1865, p. 372 *sq.*

[2] The reader is referred to the following works: J. A. Assemani, *Codex Liturg. Ecclesiæ Universæ*, 13 vols., Rome, 1749–66; Renaudot, *Liturgiarum Orient. Collectio*, 2 vols., Paris, 1716; Etheridge, *The Syrian Churches, their Early History, Liturgies, and Literature*, London, 1846; Badger, *The Nestorians and their Rituals*, 2 vols., London, 1852; Howard, *The Christians of St Thomas and their Liturgies*, Oxford, 1864; Denzinger *Ritus Orientalium, Coptorum, Syrorum, et Armenorum in administrandis sacramentis*, 2 vols., Würzburg, 1863–64; J. Morinus, *Comment. de Sacris Eccles. Ordinationibus*, &c.,

our limits. The oldest Syriac psalter in our European collections is not earlier than 600 (Brit. Mus. Add. 17110), and the series of lectionaries commences with the 9th century. Of anaphoræ or liturgies it would be easy to specify some sixty[1]. The oldest of all is a fragment of the anaphora of Diodorus of Tarsus (in the British Museum, Add. 14699, ff. 20, 21), of the 6th century, which has been edited and translated by Bickell[2].

Besides the versions of Holy Writ and other works enumerated above, the literature of Syria comprises a vast amount of matter, interesting not merely to the Orientalist but also to the classical scholar, the theologian, and the historian. Some portions of this literature we must now endeavour to pass under review.

The long series of Syrian writers is headed by the name of Bar-Daiṣān or Bardesānes, "the last of the Gnostics[3]." He was born at Edessa on

Paris, 1655, Antwerp, 1695; Bickell, *Conspectus Rei Syrorum Literariæ*, chaps. vii.–x.

[1] See a complete list in Bickell's *Conspectus*, pp. 65–68; comp. also Neale and Littledale's *Liturgies of SS. Mark, James*, &c., 2d ed., 1869, p. 146, and Appendix i.; [Maclean, *Liturgia Sanctorum Apostolorum Adaei et Maris*, Urmi, 1890].

[2] See his *Conspectus*, pp. 63, 71–72. The Syriac text is given in *Z.D.M.G.*, xxvii. (1873), pp. 608–613.

[3] See Merx, *Bardesanes von Edessa*, 1863; Hilgenfeld,

11th July 154[1], and seems to have been the son of heathen parents of rank. Of the manner of his conversion to Christianity, and how he came to deviate from orthodoxy, we are uninformed. Part of his life he spent at the court of Edessa; then he betook himself as a missionary to the rude mountaineers of Armenia, and finally settled down in the fortress of Anium, where he probably remained till his death in 222[2]. He wrote, we are told, a *History of Armenia*, which Moses of Chorene used in a Greek translation; *Hypomnemata Indica*, compiled from the oral information which he obtained from an Indian embassy passing through Edessa on its way to the Roman court; and polemical treatises against the polytheism of the heathens and the dualism of Marcion. He and his son Harmonius were poets, and their hymns were greatly admired and imitated. Even Ephraim could not help admitting their merits, whilst he reviled them[3]. Of these works, however, only a few fragments have been preserved by

*Bardesanes, der letzte Gnostiker*, 1864; Hahn, *Bardesanes Gnosticus Syrorum primus Hymnologus*, 1819.

1 So the *Chronicon Edessenum*, in Assemani, *B.O.*, i. 389, and Bar-Hebræus, *Chron. Eccles.*, i. 47; but Elias of Nisībis, as cited by Abbeloos in his notes on Bar-Hebræus, *loc. cit.*, places his birth in 134.

2 Bar-Hebræus, *Chron. Eccles.*, i. 47.

3 *E.g.*, *Opera Syr.*, ii. 439 D, 553 F, last line.

later writers[1]. The famous dialogue Περὶ εἱμαρμένης or *De Fato*, which the voice of antiquity has unanimously ascribed to Bardesānes, was in reality composed by his disciple Philip, and doubtless presents us with an accurate account of his master's teaching. The Syriac title is *Kĕthābhā dhĕ-Nāmōsē dh'Athrawāthā* (The Book of the Laws of the Countries)[2].

Of Simeon bar Ṣabbā'ē ("the Dyers' Son"), bishop of Seleucia and Ctesiphon, and Millēs, bishop of Susa, we know little beyond the fact of their martyrdom in the great persecution of the Christians by Shābhōr or Sapor II., which began in 339–340[3]. Simeon is said by 'Abhd-īshō'[4] to have written "epistles[5]," which seem to be no

1 Compare the hymn in the Syriac Acts of St Thomas (Wright, *Apocryphal Acts*, p. 274); Lipsius, *Die Apocryphen-Apostelgeschichten und -Apostellegenden*, i. 292 *sq.*

2 It was first edited by Cureton, with an English translation, in his *Spicilegium Syriacum*; see also T. & T. Clark's *Ante-Nicene Christian Library*, vol. xxii. p. 85 *sq.*, and Merx, *op. cit.*, p. 25 *sq.*

3 See S. E. Assemani, *Acta Sanctorum Martyrum*, i. 10 *sq.*, 66 *sq.*; [(Bedjan), *Acta Mart. et Sanct.*, ii. 128 *sq.*, 260 *sq.*].

4 Or 'Ĕbēdh-yēshū', bishop of Nisībis, whose bibliographical *Catalogue* has been edited by Abraham Ecchellensis, Rome, 1653, and by J. S. Assemani in his *B.O.*, iii. 1. There is an English translation of it by Badger, *The Nestorians*, ii. 361–379.

5 *B.O.*, iii. 1, 51.

longer extant. To him are also ascribed sundry hymns[1], and a work entitled *Kĕthābhā dh'Abhāhāthā* (The Book of the Fathers), which, according to Sachau, treats of the heavenly and earthly hierarchy[2]. The writings of Millēs are stated by ʿAbhd-īshōʿ (*loc. cit.*) to have been "epistles and discourses (*mēmrē*) on various subjects"; but of these time has also robbed us.

The name of Jacob (or St James) of Nisībis[3] is far more widely known. As bishop of that city he was present at the council of Nicæa. He lived to witness the outbreak of war between the Romans and the Persians, and is said to have delivered the city by his prayers from the latter power. He died in the same year (338)[4]. To him has been ascribed, on the authority of Gennadius of Marseilles[5] and of the ancient Armenian

[1] Assemani, *Acta Sanctorum Martyrum*, i. 5; Rosen, *Catalogue*, p. 14, col. 2, aa; Overbeck, *S. Ephraemi*, &c., *Opera Selecta*, p. 424.

[2] *Kurzes Verzeichniss der Sachau'schen Sammlung syrischer Handschriften*, Berlin, 1885, p. x. and No. 108, 3.

[3] Καὶ Συρίης πέδον εἶδα καὶ ἄστεα πάντα, Νίσιβιν, Εὐφράτην διαβάς, Lightfoot, *S. Ignatius*, i. 480.

[4] This date is given by the *Chronic. Edess.* (*B.O.*, i. 395), by Dionysius of Tell-Maḥrē (*ibid.*, p. 17), by the so-called *Liber Chalipharum* (in Land, *Anecd. Syr.*, i. 4), by Elias of Nisībis (see Abbeloos's note in Bar-Hebræus, *Chron. Eccles.*, ii. 31), and inferentially by Ephraim (Bickell, *S. Ephraemi Syri Carmina Nisibena*, p. 20).

[5] In his *De Viris Illustribus*, written before 496.

version[1], a collection of homilies, the Syriac text of which has only been recovered and published within the last few years. George, bishop of the Arab tribes, writing to a friend in the year 714, is aware that the author was a certain "Persian sage," *ḥakkīmā Phārsāyā*, and discusses his date and position in the church[2], but does not think of identifying him with Jacob of Nisībis. Later writers are better informed. Bar-Hebræus knows the name of Pharhādh as the author[3]; ʿAbhd-īshōʿ gives the older form of Aphrahaṭ or Ἀφραάτης[4]; and he is also cited by name by Elias of Nisībis (11th century) in his *Chronicle*[5]. The real author of the twenty-two alphabetical *Homilies* and the separate homily "On the Cluster" is now, therefore, known to have been Aphraates, a Persian Christian, who took the name of Jacob, and was subsequently famous as "the Persian

[1] Published by N. Antonelli (Rome, 1756) with a Latin translation, and reprinted in Gallandius, *Bibl. Vet. Patrum*, vol. v. The mistake has passed (no doubt through the Arabic) to the Ethiopic translation of the fifth homily; see Zotenberg, *Catal. des MSS. Éthiopiens de la Bibl. Nat.*, p. 248, col. 2, No. 17.

[2] See De Lagarde, *Anal. Syr.*, p. 108; *The Homilies of Aphraates*, ed. Wright, p. 19; Ryssel, *Ein Brief Georgs, Bischofs der Araber*, 1883.

[3] *Chron. Eccles.*, ii. 34.

[4] *B.O.*, iii. 1, 85.

[5] See Wright, *Aphraates*, p. 38.

sage." He was probably bishop of the convent of Mār Matthew near Mosul, and composed his works, as he himself tells us, in the years 337, 344, and 345, during the great persecution under Sapor II.[1]

A junior contemporary of Aphraates was Ephraim[2], commonly called Ephraem Syrus, "the prophet of the Syrians," the most celebrated father of the Syrian Church and certainly one of its most voluminous and widely read writers. He was born of heathen parents at Nisībis, but became the pupil of the bishop Jacob, and finished his education at Edessa. The incidents of his career are too well known to need recapitulation here[3]. His death took place in June 373[4]. His works

[1] Wright, *Aphraates*, pp. 440 and 507; comp. Sasse, *Prolegomena in Aphr. Sap. Pers. Sermones Homileticos*, 1878; J. Forget, *De Vita et Scriptis Aphr., Sap. Persæ*, 1882; Bickell in Thalhofer, *Bibliothek der Kirchenväter*, 102 and 103, where eight of the homilies are translated. [All the homilies have been translated by Bert, in Von Gebhardt and Harnack's series of *Texte und Untersuchungen*, vol. iii., Leipzig, 1888.]

[2] More correctly Aphrēm.

[3] See the *Acta S. Ephraemi* in the Roman ed. of his works by Peter Mobārak (Petrus Benedictus) and the Assemanis, pp. xxiii–lxiii; and comp. Bickell, *Conspectus*, p. 26, note 11.

[4] See the various authorities cited by Assemani, *B.O.*, i. 54, note; Bickell, *Carmina Nisibena*, p. 9, note; Gabriel Cardāḥī, *Liber Thesauri de Arte Poetica Syrorum*, 1875, pp. 9–13.

have been largely translated into Greek[1], Armenian, Coptic, Arabic, and Ethiopic[2]. They consist of commentaries on the Scriptures, expository sermons, and a vast mass of metrical homilies and hymns on every variety of theological subject[3]. Many of these last are composed in his favourite seven-syllable metre, in stanzas of different length; but he frequently used other metres and mixed strophic arrangements[4]. Of Ephraim's commentaries on the Old Testament but little has reached us in the original Syriac[5]. Most of what has been published in *Ephraemi Opera Syr.*, vols. i. and ii.,

[1] Even Photius speaks with respect of the rhetorical talent of Ephraim, so far as he could judge of it from these imperfect translations (ed. Bekker, p. 160).

[2] See *B.O.*, i. 149 *sq.*

[3] *Ibid.*, i. 63–149; iii. 1, 61.

[4] Compare, for instance, Bickell, *Carm. Nisib.*, Introd., p. 31. The Syrian line consists of a certain fixed number of syllables, four, five, six, seven, eight, twelve, &c. In the older writers there is no intentional rime, which first appears, we believe, among the Westerns, in Antonius Rhetor (9th century). Real metres, like those of the Greeks and Arabs, coupled in the latter case with rime, were wholly unknown to the Syrians. Hebrew poetry barely rises, as regards outward form, beyond the level of Arabic rimed prose; the Syrians, whilst destitute of rime, at least imposed upon themselves the restraint of a limited but fixed number of syllables.

[5] Genesis and Exodus in Cod. Vat. cx., and five leaves of Genesis in Cod. Vat. cxx. (see Assemani, *Catal.*, iii. p. 125).

is derived from a large *Catena Patrum*, compiled by one Severus, a monk of Edessa, in 861[1]. Of his commentary on the *Dia-ṭessarōn*, preserved only in an early Armenian translation, we have spoken above (p. 9). In the same language there is extant a translation of his commentary on the Pauline epistles[2]. Vol. ii. of the Roman edition contains some exegetical discourses (pp. 316–395), the number of which has been largely increased by Overbeck (*S. Ephraemi Syri*, &c., *Opera Selecta*, pp. 74–104). In the same work will be found two of the discourses against early heresies addressed to Hypatius and Domnus (pp. 21–73; comp. Wright, *Catal.*, p. 766, col. 2), two tracts on the love of the Most High (pp. 103–112), and the epistle to the monks who dwelt in the mountains (pp. 113–131). Of metrical writings the same book contains (pp. 339–354) the hymns against Julian the Apostate (pp. 1–20), and the conclusion of the hymns on Paradise (wanting in the Roman ed., vol. iii. 598)[3]. Other metrical

1 Cod. Vat. ciii., Brit. Mus. Add. 12144. Severus used for Genesis a commentary different from that in Cod. Vat. cx.; see Bickell, *Conspectus*, p. 19; comp. Pohlmann, *S. Ephraemi Syri Commentariorum in s. scripturam textus in codd. vatt. manuscriptus et in edit. Rom. impressus*, 2 parts, 1862–64.

2 See Bickell, *Conspectus*, p. 20.

3 The last hymn (p. 351) is genuine, as the very fact of

homilies were published by Zingerle[1]; but far more important, as having a real historical interest, are the *Carmina Nisibena*, or "Hymns relating to the City of Nisībis," edited by Bickell in 1866. These poems, which deal in great part with the history of Nisībis and its bishops and of adjacent cities (such as Anzīṭ or Hanzīṭ, Edessa, and Ḥarrān), were composed, according to Bickell (Introd., p. 6 *sq.*), between the years 350 and 370 or thereabouts[2]. A large quantity of hitherto unpublished matter is also contained in Lamy,

its being an acrostic shows (see Bickell, *Conspectus*, p. 19); whereas the metrical homily on the baptism of Constantine (pp. 355–361) is certainly spurious (Bickell, *loc. cit.*).

[1] *S. P. Ephraemi Syri Sermones duo*, Brixen, 1869 (see *B.O.*, i. 149, col. 1, No. 31); *Monumenta Syriaca ex Romanis Codd. collecta*, i. 4 (*B.O.*, *loc. cit.*, No. 30). Zingerle has rendered many of Ephraim's works into German, *e.g.*, *Die heilige Muse der Syrer: Gesänge des h. Kirchenvaters Ephraem*, 1833; *Gesänge gegen die Grübler über die Geheimnisse Gottes*, 1834; *Festkränze aus Libanons Gärten*, 1846; *Des h. Kirchenvaters Ephraem ausgewählte Schriften, aus d. Griechischen und Syrischen uebersetzt*, 6 vols., 2d ed., 1845–47; *Die Reden des h. Ephraem gegen die Ketzer*, 1850; *Reden des h. Ephraem des Syrers über Selbstverläugnung und einsame Lebensweise, mit einem Briefe desselben an Einsiedler*, 1871. Translations into English have been attempted, though with less success, by Morris (*Select Works of S. Ephraem the Syrian*, 1847) and Burgess (*Select Metrical Hymns and Homilies of Ephraem Syrus*, 1853; *The Repentance of Nineveh*, &c., 1853).

[2] Comp. Bickell, *Conspectus*, p. 28, note 21.

*S. Ephraemi Syri Hymni et Sermones*, vol. i., 1882, and vol. ii., 1886,—*e.g.*, fifteen hymns on the Epiphany, a discourse on our Lord, several metrical homilies (in particular for Passion week, the Resurrection, and New or Low Sunday), hymns on the Passover or unleavened bread (*De Azymis*) and on the Crucifixion, acts of Ephraim from the Paris MS. Ancien fonds 144, commentaries on portions of the Old Testament, other metrical homilies, and hymns on the nativity, the Blessed Virgin Mary, Lent, &c. [Vol. iii., 1889, contains a few homilies[1] and many hymns, chiefly on martyrs, before unpublished. It also contains a re-edition of the poem on the history of Joseph in ten books (see below, p. 40).] The so-called *Testament* of Ephraim[2] has been printed in the *Opera Græca*, ii. pp. 395–410 (with various readings at p. 433), and again by Overbeck (*op. cit.*, pp. 137–156)[3].

Notwithstanding his vast fecundity and great

1 [Nöldeke has shown, in *Wiener Zeitschrift für die Kunde des Morgenlandes*, iv. 245 *sq.*, that the homily on Antichrist cannot be Ephraim's.]

2 See *B.O.*, i. 141, No. 8.

3 That it has been interpolated by a later hand is shown by the long and purposeless digression on Moses and Pharaoh (*Op. Gr.*, ii. 405) and the story of Lamprotate at the end (*ibid.*, p. 409), as also by the stanzas regarding the vine which Ephraim saw growing out of his mouth when he was an infant (*ibid.*, p. 408).

popularity as a theological writer, Ephraim seems not to have had any pupils worthy to take his place. In the *Testament* we find mentioned with high commendation the names of Abhā, Abraham, Simeon, Mārā of Aggēl, and Zenobius of Gĕzīrtā[1], to whom we may add Isaac[2] and Jacob[3]. Two, on the other hand, are named with decided reprobation as heretics, namely, Paulonas (Παυλωνᾶς) or Paulinus (Παυλῖνος) and Arwadh or Arwaṭ[4]. Of these, Abhā is cited by later writers and compilers as the author of a commentary on the Gospels, a discourse on Job, and an exposition of Ps. xlii. 9[5]. Paulonas or Paulinus is probably the same who is mentioned by ʿAbhd-īshōʿ[6] as having written "*madhrāshē* or metrical homilies, discourses against inquirers, disputations against Marcion, and a treatise concerning believers and the creed." Zenobius, who was deacon of the church of Edessa, according to the same authority[7], composed treatises against Marcion and

[1] *B.O.*, i. 38, 144.

[2] *Ibid.*, i. 165.

[3] See Wright, *Catal.*, p. 992, col. 2, No. 36.

[4] Also written ܐܪܢܘܛ = Arnūṭ and ܐܘܪܝܛ = Ūriṭ. See Overbeck's text, p. 147, and the variants, p. xxx. The name seems to have been hopelessly corrupted by the scribes.

[5] See Wright, *Catal.*, pp. 831, col. 1, and 1002, col. 1.

[6] *B.O.*, iii. 1, 170.

[7] *Ibid.*, i. 168; iii. 1, 43.

Pamphylius (?), besides sundry epistles. He was also the teacher of Isaac of Antioch, of whom we shall speak shortly.

Better known than any of these disciples of Ephraim are two writers who belong to the close of this century and the beginning of the next, Balai and Cyrillōnā. The date of Balai or Balæus, chorepiscopus (as it seems) of the diocese of Aleppo, is fixed by his being mentioned by Bar-Hebræus[1] after Ephraim, but before the time of the council of Ephesus (431). Acacius, bishop of Aleppo, whom he celebrates in one of his poems, must therefore, as Bickell says[2], be the same Acacius who had a share in converting Rabbūlā to Christianity[3], and died at an extreme old age (it is said 110 years) in 432. His favourite metre was the pentasyllabic, which is known by his name, as the heptasyllabic by that of Ephraim, and the twelve-syllable line by that of Jacob of Sĕrūgh. Some of his poems have been edited by Overbeck in the often cited collection *S. Ephraemi Syri, &c., Opera Selecta*, pp. 251–336, namely, a

[1] In a passage cited by Assemani, *B.O.*, i. 166. Cardāḥī (*Liber Thes.*, pp. 25–27) places Balai's death in 460, but gives, as usual, no authority. This seems too late.

[2] *Conspectus*, p. 21; Thalhofer, *Bibliothek der Kirchenväter*, 41, p. 68.

[3] Overbeck, *S. Ephraemi Syri*, &c., *Opera Selecta*, p. 162, l. 20.

poem on the dedication of the newly built church in the town of Ḳen-neshrīn (Ḳinnesrīn), five poems in praise of Acacius, the late bishop of Aleppo, the first and eighth homilies on the history of Joseph, specimens of prayers, and a fragment on the death of Aaron[1]. [The whole ten books on the history of Joseph were published at Paris in 1887, *Histoire de Joseph par Saint Ephrem* (a 2nd edition in 1891), and also by Lamy in vol. iii. of Ephraim's works (see above).] Cyrillōnā composed a poem "on the locusts, and on (divine) chastisement, and on the invasion of the Huns[2]," in which he says: "The North is distressed and full of wars; and if Thou be neglectful, O Lord, they will again lay me waste. If the Huns, O Lord, conquer me, why do I seek refuge with the martyrs? If their swords lay me waste, why do I lay hold on Thy great Cross? If Thou givest up my cities unto them, where is the glory of Thy holy Church? A year is not yet at an end since they came forth and laid us waste and took my children captive; and lo, a second time they threaten our land that they will humble it." Now the invasion of the Huns took place in 395[3],

[1] See also Wenig, *Schola Syriaca, Chrestomathia*, pp. 160–162; Bickell, *Conspectus*, p. 46, note 5; Thalhofer, *Bibliothek*, 41, p. 67, and 44.

[2] See Wright, *Catal.*, p. 671, col. 1, No. 5, *a*.

[3] See *Chron. Edess.* in *B.O.*, i. 400, No. xl.; Dionysius

and this poem must have been written in the following year (396). The few remaining writings of Cyrillōnā, composed in various metres, have been edited by Bickell in the *Z.D.M.G.*, xxvii. p. 566 *sq.*, and translated by him in Thalhofer's *Bibliothek*, 41, pp. 9–63[1]. Bickell[2] is inclined to identify this Cyrillōnā with another writer of the same period, ʿAbhsamyā, a priest of Edessa, Ephraim's sister's son and a pupil of Zenobius; but his reasons do not seem to us sufficient. The *Chron. Edess.* (*B.O.*, i. 401) states that ʿAbhsamyā composed his hymns and discourses on the invasion of the Huns in 404; and Dionysius of Tell-Maḥrē (*B.O.*, i. 169) speaks of him in the year 397. Bar-Hebræus is less precise as to the date: after mentioning the death of Chrysostom (in 407), he adds that about this time Theodore of Mopsuestia died (429) and ʿAbhsamyā flourished, who "composed many discourses in the (heptasyllabic) metre of Mār Ephraim" on the invasion

of Tell-Maḥrē, *ibid.*, note 1; and an anonymous continuer of Eusebius in Land's *Anecd. Syr.*, i. 8, l. 2. Joshua Stylites (ed. Wright, p. 10, l. 1) specifies A. Gr. 707, which began with October 395.

[1] See also Wright, *Catal.*, pp. 670–671; Overbeck, *S. Ephraemi*, &c., *Opera Selecta*, pp. 379–381; Bickell, *Conspectus*, p. 34; Cardāḥī, *Liber Thes.*, pp. 27–29, who places his death in 400.

[2] See his *Conspectus*, p. 21; Thalhofer, *Bibl.*, 41, pp. 13, 16 (in the note).

of the Huns[1]. That 'Abhsamyā may have taken the name of Cyrillōnā at his ordination is of course possible, but it seems strange that none of these three writers should have mentioned it, if such were the case. On Bar-Hebræus's statement regarding the metre which he used in his discourses we do not insist; he might easily make a mistake in such a matter.

During the latter part of the 4th century, too, there lived in the island of Cyprus the abbot Gregory, who appears to have been sent thither from some monastery in Palestine as the spiritual head of the Syriac-speaking monks in the island[2]. He cherished friendly relations with Epiphanius, afterwards bishop of Salamis or Constantia (367–403), and a monk named Theodore. To these are addressed several of his discourses and letters; others are general exhortations to the monks under his charge[3] The discourses seem to be only portions of a work on the monastic life, which has not come down to us in a complete form, the "book" mentioned by 'Abhd-īshō' in *B.O.*, iii. 1, 191. In the letters he addresses Epiphanius as an older man speaking with authority to a younger; it is to be presumed, therefore,

[1] Bar-Hebræus, *Chron. Eccles.*, i. 133.
[2] See *B.O.*, i. 170–171.
[3] *Ibid.*, i. 172.

that they were written before Epiphanius became bishop.

With the 5th century commences the native historical literature of Syria. Previous to this time there existed martyrologies and lives of saints, martyrs, and other holy men, drawn up, in part at least, to meet the requirements of the services of the church. Such are, for example, the ancient martyrology in a manuscript of 411[1]; the *Doctrine of Addai*, in its present shape a product of the latter half of the 4th century[2]; the *Hypomnemata of Sharbēl*; and the *Martyrdoms of Bar-samyā, Bishop of Edessa, and the Deacon Ḥabbībh*, which all belong to about the same period[3]. This sort of legendary writing

[1] Brit. Mus. Add. 12150, f. 252, edited by Wright in the *Journal of Sacred Literature*, 1865–66, viii. 45, 423; see the *Acta Sanctorum*, October, vol. xii. 183–185. It can hardly be later than the middle of the 4th century.

[2] Edited in part by Cureton, in his *Ancient Syriac Documents*, from MSS. of the 5th and 6th centuries in the British Museum; and in full by Phillips from a MS. of the 6th century at St Petersburg, 1876. See also *Lettre d'Abgar ou Histoire de la Conversion des Édesséens*, translated from the Armenian version, Venice, 1868; Lipsius, *Die Edessenische Abgar-Sage*, 1880; Matthes, *Die Edessenische Abgar-Sage*, 1882; Mösinger, *Acta SS. Martyrum Edessenorum Sarbelii*, &c., No. I, 1874; [Tixeront, *Les Origines de l'Église d'Édesse*, Paris, 1888].

[3] See Cureton, *Anc. Syr. Doc.*, and Lipsius, *Die Edess. Abgar-Sage*, p. 41 *sq.*

was carried on to a much later date[1]. The *History of Bēth Sĕlōkh and its Martyrs*, for instance, can hardly have been composed before the 6th century, if so early[2]; and the *Acts of Mārī* must be still later[3]. No larger collection of such documents had, however, been attempted before the time of Mārūthā, bishop of Maiperḳaṭ[4], a man of much weight and authority, who was twice sent by the emperor Theodosius II. on embassies to the Persian monarch Yazdegerd I., and presided at the councils of Seleucia or Ctesiphon, under the catholics Isaac and Yabh-

[1] See Hoffmann, *Auszüge aus syr. Akten pers. Märtyrer.* [A large collection of martyrdoms of different dates is contained in (Bedjan's) *Acta Martyrum et Sanctorum*, of which vols. i.-iv., Paris, 1890-94, have thus far appeared. Other Syriac martyrdoms are to be found in *Analecta Bollandiana.* See also Budge, *The Martyrdom of Isaac of Tiphre* (in Trans. Soc. Bibl. Archæo. ix. 74–111); Amiaud, *La Légende Syriaque de Saint Alexis*, Paris, 1889; Feige, *Die Geschichte des Mâr 'Abhdîšô'*, &c., Kiel, 1890; and Nöldeke's paper on *Some Syrian Saints* in *Sketches from Eastern History* (Eng. trans. published by A. & C. Black, 1892).]

[2] See Mösinger, *Monumenta Syr.*, ii. 63, and Hoffmann, *op. cit.*, p. 45.

[3] See Abbeloos, *Acta S. Maris*, 1885, p. 47, where, as Nöldeke has pointed out, the writer confounds Ardashēr, the first king of the Sāsānian dynasty, with the last king of that line, Yazdegerd III., who was overthrown by the Arabs in the battle of Nihāwand, A.H. 21 (642 A.D.).

[4] Called by the Greeks Martyropolis, in Syriac Mĕdhīnath Sāhdē, and by the Arabs Maiyāfāriḳīn.

alāhā respectively[1]. He is said, too, to have been a skilful physician[2]. To him 'Abhd-īshō' assigns the following works[3],—"A book of martyrdoms, anthems and hymns on the martyrs, and a translation of the canons of the council of Nicæa, with a history of that council." The last named of these he undertook at the request of Isaac, catholicus of Seleucia, who died in 416[4]. The canons which pass under his name are those of the council of Seleucia in 410[5]. But his great work was the *Book of Martyrs*, containing accounts of those who suffered for the Christian faith under Sapor II., Yazdegerd I., and Bahrām V., to which he prefixed two discourses on the glory of the martyrs and on their torments. One of these narratives claims to have been recorded by an eye-witness, Isaiah, the son of Ḥadhbō (or Ḥadhabhū), of Arzan (Ἀρζανηνή), one of the Persian king's horsemen[6]. Portions of this work survive in the British Museum in MSS. of the

1 See *B.O.*, i. 174 *sq.*; Bar-Hebræus, *Chron. Eccles.*, i. 121, ii. 45, 49.

2 *B.O.*, iii. 1, 73, and note 4.

3 *Ibid.*, *loc. cit.*

4 *Ibid.*, i. 195.

5 See Lamy, *Concilium Seleuciæ et Ctesiphonti habitum anno* 410; comp. S. E. Assemani, *Codd. MSS. Orient. Bibl. Palat. Medic.*, p. 94.

6 *B.O.*, i. 15.

5th and 6th centuries, as well as in some of later date both there and in the Vatican. They have been edited by S. E. Assemani in the first volume of the *Acta Sanctorum Martyrum*, 1748[1]. The commentary on the Gospels mentioned by Assemani is really by Mārūthā, the maphriān of Taghrīth (Tekrīt), who is also the author of the anaphora or liturgy[2]. Of him we shall have occasion to speak afterwards (see p. 136 *infra*). It is possible too that some of the above-mentioned Acts may belong not to the work of Mārūthā but to that of Aḥā, the successor of Isaac in the see of Seleucia, who likewise wrote a history of the Persian martyrs and a life of his teacher ʿAbhdā, the head of the school in the monastery of Dōr-Ḳōnī or Dair-Ḳunnā (where the apostle Mārī was buried)[3].

About this time evil days came upon the Christian church in Syria. Paul of Samosāta, Diodore of Tarsus, and Theodore of Mopsuestia had paved the way for Nestorius. The doctrines of these writers were warmly espoused by many of the Syrian theologians; and the warfare raged

[1] See also *B.O.*, i. 181–194. There is a German translation by Zingerle, *Echte Acten der h. Märtyrer des Morgenlandes*, 2 vols., 1836.

[2] *B.O.*, i. 179.

[3] *Ibid.*, ii. 401, iii. 1, 369; also Abbeloos, *Acta S. Maris*, pp. 72 *sq.*, 88.

for many years in and around Edessa, till it ended in the total destruction of the great Persian school by the order of the emperor Zeno (488–489)[1]. Rabbūlā, a native of Ḳen-neshrīn (Ḳinnesrīn), whose father was a heathen priest but his mother a Christian, was converted to Christianity by Eusebius, bishop of Ḳen-neshrīn, and Acacius, bishop of Aleppo. He voluntarily gave up all his property, forsook his wife, and became a monk in the convent of Abraham near his native city. On the death of Diogenes, bishop of Edessa, he was appointed his successor (411–412). His admiring biographer depicts him as a model bishop, and he certainly appears to have been active and energetic in teaching and preaching and attending to the needs of the poor[2]. In the theological disputes of the day he seems at first to have sided, if not with Nestorius, at least with those who were averse to extreme measures, such as John, patriarch of Antioch, and his partisans; but afterwards he joined the opposite party, and became a warm champion of the doctrines of Cyril, which he supported at the council of Edessa (431). From this time onward he was

[1] *B.O.*, i. 353, 406.

[2] See his biography in Overbeck, *S. Ephraemi*, &c., *Opera Selecta*, p. 159 *sq.*, especially pp. 170–181; translated by Bickell, in Thalhofer's *Bibliothek*, Nos. 102–104.

a staunch opponent of Nestorianism, and even resorted to such an extreme measure as burning the writings of Theodore of Mopsuestia. Hence Ibas in his letter to Mārī speaks of him as "the tyrant of Edessa," and Andrew of Samosāta, writing to Alexander of Hierapolis in 432, complains bitterly of his persecution of the orthodox (*i.e.*, the Nestorians). He died in August 435[1]. Of the writings of Rabbūlā but little has come down to us. There is a sermon extant in manuscript[2], enjoining the bestowing of alms on behalf of the souls of the dead and prohibiting all feasting on the occasion of their commemoration. Another sermon, preached at Constantinople, is directed against the errors of Nestorius[3]. There are also extant canons and orders addressed to the monks and clergy of his diocese[4], and a number of hymns, of which Overbeck has printed some specimens[5]. He also rendered into Syriac Cyril's treatise *De Recta in Dominum nostrum J. C. Fide ad Theodosium Imperatorem*[6] from a copy which

[1] *B.O.*, i. 403.

[2] *Codd. MSS. Orient. Bibl. Palat. Medic.*, p. 107.

[3] See Overbeck, *S. Ephraemi*, &c., *Opera Selecta*, pp. 239–244; translated by Bickell.

[4] *Ibid.*, pp. 210–221.

[5] *Ibid.*, pp. 245–248, 362–378.

[6] See Wright, *Catal.*, p. 719.

was sent to him by the author[1]. His biographer intended to translate into Syriac a collection of forty-six of his letters, written in Greek "to priests and emperors and nobles and monks[2]"; but of these only a few remain, *e.g.*, to Andrew of Samosāta, condemning his treatise against the twelve anathemas of Cyril[3]; to Cyril, regarding Theodore of Mopsuestia[4]; and to Gemellinus of Perrhē, about certain monks and other persons who misused the sacred elements as ordinary food[5].

Rabbūlā was succeeded in the see of Edessa (435) by Īhībhā or Hībhā (Græcized Ibas)[6], who in his younger days had been one of the translators of Theodore's works in the Persian school[7]. This, with his letter to Mārī the Persian[8] and other utterances, led to his being charged with Nestorianism. He was acquitted by the two synods of Tyre and Beirūt, but condemned by

1 Comp. the letter of Cyril to Rabbūlā, Overbeck, *op. cit.*, pp. 228–229.

2 See Overbeck, *op. cit.*, p. 200.

3 *Ibid.*, p. 222.

4 *Ibid.*, p. 223, a fragment.

5 *Ibid.*, pp. 230–238. The shorter fragment should follow the longer one.

6 *B.O.*, i. 199.

7 *Ibid.*, iii. 1, 85; Wright, *Catal.*, pp. 107, col. 2, 644, col. 1.

8 See Labbe, *Concil.*, ix. 51; Mansi, vii. 241.

the second council of Ephesus (449)[1], and Nonnus was substituted in his room. He was restored, however, at the end of two years by the council of Chalcedon, and sat till October 457, when he was succeeded by Nonnus[2], who in his turn was followed by Cyrus in 471. Besides the writings above-mentioned, 'Abhd-īshō' attributes to Ibas[3]

[1] The so-called ληστρικὴ σύνοδος or *latrocinium Ephesinum*. Of the first session of this council a portion is extant in Syriac in Brit. Mus. Add. 12156, ff. 51b–61a (written before 562), containing the acta in the cases of Flavian of Antioch and Eusebius of Dorylæum. Add. 14530 (dated 535) contains the second session, comprising the acta in the cases of Ibas, his nephew Daniel of Ḥarrān, Irenæus of Tyre, Aquilinus of Byblus, Sophronius of Tellā or Constantina, Theodoret of Cyrrhus, and Domnus of Antioch. These documents have been translated into German by Hoffmann, *Verhandlungen der Kirchenversammlung zu Ephesus am* xxii. *August* CDXLIX., &c., 1873; into French by Martin, *Actes du Brigandage d'Éphèse*, 1874; and into English (with the assistance of a German scholar) by the Rev. S. G. F. Perry, *The Second Synod of Ephesus*, 1881. See also Martin, *Le Pseudo-Synode connu dans l'Histoire sous le nom de Brigandage d'Éphèse*, &c., 1875; and Perry, *An Ancient Syriac Document purporting to be the record in its chief features of the Second Synod of Ephesus*, &c., part i., 1867. Mr Perry printed a complete edition of the Syriac text at the Clarendon Press, Oxford, but no one seems to know what has become of the copies. The copies of the English translation were purchased at the sale of Mr Perry's library by Mr Quaritch.

[2] *B.O.*, i. 257.

[3] *Ibid.*, iii. 1, 86. These are of course utterly ignored by Assemani in vol. i.

"a commentary on Proverbs, sermons and metrical homilies (*madhrāshē*), and a disputation with a heretic"; but none of these appear to have come down to us.

During this stormy period the name of Acacius, bishop of Āmid, is mentioned as the author of certain epistles[1]. The great event of his life, which is referred by Socrates (bk. vii. 21) to the year 422, is thus briefly recorded in the *Martyrologium Romanum Gregorii XIII.* (Malines, 1859), 9th April: "Amidæ in Mesopotamia sancti Acatii episcopi, qui pro redimendis captivis etiam ecclesiæ vasa conflavit ac vendidit." The said captives were Persian subjects, who were thus ransomed and sent back to their king and country[2]. Acacius was doubtless a favourer of Nestorianism, for his letters were thought worthy of a commentary by Mārī, bishop of Bēth Hardashēr[3], the correspondent of Ibas[4].

About the same time rose one of the stars of Syriac literature, Isaac, commonly called the

[1] *B.O.*, iii. 1, 51.

[2] *Ibid.*, i. 195–196.

[3] Bēth Hardashēr or Bēth Hartashēr, in Persian Weh-Ardashēr or Beh-Ardashēr, Arabicized Bahurasīr, close by Seleucia, on the right bank of the Tigris. See Hoffmann, *Verhandlungen der Kirchenversammlung zu Ephesus*, &c., p. 93, note 160.

[4] *B.O.*, iii. 1, 172.

Great, of Antioch[1]. He was a native of Āmid, but went as a young man to Edessa, where he enjoyed the teaching of Zenobius, the disciple of Ephraim[2]. Thence he removed to Antioch, where he lived as priest and abbot of one of the many convents in its immediate neighbourhood. In his younger days he would seem to have travelled farther than most of his countrymen, as it is stated that he visited Rome and other cities[3]. With this agrees what is recorded by Dionysius of Tell-Maḥrē[4] as to his having composed poems on the secular games celebrated at Rome in 404, and on the capture of the city by Alaric in 410, which shows that he took a more than ordinary interest in the Western capital. Isaac died in or about

[1] *B.O.*, i. 207–234; Bickell, in Thalhofer's *Bibliothek*, No. 44, and *Conspectus*, p. 22.

[2] That he is identical with Isaac, the disciple of Ephraim (as some have supposed), seems wholly unlikely. He may possibly have seen Ephraim in the flesh, but this is very doubtful, considering the date of his own death. Even Jacob of Edessa appears to have got into some confusion on this subject (see Wright, *Catal.*, p. 603, col. 2).

[3] Land, *Anecd. Syr.*, iii. 84.

[4] *B.O.*, i. 208–209; see *Dionysii Telmahharensis Chronici liber I.*, ed. Tullberg, 1850, p. 52, and *Eusebii Canonum Epitome ex Dionysii Telm. Chronico petita*, by C. Siegfried and H. Gelzer, 1884, p. 29. The difficulty was first cleared up by Scaliger, who in his *Thesaurus Temporum*, *Animadv.* No. MDLXIV., proposed σηκλαρίων.

460, soon after the destruction of Antioch by the earthquake of 459, on which he wrote a poem[1]. Isaac's works are nearly as voluminous and varied as those of Ephraim, with which indeed they are often confounded in MSS. and in the Roman edition[2]. They were gathered into one corpus by the Jacobite patriarch John bar Shūshan or Susanna, who began in his old age to transcribe and annotate them, but was hindered from completing his task by death (1073)[3]. Assemani has given a list of considerably more than a hundred metrical homilies from MSS. in the Vatican[4]. Of these part of one on the Crucifixion was edited by Overbeck[5], and another on the love of learning by Zingerle[6]. But it has been left to Bickell to collect and translate all the extant writings of this Syrian father and to commence the publication of them. Out of nearly 200 metrical

[1] *B.O.*, i. 211. [2] See Bickell, *Conspectus*, p. 23, note.

[3] *B.O.*, i. 214-215, ii. 355; Bar-Hebræus, *Chron. Eccles.*, i. 447.

[4] *B.O.*, i. 214-234.

[5] *S. Ephraemi Syri*, &c., *Opera Selecta*, pp. 379–381. [This homily may be Cyrillōnā's or Balai's: see above, p. 41, n. 1, and Bickell in *Z.D.M.G.*, xxvii. p. 571, n. 1.]

[6] *Monumenta Syriaca*, i. 13–20; see also some extracts in Zingerle's *Chrestom. Syr.*, pp. 299 *sq.*, 387 *sq.* Zingerle has translated large portions of the homilies on the Crucifixion into German in the *Tübinger Theolog. Quartalschrift*, 1870, 1. Further, Cardāḥī, *Liber Thes.*, pp. 21–25.

homilies his first volume contains in 307 pages only fifteen, and his second brings us in 353 pages only as far as No. 37[1]. Some of these poems have a certain historical value, such as the second homily on fasting, probably written soon after 420[2], the two homilies on the destruction of the town of Bēth Ḥūr by the Arabs (*c.* 457)[3], and the two against persons who resort to soothsayers[4]. Others possess some interest as bearing on the theological views of the author, who combats the errors of Nestorius and Eutyches[5]. One of the longest and most wearisome is a stupendous poem of 2137 verses on a parrot which proclaimed *ἅγιος ὁ Θεός* in the streets of Antioch[6]. Another on repentance runs to the length of 1929 verses. In prose Isaac seems to have written very little; at least Bickell[7] mentions only "various questions and answers, an ascetic narrative and ascetic rules."

Concerning Isaac's contemporary Dādhā we know but little[8]. He was a monk from the

[1] *S. Isaaci Antiocheni, Doctoris Syrorum, Opera Omnia*, ed. G. Bickell, part i., 1873; part ii., 1877. We hope soon to receive the remaining parts at his hands.

[2] *B.O.*, i. 227; Bickell, i. 280.

[3] *B.O.*, i. 225; Bickell, i. 207, 227.

[4] Bickell, ii. 205 *sq.*

[5] See Bickell's translations in Thalhofer's *Bibliothek*, 44.

[6] Bickell, i. 85.

[7] *Opera*, i. p. viii.

[8] See Land, *Anecd. Syr.*, iii. 84.

neighbourhood of Āmid, who was sent by the people of that city to Constantinople on account of the ravages of war and famine, to obtain remission of the taxes or some similar relief, and was well received by the emperor. He is said to have written about three hundred tracts on various topics connected with the Scriptures and on the saints, besides poems (*madhrāshē*).

Here, too, we may record the name of Simeon the Stylite, who died in 459 or soon after[1]. The Monophysites contend that he held their theological views, and accordingly we find in a MS. of the 8th century a letter of his to the emperor Leo regarding Theodoret of Cyrrhus, who had come to him and tried to pervert him to the opinions of the Dyophysites[2], and in another MS., of about the same age, three letters to the emperor Leo, to the abbot Jacob of Kaphrā Rĕḥīmā, and to John I., patriarch of Antioch, all tending to prove that he rejected the council of Chalcedon[3]. A third MS., of the 6th century, contains certain "precepts and admonitions" addressed by him to the brethren[4].

1 See Bar-Hebræus, *Chron. Eccles.*, i. 142, 181, and note 2; *B.O.*, i. 252, 405.

2 Wright, *Catal.*, p. 951, No. xxix.

3 *Ibid.*, p. 986, No. 33.

4 *Ibid.*, p. 1153, col. 1.

There is extant in very old MSS.[1] a *Life* of Simeon, full of absurd stories, which has been edited by S. E. Assemani in the *Acta Sanctorum Martyrum*, vol. ii. 268 *sq.*; [and again (from Brit. Mus. Add. 14484) in (Bedjan's) *Acta Martyrum et Sanctorum*, vol. iv. 507 *sq.*]. At the end of it there is a letter by one Cosmas[2], priest of the village of Panīr, written in the name of his congregation to the Stylite, promising implicit obedience to all his precepts and orders, and requesting his prayers on their behalf; but there is nothing whatever to show that this Cosmas was the author of the *Life* or had any share in writing it[3].

About this time we find Dādh-īshō', the catholicus of Seleucia (421–456)[4], composing his commentaries on the books of Daniel, Kings, and Bar-Sīrā or Ecclesiasticus[5]. But the chief seat of Nestorian scholarship and literary activity was still the Persian school of Edessa, where

[1] *E.g.*, Cod. Vat. clx., transcribed 473; Brit. Mus. Add. 14484, of the 6th century.

[2] *B.O.*, i. 237.

[3] Assemani is also mistaken in supposing that the *Life* was composed at the request of Simeon, the son of Apollonius, and Bar-Ḥāṭar (?), the son of Ūdhān (Uranius?). These are merely the persons who paid for the writing of this portion of Cod. Vat. clx.

[4] See Bar-Hebræus, *Chron. Eccles.*, ii. 57, note 1.

[5] *B.O.*, iii. 1, 214.

Bar-ṣaumā and other teachers were actively engaged in defending and propagating their peculiar tenets. Bar-ṣaumā, if we may believe the scurrilous Monophysite Simeon of Bēth Arshām[1], was originally the slave of one Mārā of Bēth Ḳardū[2], and bore at Edessa the nickname of *Sāḥē bēth ḳĕnaiyā*[3]. He was at Edessa in 449, when his expulsion was called for by the rabble[4]. In what year it actually took place we do not know, but we afterwards find him busy in the East under the catholicus Bābhōyah or Babuæus (from about 457 to 483)[5] and his successor Acacius (from about 484 to 496), during which period he was bishop of Nisībis[6]. Of his personal character and work this is not the place to attempt to form a judgment; but the reader

[1] *B.O.*, i. 351.

[2] On the left bank of the Tigris, over against Jazīrat Ibn 'Omar.

[3] "The Swimmer, or Bather, among the Reeds," meaning "the wild boar." See Hoffmann, *Verhandl. d. Kirchenversam. zu Ephesus*, &c., p. 91, note 114.

[4] Hoffmann, *op. cit.*, p. 14; Bar-Hebræus, *Chron. Eccles.*, ii. 55, note 1.

[5] Bar-Hebræus, *Chron. Eccles.*, ii. 57, note 1.

[6] See *B.O.*, iii. 1, 66, note 7, compared with i. 351, note 4, and ii. 407, note 2. [Guidi has shown from the Syriac *Synodicum* that Bar-ṣaumā was bishop of Nisībis in 485 but that his successor Hosea was in office in 496 (*Z.D.M.G.*, xliii. 412; *Gli statuti della Scuola di Nisibi*, Rome, 1890, p. 3).]

should beware of placing implicit trust in the statements of bitter and unscrupulous theological opponents like Simeon of Bēth Arshām, Bar-Hebræus, and Assemani. Bar-ṣaumā does not appear to have written much, as 'Abhd-īshō'[1] mentions only parænetic and funeral sermons, hymns of the class called *turgāmē*[2], metrical homilies (*madhrāshē*), letters, and an anaphora or liturgy.

A fellow-worker with him both at Edessa and Nisībis was Narsai (or Narsē), of Ma'allĕthā or Ma'althāyā[3], whom Simeon of Bēth Arshām calls "the Leper[4]," whereas his co-sectarians style him "the Harp of the Holy Spirit." He was especially famous as a writer of hymns and other metrical compositions, his favourite metre being that of six syllables[5]. He fled from Edessa to escape the wrath of the bishop Cyrus (471–498), probably in the year 489, and died at Nisībis early in the next century[6]. Narsai's works, as

[1] *B.O.*, iii. 1, 66.

[2] See Badger, *The Nestorians*, ii. 19.

[3] Hoffmann, *Auszüge*, p. 208; Badger, *The Nestorians*, i. 174.

[4] Perhaps in a spiritual sense only, though Assemani thinks otherwise; see *B.O.*, i. 352 and note 5, 354; iii. 1, 63.

[5] *B.O.*, iii. 1, 65, note 6.

[6] See Bar-Hebræus, *Chron. Eccles.*, ii. 77; *B.O.*, ii. 407.

enumerated by 'Abhd-īshō'[1], consist of commentaries on the first four books of the Pentateuch, Joshua, Judges, and Ecclesiastes, Isaiah and the twelve minor prophets, Jeremiah, Ezekiel, and Daniel, twelve volumes of metrical discourses (360 in number)[2], a liturgy, expositions of the order of celebrating the Eucharist and of baptism, parænetic and funeral sermons, hymns of several sorts[3], and a book entitled *On the Corruption of Morals.*

Mārī the Persian has been already mentioned as the correspondent of Ibas. Besides the commentary on the epistles of Acacius (see above, p. 51), he wrote a commentary on the book of Daniel and a controversial treatise against the magi[4] of Nisībis[5]. Acacius, catholicus of Seleucia

[1] *B.O.*, iii. 1, 65, 66.

[2] Some of these are probably contained in the Berlin MSS. Sachau 174–176 (*mēmrē dha-mĕdhabbĕrānūthā*, on the life of our Lord) and 219 (two poems on Joseph, and two others).

[3] Two of them are often found in the Nestorian Psalter. See, for example, Brit. Mus. Add. 7156 (Rosen, *Catal.*, p. 12, col. 2, No. 3a, c) and Add. 17219 (Wright, *Catal.*, p. 134, col. 2, No. 3 a, c).

[4] *Mĕghūshē*, from *magu*, *mag*, the Persian priesthood, the head of whom in each district was the *magupat*, *mogpet*, or *mōbedh*. See Nöldeke, *Geschichte der Perser und Araber zur Zeit der Sasaniden*, p. 450.

[5] *B.O.*, iii. 1, 171.

(*c.* 484–496), composed discourses on fasting and on the faith, as also against the Monophysites, and translated into Persian for the king Ḳawādh a treatise on the faith by Elisha, bishop of Nisībis, the successor of Bar-ṣaumā[1]. Assemani tries hard to cleanse Acacius from the stain of Nestorianism, but, as Abbeloos remarks[2], "vereor ne Æthiopem dealbare voluerit; nam omnia tum Jacobitarum tum Nestorianorum monumenta, quæ ipse recitat, contrarium testantur." Mīkhā or Micah, another member of the band of exiled Edessenes[3], became bishop of Lāshōm[4]. He wrote a commentary on the books of Kings, a discourse on his predecessor Sabhr-īshō', another on a person whose name is written Ḳnṭropos[5], and a tract entitled *The Five Reasons of the Mautĕbhē*[6]. To these writers may

[1] *B.O.*, iii. 1, 389. Elisha is called by some authorities Hosea; *ibid.*, ii. 407, iii. 1, 429. [So the Syriac *Synodicon* as cited by Guidi in *Z.D.M.G.*, xliii. 412, and *Gli statuti della Scuola di Nisibi*, p. 3.]

[2] Bar-Hebræus, *Chron. Eccles.*, ii. 74, note 2.

[3] *B.O.*, i. 352–353. His enemies gave him the nickname of Dagon.

[4] Now Lāsim, a short distance south-west of Dāḳūḳ or Tā'ūḳ, in Bēth Garmai; see Hoffmann, *Auszüge*, p. 274.

[5] Vocalized Ḳenṭropos or Ḳanṭropos; *B.O.*, iii. 1, 170, l. 2.

[6] Meaning probably the division of the Psalter into three kathismata (Bickell, *Conspectus*, p. 92); see *B.O.*, iii. 1, 71, note 2.

be added two others,—Yazīdādh[1], who is also said to have belonged to the Edessene school and to have compiled "a book of collectanea (*lukkāṭē*)[2]," and Ara, who wrote a treatise against the magi or Persian priesthood, and another against the followers of Bardesānes with the contemptuous title of *Ḥabhshōshyāthā* or "the Beetles[3]."

The Persian school at Edessa was, as we have already hinted, the chief seat of the study of Greek during the early days of the Syrian literature. Of the most ancient translators we know nothing; but the oldest MSS. are Edessene, viz., the famous MS. in the British Museum, Add. 12150, dated towards the end of 411, and the equally well known codex at St Petersburg, written in 462. The former contains the *Recognitiones* of Clement, the discourses of Titus of Bostra against the Manichees, the *Theophania* of Eusebius, and his history of the confessors in Palestine; the latter, the *Ecclesiastical History* of Eusebius. Now, as the text presented by these MSS. has evidently passed through the hands of several successive scribes, it seems to

[1] For Yazed-dādh or Īzad-dādh, like Yazed-panāh, Yazed-bōzedh; see Hoffmann, *Auszüge*, p. 88, note 796.

[2] *B.O.*, iii. 1, 226.

[3] Of Ara we seem to know absolutely nothing; his very *floruit* is uncertain, and he may have belonged to the previous century; *B.O.*, iii. 1, 230.

follow that these books were translated into Syriac in the lifetime of the authors themselves, or very soon after, for Eusebius died in 340 and Titus in 371. Very likely the one or the other may have had a friend at the chief seat of Syriac learning who was willing to perform for him the same kind office that Rabbūla undertook for Cyril[1]. A little later on our information becomes fuller and more exact. Ma'nā[2], a Persian by race[3], from the town of Bēth Hardashēr, was resident at Edessa in the earlier part of the 5th century, and is mentioned by Simeon of Bēth Arshām among the distinguished Nestorian scholars whom he holds up to ridicule[4]. His nickname was *Shāthē ḳeṭmā*, "the

[1] See above, p. 48, and compare Merx, "De Eusebianæ Historiæ Eccles. Versionibus, Syriaca et Armeniaca," in *Atti del IV. Congresso Internazionale degli Orientalisti*, Florence, 1880, i. 199 *sq.*, especially pp. 201–202. It may here be mentioned that the literature of Armenia is largely indebted in its earliest days to that of Syria, not only for the translation of Eusebius's *Eccles. History*, but for such works as the *Doctrine of Addai* and the *Homilies* of Aphraates, wrongly ascribed to Jacob of Nisībis.

[2] So the name is written by Mārī bar Shĕlēmōn, whom Assemani follows, *B.O.*, iii. 1, 376, pronouncing it, however, Ma'nē or Maanes. Elias of Nisībis also gives Ma'nā (Bar-Hebræus, *Chron. Eccles.*, ii. 53, note 2); but Bar-Hebræus himself (*loc. cit.*) has Maghnā, which Abbeloos latinizes Magnes.

[3] His Persian name is unknown to us.

[4] *B.O.*, i. 352.

Drinker of Ashes." Ma'nā devoted himself to the task of translating into Syriac the commentaries of Theodore of Mopsuestia during the lifetime of that great theologian, who did not die till 429. He must, however, have withdrawn from Edessa at a comparatively early period, as he was bishop of Persis[1] prior to 420, in which year (the last of his reign) Yazdegerd I. made him catholicus of Seleucia, in succession to Yabh-alāhā[2]. He had, it appears, translated a number of books from Syriac into Persian (Pahlavī), and thus probably ingratiated himself with the king[3]. However, he soon fell under the royal displeasure, was degraded from his office, and ordered to retire to Persis, where he resumed his former duties[4], and so incurred the anger of Yazdegerd's successor, Pērōz[5]. Ma'nā's work, the exact extent of which is not known to us, was carried on and completed by other members of the Persian school,—such as Acacius the catholicus and Yazīdādh; John of Bēth Garmai, afterwards bishop of Bēth Sārī (or Sĕrāi ?), and Abraham the Mede, disciples of Narsai; Mīkhā, afterwards bishop of Lāshōm in Bēth Garmai; Paul bar Ḳaḳai (or Ḳaḳī), after-

1 Bar-Hebræus, *Chron. Eccles.*, ii. 55, 63.

2 *B.O.*, ii. 401. 3 *Ibid.*, iii. 1, 376.

4 Bar-Hebræus, *Chron. Eccles.*, ii. 63.

5 *B.O.*, ii. 402; iii. 1, 377.

wards bishop of Lādhān in al-Ahwāz; ʻAbhshoṭā (?) of Nineveh, and others[1],—who are expressly said to "have taken away with them" (*appēḳ ʻammĕhōn*) from Edessa, and disseminated throughout the East, the writings of Theodore and Nestorius[2]. Ibas himself was one of these translators in his younger days (see above, p. 49). About the same time with Maʻnā's translations began the Aristotelian studies of the Syrian Nestorians. To understand and translate the writings of their favourite Greek theologians, Paul of Samosāta, Diodore of Tarsus, Theodore of Mopsuestia, and Nestorius himself, not to mention Theodoret[3] of Cyrrhus, required a considerable knowledge of the Aristotelian logic. Hence the labours of Probus (Πρόβος, in Syriac *Prōbhos, Prōbhā,* or *Prōbhē*), who translated and commented on the Περὶ ἑρμηνείας[4], and probably treated in a similar manner other parts of the

[1] *B.O.*, i. 351–354.

[2] *Ibid.*, i. 350; iii. 1, 226, note 8.

[3] His *Eranistes* (of which the fourth book is a *demonstratio per syllogismos* of the incarnation) appears as the name of an *author* in ʻAbhd-Ishōʻ's *Catalogue* (*B.O.*, iii. 1, 41), under the form of Eranistatheos, or something similar.

[4] See Hoffmann, *De Hermeneuticis apud Syros Aristoteleis*, 1869. MSS.,—Berlin, Alt. Best. 36, 9, 10; Brit. Mus. Add. 14660. The translation may possibly be even anterior to Probus.

*Organon*[1]. It is not easy to fix his date precisely. 'Abhd-īshō'[2] makes him contemporary with Ibas and another translator named Kūmī [or Kumai]. If the Berlin MS. Sachau 226 can be trusted, he was archdeacon and archiater at Antioch. Hoffmann[3] has assigned reasons for supposing him not to be anterior to the Athenian expositor Syrianus (433–450 ?).

Whilst the Nestorians were thus making rapid progress all over the East, another heresy was spreading in the West. Eutyches had found followers in Syria, among others Bar-ṣaumā the archimandrite, a man famous for his piety and asceticism[4], who represented the abbots of Syria

[1] Berlin, Sachau 226, 1, is described as "Isagoge des Porphyrius, von Probus, Presbyter, Archidiacon, und Archiater in Antiochien"; and in the same MS., No 8, is "Erklärung der Analytica von Probus," with an "Einleitung in d. Erkl. d. Anal. von Probus," No. 7.

[2] *B.O.*, iii. 1, 85.

[3] *Op. cit.*, pp. 144–145. The name of Fūbrī or Phubrius, which appears as a variation of Probus in Hottinger's *Bibl. Orient.*, in Assemani (*B.O.*, iii. 1, 85, note 5), in Renan (*De Philosophia Peripatetica apud Syros*, p. 14), and in other books on this subject, has nothing to do with that of Probus, but is an error for Ḳuwairī, Abū Isḥāḳ Ibrāhīm, a Syro-Arabian Aristotelian who lived about the beginning of the 10th century. See the *Fihrist*, p. 262; Ibn Abī Oṣaibi'ah, i. 234; Wüstenfeld, *Gesch. d. Arab. Aerzte*, p. 24, No. 62, "Futherī oder Fubrī."

[4] All "hypocrisy" in the eyes of Assemani, *B.O.*, ii. 2; "scelestissimus pseudo-monachus," p. 9.

at the second council of Ephesus[1], and was afterwards condemned by the council of Chalcedon[2]. He died in 458[3]. His life was written by his disciple Samuel, in much the same style as that of Simon Stylites, and is extant in several MSS. in the British Museum[4]. His memory has always been held in the greatest reverence by the Jacobites. The Armenians, according to Assemani[5], keep his commemoration on the 1st of February, the Syrians and Copts on the 3rd. The decisions of the council of Chalcedon produced an immediate and irreparable breach in the Eastern Church; and the struggle of the rival factions was carried on with desperate fury alike at Constantinople, Antioch, and Alexandria. In Syria the persecution of the Monophysites was violent during the years 518–521, under the emperor Justin, and again in 535 and the following years, under Justinian, when they seemed in a fair way of being completely crushed by brute force.

[1] Bar-Hebræus, *Chron. Eccles.*, i. 161–165; Hoffmann, *Verhandl. d. Kirchenversammlung zu Ephesus*, &c., p. 4, l. 39.

[2] Bar-Hebræus, *loc. cit.*, 179.

[3] *Ibid.*, 181.

[4] *B.O.*, ii. 296, also p. cxlviii. No. 3; Wright, *Catal.*, p. 1123.

[5] *B.O.*, ii. 9; comp. Wright, *Catal.*, p. 175, col. 2, No. 3, and p. 311, No. cclxxxvii.

The first name to be mentioned here, as belonging to both the 5th and 6th centuries, is that of Jacob of Sĕrūgh, one of the most celebrated writers of the Syrian Church[1], "the flute of the Holy Spirit and the harp of the believing church." There are no less than three biographies of him extant in Syriac,—the first, by his namesake Jacob of Edessa[2]; the second, anonymous[3]; the third, a lengthy metrical panegyric, said to have been written for his commemoration[4] by a disciple of his named George[5]. This, however, seems, from the whole tone of the composition, to be unlikely, and Bickell is probably right in supposing the author to be George, bishop of Sĕrūgh, a contemporary of Jacob of Edessa[6].

1 *B.O.*, i. 283 *sq.*; Matagne, in *Acta Sanctorum*, October, vol. xii. 824, 927; Abbeloos, *De Vita et Scriptis S. Jacobi Batnarum Sarugi in Mesopotamia epi*, 1867; Bickell, *Conspectus*, p. 25; Bickell in Thalhofer, *Bibl. d. Kirchenväter*, 58; Martin, "Lettres de Jacques de Saroug aux Moines du Couvent de Mar Bassus, et à Paul d'Édesse," in *Z.D.M.G.*, xxx. (1876), p. 217.

2 *B.O.*, i. 286, 299; Martin, in *Z.D.M.G.*, xxx. p. 217, note 3.

3 Abbeloos, *op. cit.*, p. 311.

4 See Wright, *Catal.*, p. 311, No. ccclxxxix. The Armenians hold it on 25th September, the Jacobites on 29th June, 29th July, and 29th October.

5 Abbeloos, *op. cit.*, p. 24; *B.O.*, i. 286, 340.

6 See Bickell in Thalhofer, *Bibl.*, 58, p. 198.

Jacob was born at Kurtam, "a village on the river Euphrates," probably in the district of Sĕrūgh, in 451. His father was a priest, and, as his parents had been childless for many years, his birth was regarded as a reward for their alms, prayers, and vows. Whether he was educated at Edessa or not, he soon acquired a great reputation for learning and eloquence. He appears to have led a life of quiet work and study, and to have devoted himself in particular to literary composition. He became periodeutes of Ḥaurā in Sĕrūgh, whence we find him writing to the Christians of Najrān, and to the city of Edessa when threatened by the Persians[1]. As periodeutes he is mentioned in eulogistic terms by Joshua the Stylite[2] (503). In 519, when sixty-eight years old, he was made bishop of Baṭnān, the chief town of Sĕrūgh, where he died on 29th November 521. Jacob's prose writings are not numerous[3]. A liturgy is ascribed to him, and an order of baptism, the former of which has been translated by Renaudot[4] the latter edited by J. A. Assemani[5]. Further, he composed six festal homilies, one of which has

[1] Wright, *Catal.*, p. 520, Nos. 15, 16.
[2] *Chronicle*, ed. Wright, ch. liv. Joshua wrote in 507.
[3] *B.O.*, i. 300–305.
[4] *Liturgg. Orientt. Collectio*, ii. 356.
[5] *Cod. Liturg. Eccl. Univers.*, ii. 309, iii. 184.

been published by Zingerle[1], who has also translated the whole of them into German[2]; a discourse showing that we should not neglect or despise our sins[3]; another for the night of Wednesday in the third week of Lent[4]; and some short funeral sermons[5]. To him we also owe a life of Mār Ḥannīnā (died in 500), addressed to one Philotheus[6]. Of his letters a considerable number have been preserved, particularly in two MSS. in the British Museum, Add. 14587 and 17163, ff. 1–48[7]. Of these Martin has edited and translated the three epistles to the monks of the convent of Mār Bassus at Ḥārim[8], with a reply by the monks, and another letter to Paul, bishop of Edessa, from all of which it is evident that Jacob always was a Monophysite, and continued such to his death[9]. The letter to Stephen bar Ṣūdh-ailē is given, with an English version, by Frothing-

[1] *Mon. Syr.*, i. 91.

[2] *Sechs Homilien des h. Jacob von Sarug*, 1867.

[3] Wright, *Catal.*, p. 826, No. 16; comp. the Index, p. 1293, col. 1.

[4] *Ibid.*, p. 844, No. 32.

[5] *Ibid.*, p. 364, col. 2.

[6] *Ibid.*, p. 1113, No. 14; p. 1126, No. 16.

[7] *Ibid.*, Nos. dclxxii., dclxxiii., and comp. the Index, p. 1293, col. 1.

[8] *Ibid.*, p. 602, col. 2.

[9] See Martin, *Z.D.M.G.*, xxx. (1876), pp. 217–219.

ham[1]; and that to the Ḥimyarite Christians of Najrān has been edited and translated by Schröter in the *Z.D.M.G.*, xxxi. (1877), p. 360 *sq.* It belongs to the year 519 or 520[2]. According to Bar-Hebræus[3], he also wrote "a commentary on the six centuries of Evagrius, at the request of Mār George, bishop of the (Arab) tribes, who was his disciple." As George, bishop of the Arab tribes, was a contemporary of Jacob of Edessa, this statement seems to rest on some misapprehension; at all events no such work now exists. The paucity of Jacob's prose writings is more than compensated by a flood of metrical compositions, mostly in dodecasyllabic verse, or the four-syllable line thrice repeated. "He had," says Bar-Hebræus[4], "seventy amanuenses to copy out his metrical homilies, which were 760[5] in number, besides commentaries and letters and odes (*madhrāshē*) and hymns (*sughyāthā*)." Of these

[1] See his *Stephen bar Sudaili the Syrian Mystic and the Book of Hierotheos*, Leyden, 1886, p. 10 *sq.*

[2] See Guidi, *La Lettera di Simeone Vescovo di Bêth-Arśâm sopra i Martiri Omeriti*, 1881, p. 11.

[3] *Chron. Eccles.*, i. 191.

[4] *Loc. cit.*

[5] Jacob of Edessa says 763, of which that on the chariot of Ezekiel was the first, and that on Mary and Golgotha the last, which he left unfinished; see *B.O.*, i. 299; Abbeloos, *De Vita*, &c., p. 312.

homilies more than the half have perished, but nearly 300 are still preserved in European collections[1]. Very few of them have as yet been published, though many of them are by no means devoid of interest[2]. Indeed Jacob is on the whole

[1] Comp. *B.O.*, i. 305–339; Abbeloos, *op. cit.*, pp. 106–113.

[2] Zingerle has given extracts in the *Z.D.M.G.*, xii., xiii., xiv., xv., and xx., and in his *Chrest. Syr.*, pp. 360–386. The homily on Simeon Stylites has been published by Assemani in the *Acta S. Martyrum*, ii. 230 *sq.*, [and has anew appeared in vol. iv. 650 *sq.* of (Bedjan's) *Acta Martyrum et Sanctorum*]; that on virginity, fornication, &c., by Overbeck, *S. Ephraemi Syri*, &c., *Opera Selecta*, p. 385 *sq.*; that on Alexander the Great (perhaps spurious) by Knös, *Chrest. Syr.*, 1807, p. 66 *sq.* [and (a better edition) by Budge, *Zeitschrift f. Assyriologie*, vi. 359–404], (there is a German translation by A. Weber, *Des Môr Yakūb Gedicht über den gläubigen König Alexsandrûs*, 1852); on Ḥabbībh and on Guryā and Shamūnā, Edessene martyrs, with a *sūghīthā* on Edessa, by Cureton, *Ancient Syriac Documents*, pp. 86–98 [and in *Acta Martyrum et Sanctorum*, vol. i. 131 *sq.*, 160 *sq.*]; on Sharbēl by Mösinger, *Mon. Syr.*, ii. 52, and on the chariot of Ezekiel, with an Arabic translation, *ibid.*, p. 76; two on the Blessed Virgin Mary by Abbeloos, *De Vita*, &c., pp. 203–301; on Jacob at Bethel, on our Lord and Jacob, the church and Rachel, Leah and the synagogue, on the two birds (Lev. xiv. 4), on the two goats (Lev. xvi. 7), and on Moses' vail (Exod. xxxiv. 33) by Zingerle, *Mon. Syr.*, i. 21–90; on Tamar by J. Zingerle, 1871; on the palace which St Thomas built for the king of India in Heaven (perhaps spurious) by Schröter, in *Z.D.M.G.*, xxv. 321, xxviii. 584; on the fall of the idols by Martin, in *Z.D.M.G.*, xxix. 107; on the baptism

far more readable than Ephraim or Isaac of Antioch.

Very different from the gentle and studious bishop of Sĕrūgh was his contemporary and neighbour, the energetic and fiery Philoxenus of Mabbōgh. Aksĕnāyā or Philoxenus was a native of Taḥal, somewhere in Bēth Garmai, and studied at Edessa in the time of Ibas[1]. He was ordained bishop of Hierapolis or Mabbōgh (Manbij) by Peter the Fuller, patriarch of Antioch, in 485, and devoted his life to the advocacy of Monophysite doctrine. Twice he visited Constantinople in the service of his party, and suffered much (as was to be expected) at the hands of its enemies, for thus he writes in later years to the monks of the convent of Sĕnūn near Edessa; "What I endured from Flavian and Macedonius, who were archbishops of Antioch and of the capital, and previously from Calendion, is known and spoken of everywhere. I keep silence both as to what

of Constantine (perhaps spurious) by Frothingham, in the *Atti della Accademia dei Lincei* for 1881–82 (Rome, 1882). Bickell has translated into German (in Thalhofer, *Bibl.*, 58) the first homily on the Blessed Virgin Mary, that on Jacob at Bethel, on Moses' vail, and on Guryā and Shamūnā. Some of Jacob's homilies are extant in Arabic, and even in Ethiopic. His prayer as a child see in Overbeck, *op. cit.*, p. 382.

[1] *B.O.*, i. 353.

was plotted against me in the time of the Persian war among the nobles by the care of the aforesaid Flavian the heretic, and also as to what befell me in Edessa, and in the district of the Apameans, and in that of the Antiochians, when I was in the convent of the blessed Mār Bassus, and again in Antioch itself; and when I went up on two occasions to the capital, like things were done to me by the Nestorian heretics[1]." He succeeded at last in getting rid of his enemy Flavian in 512, and in the same year he presided at a synod in which his friend Severus was ordained patriarch of Antioch[2]. His triumph, however, was but short-lived, for Justin, the successor of Anastasius, sentenced to banishment in 519 fifty-four bishops who refused to accept the decrees of the council of Chalcedon, among whom were Severus, Philoxenus, Peter of Apamea, John of Tellā, Julian of Halicarnassus, and Mārā of Āmid. Philoxenus was exiled to Philippopolis in Thrace[3], and afterwards to Gangra in Paphlagonia, where he was murdered about the year 523. The Jacobite Church commemorates him on 10th December,

[1] *B.O.*, ii. 15; comp. the mention of him at Edessa by Joshua the Stylite in 498, *Chronicle*, ed. Wright, chap. xxx.

[2] *Ibid.*, pp. 17, 18.

[3] He was living there when he wrote to the monks of Sĕnūn in 522; *B.O.*, ii. 20.

18th February, and 1st April. Philoxenus, however, was something more than a man of action and of strife: he was a scholar and an elegant writer. Even Assemani, who never misses an opportunity of reviling him[1], is obliged to own (*B.O.*, ii. 20) "scripsit Syriace, si quis alius, elegantissime, atque adeo inter optimos hujusce linguæ scriptores a Jacobo Edesseno collocari meruit." [Until the recent edition of his homilies by Budge] scarcely any of his numerous works had been printed[2]. To him the Syriac Church owed its first revised translation of the Scriptures (see above, p. 13); and he also drew up an anaphora[3] and an order of baptism[4]. Portions of his commentaries on the Gospels are contained in two MSS. in the British Museum[5]. Besides sundry sermons, he composed thirteen homilies on the Christian life and character, of which there are several ancient copies in the British Museum. [Of these homilies a fine edition by Budge has now appeared, based on the Brit. Mus. MSS. of

[1] "Scelestissimus hæreticus" (*B.O.*, ii. 11); "flagitiosissimus homo" (p. 12); "ecclesiam Dei tanquam ferus aper devastaverit" (p. 18).

[2] *B.O.*, ii. 23 *sq.*; Wright, *Catal.*, Index, p. 1315.

[3] Renaudot, ii. 310; *B.O.*, ii. 24.

[4] *B.O.*, ii. 24.

[5] Add. 17126, dated 511, and Add. 14534, probably of equal age.

the 6th and 7th centuries[1].] Of his controversial works the two most important are a treatise *On the Trinity and the Incarnation* in three discourses[2], and another, in ten discourses, showing "that one (Person) of the Trinity became incarnate and suffered[3]"; but there are many smaller tracts against the Nestorians and Dyophysites[4]. His letters are numerous and may be of some value for the ecclesiastical history of his time. Assemani enumerates and gives extracts from several of them[5], but none of them have as yet been printed in full, with the exception of that to Abū Nafīr of Ḥērtā (al-Ḥīrah)[6], to the monks of Tell-'Addā[7], and to the priests Abraham and

[1] [*The Discourses of Philoxenus, Bishop of Mabbogh*, A.D. 485–519, vol. i., London, 1894. Vol. ii., which is still in course of preparation, is to contain an English translation, with illustrative extracts from the unpublished works of Philoxenus.]

[2] The Vatican MS. (Assemani, *Catal.*, iii. p. 217, No. cxxxvii.) is dated 564; see *B.O.*, ii. 25 *sq.*

[3] *B.O.*, ii. 27 *sq.* The Vatican MS. is dated 581; that in the British Museum Add. 12164 is at least as old.

[4] See *B.O.*, ii. 45, Nos. 15–17, and Wright, *Catal.*, p. 1315.

[5] *B.O.*, ii. 30–46. Others may be found in Wright, *Catal.*, p. 1315.

[6] See Martin, *Grammatica Chrestomathia et Glossarium Linguæ Syriacæ*, p. 71.

[7] Ign. Guidi, *La Lettera di Filosseno ai Monaci di Tell 'Addâ (Teleda)*, Reale Accademia dei Lincei, anno cclxxxii.,

Orestes of Edessa regarding Stephen bar Ṣūdh-ailē[1].

Contemporary with Jacob of Sĕrūgh and Philoxenus of Mabbōgh was the pantheist Stephen bar Ṣūdh-ailē[2], with whom both of these writers corresponded[3], and regarding whom the latter wrote the above-mentioned letter to the priests Abraham and Orestes. This man was the author of the work entitled *The Book of Hierotheus*, which he published under the name of Hierotheus, the teacher of St Dionysius of Athens[4], and

1884–85, Rome, 1886. In the Ethiopic literature there is extant a book entitled *Fīlĕksĕyūs*, *i.e.*, Philoxenus, from the name of its author, "Philoxenus the Syrian, bishop of Manbag" (see, for example, Wright, *Catal.*, p. 177). It is a series of questions and answers on the *Paradise* of Palladius, like the Syriac work described in Wright, *Catal.*, p. 1078.

1 See *B.O.*, ii. 30; Frothingham, *Stephen bar Sudaili*, p. 28 *sq.*

2 So in a MS. of the 7th century (Brit. Mus. Add. 17163; see Wright, *Catal.*, p. 524). The MSS. of Bar-Hebræus (*Chron. Eccles.*, i. 221) have ܨܘܕܗܝܠܐ or ܨܘܕܝܗܝܠܐ. Assemani writes ܨܘܕܝܠܐ (*Sudaili*). "Hunt the deer" can of course be only a nickname of the father. See Frothingham, *op. cit.*, p. 56 *sq.*

3 *B.O.*, i. 303, ii. 32; comp. Bar-Hebræus, *Chron. Eccles.*, i. 221.

4 *B.O.*, ii. 120, 290, 302; Frothingham, *op. cit.*, p. 63 *sq.* The existence of any Greek text seems to be very doubtful, see Frothingham, p. 70.

exercised a strong influence on the whole pseudo-Dionysian literature[1]. Theodosius, patriarch of Antioch (887–896), wrote a commentary on the *Hierotheus*[2]. Bar-Hebræus too made copious extracts from it, which he arranged and illustrated with a commentary chiefly derived from that of Theodosius[3].

At the same time with Jacob of Sĕrūgh and Philoxenus, and in the same neighbourhood, lived one of the earliest and best of the Syrian historians, the Stylite monk Yēshū' or Joshua. Of him we know nothing but that he originally belonged to the great convent of Zuḳnīn near Āmid, that at the beginning of the 6th century he was residing at Edessa, and that he dedicated his *Chronicle* of the Persian War[4] to an abbot named Sergius. His approving mention of Jacob[5] and Philoxenus[6] shows that he was a Monophysite. Joshua's *Chronicle* would have been entirely lost to us, had it not been for the thoughtfulness of a

[1] *B.O.*, iii. 1, 13; Frothingham, *op. cit.*, pp. 2 and 81.

[2] See MS. Brit. Mus. Add. 7189 (apparently the very copy used by Bar-Hebræus); Rosen, *Catal.*, p. 74 *sq.*; Frothingham, *op. cit.*, p. 84.

[3] Brit. Mus. Or. 1017 (Wright, *Catal.*, pp. 893–895); Bibl. Nation., Anc. fonds 138 (Zotenberg, *Catal.*, pp. 175–176); Frothingham, *op. cit.*, p. 87.

[4] Ed. Wright, p. ix.

[5] *Ibid.*, chap. liv.

[6] *Ibid.*, chap. xxx.

later writer, Dionysius of Tell-Maḥrē (d. 845), who incorporated it with his account of the reign of Anastasius in the smaller redaction of his own *History*. It was first made known to us by Assemani (*Bibl. Orient.*, i. 260–283), who gave a copious analysis with some extracts; and it is now generally acknowledged to be one of the best, if not actually the best, account of the great war between the Persian and Byzantine empires during the reigns of Ḳawādh and Anastasius (502–506)[1]. To the indefatigable Abbé Martin belongs the credit of publishing the *editio princeps* of the Syriac text[2]. The work was written in the year 507, immediately after the conclusion of the war, as is shown by the whole tone of the last chapter; and it is much to be regretted that the author did not carry out his intention of continuing it, or, if he did, that the continuation has perished.

The interest which Jacob of Sĕrūgh took in every branch of literature was the means of bringing into notice a hymn-writer of humble

[1] See, for example, the use that has been made of it in De Saint-Martin's notes to Lebeau's *Hist. du Bas-empire*, vol. vii.

[2] *Chronique de Josué le Stylite*, 1876, in vol. vi. of the *Abhandlungen für d. Kunde d. Morgenlandes*. Another edition was published by Wright, *The Chronicle of Joshua the Stylite*, 1882.

rank, the deacon Simeon Ḳūḳāyā, a potter by trade, as his name denotes. This man lived in the village of Gēshīr[1], not far from the convent of Mār Bassus, and while he worked at his wheel composed hymns, which he wrote down on a tablet or a scroll, as might be convenient. Jacob heard of him from the monks, paid him a visit, admired his hymns, and took away some of them with him, at the same time urging the author to continue his labours[2]. A specimen of these *Ḳūḳāyāthā* has been preserved in the shape of nine hymns on the nativity of our Lord, Brit. Mus. Add. 14520, a MS. of the 8th or 9th century[3].

About the same time flourished Simeon, bishop of Bēth Arshām[4], commonly called *Dārōshā Phārsāyā* or "the Persian Disputant." This keen Monophysite[5] was one of the few representatives

1 ܓܐܫܝܪ or ܓܝܫܝܪ.

2 See the narrative by Jacob of Edessa in Wright, *Catal.*, p. 602; and comp. *B.O.*, i. 121, ii. 322; Bar-Hebræus, *Chron. Eccles.*, i. 191.

3 Wright, *Catal.*, p. 363.

4 A village near Seleucia and Ctesiphon; Bar-Hebræus, *Chron. Eccles.*, ii. 85.

5 Assemani has tried to whitewash him, but with little success; *B.O.*, i. 342 *sq.* If he had had before him the account of Simeon by John of Ephesus (Land, *Anecd. Syr.*, ii. 76–88), he would probably have abandoned the attempt

of his creed in the Persian territory, and exhibited a wonderful activity, mental and bodily, on behalf of his co-religionists, traversing the Babylonian and Persian districts in all directions, and disputing with Manichees, Daisanites, Eutychians, and Nestorians[1]. After one of these disputations, at which the Nestorian catholicus Bābhai (498–503) was present[2], Simeon was made bishop, a dignity which he had declined on several previous occasions. He visited Ḥērtā (al-Ḥīrah) more than once, and died during his third residence at Constantinople, whither he had come to see the empress Theodora[3]. Assemani states, on the authority of Dionysius of Tell-Maḥrē, that he was bishop of Bēth Arshām from 510 to 515, but the Syriac passage which he quotes merely gives the *floruit* of 510. If, however, the statements of John of Ephesus, who knew him personally, be correct, he was probably made bishop before 503, the date of Bābhai's decease[4]. His death must have taken place before 548, in which year Theodora departed this life. Besides an anaphora[5], we

in disgust. See Guidi, *La Lettera di Simeone Vescovo di Bêth-Aršâm sopra i Martiri Omeriti*, 1881, pp. 4–7.

[1] See Bar-Hebræus, *Chron. Eccles.*, ii. 85, i. 189; comp. *B.O.*, i. 341, ii. 409, iii. 1, 403.

[2] Land, *Anecd. Syr.*, ii. 82, l. 12.

[3] *Ibid.*, ii. 87, last line.

[4] *B.O.*, iii. 1, 427.

[5] *Ibid.*, i. 345.

possess only two letters of Simeon, which are both of considerable interest. The one is entitled *On Bar-ṣaumā and the Sect of the Nestorians*[1]; it deals with the origin and spread of Nestorianism in the East, but from the bitterest and narrowest sectarian point of view[2]. The other, which is much more valuable, is addressed to Simeon, abbot of Gabbūlā[3], and treats of the persecution of the Christians at Najrān by Dhū Nuwās, king of al-Yaman, in the year 523[4]. It is dated 524, in which year the writer was himself at Ḥērtā (al-Ḥīrah).

To the same age and sect as Simeon belonged John bar Cursus (Κοῦρσος)[5], bishop of Tellā or

[1] *B.O.*, i. 346.

[2] First printed in *B.O.*, i. 346 *sq.*, from the Vatican MS. cxxxv. (*Catal.*, iii. 214).

[3] Al-Jabbūl. Or is it Jabbul, on the east bank of the Tigris, between an-Nu'māniyah and Wāsiṭ?

[4] First printed in *B.O.*, i. 364 *sq.*, according to the text offered by John of Ephesus in his *History*. There is, however, a longer and better text in a MS. of the Museo Borgiano and in Brit. Mus. Add. 14650, from which it has been reedited (with an excellent introduction, translation, and notes) by Guidi, *La Lettera di Simeone*, &c., Reale Accademia dei Lincei, 1881. To this work the reader is referred for all the documents bearing on the subject. [Another edition of the text, following Guidi's, in (Bedjan's) *Acta Martyrum et Sanctorum*, i. 372 *sq.*]

[5] The name of the father is also given as Curcus and Cyriacus. Assemani's Barsus (*B.O.*, ii. 54) is a misreading.

Constantina. He was a native of Callinīcus (ar-Raḳḳah), of good family, and was carefully educated by his widowed mother, who put him into the army at the age of twenty. He would not, however, be hindered from quitting the service after a few years and becoming a monk. Subsequently, in 519, he was raised to the dignity of bishop of Tellā, whence he was expelled by Justin in 521. In 533 he visited Constantinople, and on his return to the East was seized by his enemies in the mountains of Sinjār, and dragged to Nisībis, Rās'ain, and Antioch, where he died in 538, at the age of fifty-five, having been for a year and six days a close prisoner in the convent of the Comes Manassē by order of the cruel persecutor Ephraim, patriarch of Antioch (529–544). His life was written by his disciple Elias (of Dārā ?)[1]. The Jacobite Church commemorates him on the 6th of February. Canons by John of Tellā are extant in several MSS. in the British Museum and elsewhere[2]. The questions put to him by Sergius with his replies have been published by Lamy[3]. His creed or confession of faith, addressed

[1] There are two copies in the British Museum, edited by Kleyn, *Het Leven van Johannes van Tellā door Elias*, 1882; see also the *Life* by John of Asia in Land, *Anecd. Syr.*, ii. 169.

[2] *B.O.*, ii. 54.

[3] *Dissert. de Syrorum Fide et Disciplina in Re Eucharistica*, 1859, pp. 62–97.

to the convents in and around Tellā, is found in Brit. Mus. Add. 14549 (*Catal.*, p. 431), and an exposition of the Trisagion in Cod. Vat. clix. (*Catal.*, iii. 314) and Bodl. Marsh. 101 (Payne Smith, *Catal.*, p. 463, No. 20).

Another of the unfortunate Monophysite bishops whom Justin expelled from their sees (in 519) was Mārā of Āmid, the third bishop of the name. He was banished, with his syncelli and with Isidore, bishop of Ḳen-neshrīn (Ḳinnesrīn), in the first instance to Petra, but was afterwards allowed to go to Alexandria[1], where he died in about eight years[2]. According to Assemani (*Bibl. Orient.*, ii. 52; comp. p. 169), Mārā wrote a commentary on the Gospels. It would seem, however, from a passage of Zacharias Rhetor[3], that Mārā merely prefixed a short prologue in Greek to a copy of the Gospels which he had procured at Alexandria[4], and that this MS. contained (as might be expected) the pericope on the woman taken in adultery (John viii. 2–11). That the Syriac translations of the prologue and pericope were made by himself is nowhere stated.

Yet another sufferer at the hands of Justin

[1] See Land, *Anecd. Syr.*, ii. 105.

[2] *Ibid.*, p. 108.

[3] *Ibid.*, iii. 250 *sq.*

[4] Compare what is said of his fine library and of its ultimate deposition at Āmid, *ibid.*, p. 245.

was John bar Aphtōnyā (Aphtonia, his mother's name)[1]. He was abbot of the convent of St Thomas at Seleucia (apparently in Pieria, on the Orontes), which was famous as a school for the study of Greek literature. Being expelled thence, he removed with his whole brotherhood to Ḳenneshrē (the Eagles' Nest) on the Euphrates, opposite Europus (Jerābīs), where he founded a new convent and school that more than rivalled the parent establishment, for here Thomas of Heraclea, Jacob of Edessa, and others received their training in Greek letters[2]. His *Life*, written by a disciple, is extant in Brit. Mus. Add. 12174[3]. According to Dionysius of Tell-Maḥre, as quoted by Assemani (*loc. cit.*), he died in 538. He wrote a commentary on the Song of Songs, some extracts from which are preserved in a *Catena Patrum* in the British Museum (Add. 12168, f. 138a), a considerable number of hymns[4], and a biography of Severus of Antioch[5], which

[1] *B.O.*, ii. 54.

[2] See Bar-Hebræus, *Chron. Eccles.*, i. 267, 289, and comp. pp. 258, 295, 321; Hoffmann, *Auszüge*, p. 162, note 1260.

[3] Wright, *Catal.*, p. 1124, No. 5.

[4] See for example, Brit. Mus. Add. 17134 (Wright, *Catal.*, p. 330).

[5] Cited in Brit. Mus. Add. 14731 (Wright, *Catal.*, p. 855).

must have been his last work, as he survived Severus only about nine months.

We now come to the man who was the real founder of the Jacobite Church in Asia, and from whom the Jacobites took their name, Jacob bar Theophilus, surnamed "Burdĕʿānā[1]," because his dress consisted of a *bardaʿthā* or coarse horse-cloth, which he never changed till it became quite ragged[2]. What Assemani could learn regarding him he has put together in the *Bibl. Orient.*, ii. 62–69[3]; since then our sources of information have been largely increased, especially by the publication of the *Ecclesiastical History* of John of Ephesus by Cureton and of the same writer's *Lives* in Land's *Anecd. Syr.*, ii.[4] On a careful study of these is based Kleyn's excellent book *Jacobus Baradæüs, de Stichter der Syrische Monophysietische Kerk*, 1882. Jacob was the son of Theophilus bar Maʿnū, a priest of Tellā or Constantina, and the child of his old age. After

1 Usually corrupted into Baradæus; the form Burdĕʿāyā seems to be incorrect; see Bar-Hebræus, *Chron. Eccles.*, ii. 97.

2 See Land, *Anecd. Syr.*, ii. 375.

3 Comp. also ii. 326, 331.

4 The life at p. 249 is of course by John of Asia; that at p. 364 can hardly be called his in its present form, though he may have collected most of the materials; see Kleyn, *op. cit.*, p. 34, 105 *sq.*

receiving a good education, he was entered at the monastery of Pĕsīltā (or the Quarry)[1], close by the village of Gummĕthā in Mount Īzalā (or Īzlā)[2], not far from Tellā. About 527–528 he and another monk of Tellā, named Sergius, were sent to Constantinople in defence of their faith, and, being favourably received by the empress Theodora, they remained there fifteen years. Meantime the persecutions of the Monophysites, more especially that of 536–537 by Ephraim of Antioch, seemed to have crushed their party, despite all the efforts of the devoted John of Tellā and John of Hephæstus[3]. This state of matters excited the religious zeal of al-Ḥārith ibn Jabalah, the Arab king of Ghassān, who came to Constantinople in 542–543, and urged Theodora to send two or three bishops to Syria. Accordingly two were consecrated by Theodosius, the exiled patriarch of Alexandria, namely, Theodore as bishop of Bostra, with jurisdiction over the provinces of Palestine and Arabia, and Jacob as bishop of Edessa, with jurisdiction over all Syria and Asia. From this time forward Jacob's life was one of ceaseless toil and hardship. He visited in person and on foot almost every part of his

[1] Land, *op. cit.*, p. 365, ll. 6, 7.
[2] *Ibid.*, p. 372, l. 2.
[3] *Ibid.*, p. 176.

vast diocese, consecrating deacons and priests, strengthening the weak, and bringing back those who had erred from the true faith. But to restore the Monophysite Church bishops were necessary, and the consecration of a bishop required the presence of at least three others. Selecting a priest named Conon from Cilicia and another named Eugenius from Isauria, he travelled with them to Constantinople and thence to Alexandria with letters of recommendation from the patriarch Theodosius. At Alexandria Conon was ordained bishop of Tarsus in Cilicia and Eugenius bishop of Seleucia in Isauria, whilst Antoninus and Antonius were consecrated for dioceses in Syria. On his return to Syria other bishops were appointed to sees there and in Asia, among the latter the historian John of Ephesus; and so the work progressed, till at last Jacob's efforts were crowned by the enthroning of his old friend Sergius as patriarch of Antioch (in 544). Sergius died in 547, and the see remained vacant for three years, after which, by the advice of Theodosius, Jacob and his bishops chose Paul, an abbot of Alexandria, to be their patriarch. Of the subsequent internal strifes among the Monophysites themselves we cannot here speak. The aged Jacob set out once more in the year 578 to visit Damian, patriarch of Alexandria, but died on the Egyptian frontier in the convent of Mār Romanus or of Casion. Here his remains rested in peace till 622, when they were stolen by the emissaries of Zacchæus, bishop of Tellā, and buried with much pomp in the monastery of Pĕsīltā[1]. His commemoration takes place on 28th November, 21st March, and 31st July. Jacob's life was too active and busy to admit of his writing much. We may mention an anaphora[2], sundry letters[3], a creed or confession of faith, preserved in Arabic and a secondary Ethiopic translation[4], and a homily for the feast of the Annunciation, also extant only in an Arabic translation[5].

Conspicuous among the scholars of this age for his knowledge of Greek, and more especially of the Aristotelian philosophy, was Sergius, priest and archiater of Rās'ain. He was, however, if Zacharias Rhetor may be trusted, a man of loose

[1] See the account of this "translation" by Cyriacus, bishop of Mardē (Māridīn), in Brit. Mus. Add. 12174 (Wright, *Catal.*, p. 1131).

[2] Translated by Renaudot, ii. 333.

[3] Translated from the *Greek* originals in Brit. Mus. Add. 14602; see Wright, *Catal.*, p. 701; Kleyn, *op. cit.*, pp. 164–194.

[4] See the Arabic text in Kleyn, *op. cit.*, p. 121 *sq.*; the Ethiopic version has been edited by Cornill in *Z.D.M.G.*, xxx. 417 *sq.*

[5] Bodl. Hunt. 199 (Payne Smith, *Catal.*, p. 448, No. 5).

morals and avaricious[1]. He journeyed in 535 from Rās'ain to Antioch to lodge a complaint before the patriarch Ephraim against his bishop Asȳlus[2]. Just at this time the exiled Severus of Antioch and Theodosius of Alexandria, as well as the Stylite monk Zĕ'ōrā, were living with Anthimus of Constantinople under the protection of the empress Theodora. This alarmed Ephraim, who seems to have found a willing tool in Sergius. At any rate he sent him to Rome with letters to Agapetus, who travelled with him to Constantinople in the spring of 536, and procured the deposition and banishment of the Monophysites. Sergius died at Constantinople almost immediately afterwards, and Agapetus followed him in a few days, wherein John of Ephesus and Zacharias Rhetor clearly see the judgment of Heaven[3]. As a man of letters Sergius was to the Monophysites what Probus was to the Nestorians: he was the first[4] to make them acquainted with the works of

1 Land, *Anecd. Syr.*, iii. 289, ll. 13–15; comp. Bar-Hebræus, *Chron. Eccles.*, i. 207.

2 Bar-Hebræus (*Chron. Eccles.*, i. 205) has Ascolius (see also *B.O.*, ii. 323), but Asȳlus is correct; see *Anecd. Syr.*, iii. 289, l. 6, and Kleyn, *Johannes van Tella*, p. 59, l. penult.

3 Land, *Anecd. Syr.*, ii. 19; iii. 290.

4 Bar-Hebræus, *Chron. Syr.*, 62 (trans., p. 59) [ed. Bedjan, p. 57]; see also the *Hist. Dynast.*, 150 (trans., p. 94) and 264 (trans., p. 172).

Aristotle by means of translations and commentaries. ʽAbhd-īshōʽ, it is true, gives Sergius a place in his catalogue of Nestorian writers[1], and states that he composed "expositions of logic" or "dialectics"; but he merely does so in the same way and on the same grounds that he registers the name of Jacob of Edessa as the author of "annals and a chronicle[2]." The books were too valuable for him to insist on the heresy of the writers. In the case of Sergius there was an additional reason. The man was well known in the East[3], many of his works being dedicated to his friend and pupil Theodore, afterwards Nestorian bishop of Marū or Merv (see p. 119 *infra*)[4]. What remains of Sergius's labours is mostly contained in a single MS. of the 7th century (Brit. Mus. Add. 14658)[5]. Of translations from the Greek we find in this volume the *Isagoge* of Porphyry, followed by the so-called *Tabula Por-*

[1] *B.O.*, iii. 1, 87.

[2] *Ibid.*, 229.

[3] He may even be identical with the Sergius mentioned by Agathias as residing at the Persian court, where he translated into Greek a history of the kings of Persia; see *B.O.*, iii. 1, 87, note 3; Renan, *De Philosophia Peripatetica apud Syros*, 1852, pp. 24–25.

[4] *B.O.*, iii. 1, 147; Renan, *op. cit.*, p. 29.

[5] Wright, *Catal.*, p. 1154 *sq.*; comp. Renan, *op. cit.*, p. 25 *sq.*; *Journ. Asiat.*, 1852, 4th series, vol. xix. p. 319 *sq.*

*phyrii*[1], the *Categories* of Aristotle[2], the Περὶ κόσμου πρὸς Ἀλέξανδρον[3], and a treatise on the soul,—not the well-known Περὶ ψυχῆς, but a wholly different tractate in five short sections. It also contains Sergius's own treatise on logic, addressed to Theodore, which is unfortunately

[1] There is a fragment of the *Isagoge* also in Brit. Mus. Add. 1618 (Wright, *Catal.*, p. 738).

[2] In the Vatican MS. clviii. (*Catal.*, iii. 306, No. vi.) this translation is wrongly ascribed to Jacob of Edessa, who could hardly have been more than a boy at the time when the MS. in the British Museum was transcribed. Besides, the version is not in his style. The Paris MS. Ancien fonds 161 naturally repeats this mistake (Zotenberg, *Catal.*, p. 202). In *Catal. Bibl. Palat. Medic.*, cod. cxcvi., it is likewise erroneously attributed to Ḥonain ibn Isḥāḳ (comp. Renan, *De Philos. Peripat. ap. Syros*, p. 34, note 3). The Berlin MS. Alt. Best. 36 contains as No. 7 a treatise of Sergius on the *Categories* addressed to Philotheus.

[3] Edited by Lagarde, *Anal. Syr.*, p. 134 *sq.*; see V. Ryssel, *Ueber den textkritischen Werth d. syr. Uebersetzungen griechischer Klassiker*, part i. 1880, part ii. 1881. In part i. p. 4 Professor Ryssel speaks of this version as "ein Meisterwerk der Uebersetzungskunst"; and in part ii. p. 10 he says: "Die Uebersetzung der Schrift περὶ κόσμου schliesst sich aufs engste an den Text des griechischen Originales an. Dass wir deshalb diese Uebersetzung als eine im besten Sinne wortgetreue bezeichnen können, zeigt schon eine Vergleichung mit der lateinischen Bearbeitung des Apulejus von Madaura." This opinion serves to rectify the judgment of Ibn Abī Oṣaibiʿah (i. 204) that Sergius was only a mediocre translator, and that his work needed revision by the later Ḥonain ibn Isḥāḳ.

imperfect; a tract on negation and affirmation; a treatise, likewise addressed to Theodore, *On the Causes of the Universe, according to the views of Aristotle, showing how it is a circle;* a tract *On Genus, Species, and Individuality;* and a third tract addressed to Theodore, *On the Action and Influence of the Moon*, explanatory and illustrative of Galen's Περὶ κρισίμων ἡμερῶν, bk. iii.[1], with a short appendix "On the Motion of the Sun." Here too we find part (sections 11, 12) of his version of the *Ars Grammatica* of Dionysius Thrax, a larger portion (sections 11–20) being contained in Brit. Mus. Add. 14620 (Wright, *Catal.*, p. 802)[2]. There is a scholion of Sergius on the term σχῆμα in the Brit. Mus. Add. 14660 (see Wright, *Catal.*, p. 1162). In his capacity of physician, Sergius translated part of the works of Galen. Brit. Mus. Add. 14661 contains books vi.–viii. of the treatise *De Simplicium Medicamentorum Temperamentis ac Facultatibus* (Wright,

[1] See Sachau, *Inedita Syr.*, pp. 101–126.

[2] This identification is due to Merx; see *Dionysii Thracis Ars Grammatica*, ed. Uhlig, p. xliv. *sq.* Merx has treated of an old, but independent, Armenian version in the same book, p. lvii. *sq.* [The Syriac text is given in the appendix to Merx's *Historia artis grammaticae apud Syros.* Merx however maintains that the work was not translated by Sergius, and that several other of the contents of Brit. Mus. Add. 14658 are not his (*op. cit.*, p. 7 *sq.*).]

*Catal.*, p. 1187)[1], addressed to Theodore; and in Brit. Mus. Add. 17156 there are three leaves, two of which contain fragments of the *Ars Medica*, and one of the treatise *De Alimentorum Facultatibus* (Wright, *Catal.*, p. 1188)[2]. As one of the clergy, he wasted his time in making a translation of the works which passed under the name of Dionysius the Areopagite[3]. Brit. Mus. Add. 12151[4] contains this version with the introduction and notes of Phocas bar Sergius of Edessa[5], a writer of the 8th century, as appears from his citing Athanasius II. and Jacob of Edessa. In Brit. Mus. Add. 22370[6] we find Sergius's own introduction and the commentary of a later writer, Theodore bar Zarūdī[7].

[1] See Merx's article in *Z.D.M.G.*, xxxix. (1885), p. 237 *sq.*

[2] See Sachau, *Ined. Syr.*, pp. 88–94.

[3] See Frothingham, *Stephen bar Sudaili*, p. 3.

[4] See Wright, *Catal.*, p. 493.

[5] *B.O.*, i. 468. Assemani erroneously places him before Jacob of Edessa.

[6] See Wright, *Catal.*, p. 500.

[7] There are also old MSS. of Sergius's version in the Vatican; *Catal.*, iii. Nos. cvii. (p. 56), ccliv. (p. 542). Bar-Hebræus states (*Hist. Dynast.*, p. 158; transl., p. 99) that Sergius translated into Syriac the *Syntagma* of the Alexandrian priest and physician Aaron, and added to it two books; but Steinschneider (*Al-Fārābī*, p. 166, note 2) says that this is a mistake, and that the real author of the two additional books was the Arabic translator Māsarja-

If Sergius was the Probus of the Monophysites, their Maʿnā was Paul, bishop of Callinīcus (ar-Raḳḳah)[1], who, being expelled from his see in 519, betook himself to Edessa and there devoted himself to the task of translating the works of Severus into Syriac. We know for certain[2] that he edited versions of the correspondence of Severus and Julian of Halicarnassus on the corruptibility or incorruptibility of the body of Christ, with a discourse of Severus against Julian[3]; of the treatise against the *Additions* or *Appendices* of Julian[4], and against the last apology of Julian[5];

waihi or Māsarjis. The translator of the Geoponica, *Al-Falāḥah ar Rūmīyah* (Leyden, cod. 414 Warn.; *Catal.*, iii. 211) and joint translator of the Μεγάλη σύνταξις of Ptolemy (Leyden, cod. 680 Warn.; *Catal.*, iii. 80), by name Serjis or Serjūn (Sergius or Sergōnā) ibn ar-Rūmī, seems to be a quite different person of later date.

[1] *B.O.*, ii. 46. He is to be distinguished from his namesake and contemporary, Paul, bishop of Edessa, who was banished to Euchaita in 522 (*B.O.*, i. 409–411), restored to his see in 526 (*ibid.*, p. 413), and died in the following year; whereas Paul of Callinīcus was working at Edessa in 528 (see p. 135, *infra*).

[2] Thanks in part to a note at the end of Cod. Vat. cxl. (*Catal.*, iii. 223; comp. *B.O.*, *loc. cit.*).

[3] Completed in 528; Cod. Vat. cxl.; Brit. Mus. Add. 17200 (Wright, *Catal.*, p. 554).

[4] Cod. Vat. cxl.; Brit. Mus. Add. 12158 (Wright, *Catal.*, p. 556), dated 588.

[5] Brit. Mus. Add. 12158.

of that against the Manichees; and of the *Philalethes*[1]. Probably by him are the older translation of the *Homiliæ Cathedrales*[2] and that of the correspondence of Sergius Grammaticus and Severus regarding the doctrine of the two natures in Christ[3], possibly, too, the translation of the treatise against John Grammaticus of Cæsarea[4] and of some other works which are known to us only by a few scattered citations[5]. Hence he is called by the Jacobites *Mĕphashshĕḳānā dhakhĕthābhē*, "the Translator of Books[6]."

This seems the proper place to make mention of a most important though anonymous work, the translation of the so-called *Civil Laws of the Emperors Constantine, Theodosius and Leo*, which lies at the root of all subsequent Christian Oriental legislation in ecclesiastical, judicial, and private

[1] There is a long extract from this work in Cod. Vat. cxl. (*Catal.*, iii. 232).

[2] Brit. Mus. Add. 14599, dated 569; Cod. Vat. cxlii., dated 576; cxliii., dated 563; cclvi.

[3] Brit. Mus. Add. 17154.

[4] Brit. Mus. Add. 17210–11, 12157.

[5] Compare, for example, Wright, *Catal.*, p. 1323. The translation of the *Octoëchus* is the work, not of Paul of Callinīcus, but of an abbot Paul, who executed it in the island of Cyprus (see p. 135 *infra*).

[6] The passage quoted by Assemani (*B.O.*, i. 409, note 2) seems, however, to confound him with his namesake of Edessa.

matters[1]. The Syriac version, made from a Greek original, exists in two manuscripts[2], the older of which undeniably belongs to the earlier part of the 6th century. The work itself appears, according to the researches of Bruns (*op. cit.*, pp. 318–319), to date from the time of the emperor Basilicus (A.D. 475–477), who was a favourer of the Monophysites; the Syriac translation is ascribed to a Monophysite monk of Mabbōgh or Hierapolis (*ibid.*, p. 155). The Paris MS. probably represents a Nestorian revision of the 9th or 10th century at (Baghdad) Baghdādh (*ibid.*, p. 166). [A third Syriac recension, which must have differed very considerably from the other two, is known from an imperfect Cambridge MS.[3]] The oldest MS. of the secondary Arabic version is dated 1352 (*ibid.*, p. 164), but it has been traced back to the time of the Nestorian lawyer

[1] *B.O.*, iii. 1, 267, note 6, 278, 338–339, 351, col. 2; comp. Bruns and Sachau, *Syrisch-Römisches Rechtsbuch*, 1880, pp. 175–180.

[2] Brit. Mus. Add. 14528 (Wright, *Catal.*, p. 177), and Paris, Suppl. 38 (Zotenberg, *Catal.*, p. 75, col. 1, No. 46). The text of the former was first published by Land (*Anecd. Syr.*, i. 30–64), with a Latin translation. Both have been edited and translated, along with the Arabic and Armenian versions, with translations and a learned apparatus, by Bruns and Sachau, *op. cit.*

[3] [Only the last four sections remain; printed (for private circulation) in Wright's *Notulæ Syriacæ*, 1887.]

Abu 'l-Faraj ʿAbdallāh ibn aṭ-Ṭaiyib (who died 1043), whether made by him or not (*ibid.*, p. 177). It belongs to the same class as the London Syriac, but is based on a better text, such as that of the fragment in Brit. Mus. Add. 18295 (*ibid.*, p. 172)[1]. Of the secondary Armenian translation the same is to be said as of the Arabic. The oldest MS. of it dates from 1328, but it probably goes as far back as the end of the 12th century (*ibid.*, p. 164). The Georgian version, of which there is a MS. at St Petersburg, is most likely an offshoot of the Armenian.

Another scholar, besides Sergius, whom ʿAbhd-īshōʿ wrongly claims as a Nestorian, is Aḥū-dh'emmēh, metropolitan of Taghrīth (Tekrīt). He appears, on the contrary, to have been the head of the Monophysites in the Persian territory. According to Bar-Hebræus[2], he was appointed by Christopher, catholicus of the Armenians, to be bishop of Bēth ʿArbāyē[3], but was promoted by Jacob Burdĕʿānā in 559 to the see of Taghrīth, where he ordained many priests and founded two monasteries. Among his numerous converts from heathenism was a youthful member of the

1 Wright, *Catal.*, p. 1184.

2 *Chron. Eccles.*, ii. 99; comp. *B.O.*, ii. 414, iii. 1, 192, note 3.

3 Bā-ʿarbāyā, the district between Nisībis and the Tigris.

royal family of Persia, whom he baptized by the name of George. This excited the anger of Khosrau I. Anōsharwān, who ordered the bishop to be beheaded (2d August 575). As a writer Aḥū-dh'emmēh seems to have been more of a philosopher than a theologian[1]. He wrote against the Persian priesthood and against the Greek philosophers, a book of definitions, a treatise on logic, on freewill in two discourses, on the soul and on man as the microcosm, and a treatise on the composition of man as consisting of soul and body[2]. He is also mentioned by later authors as a writer on grammar[3].

[Here may be mentioned the *Mĕ'ārath Gazzē* ('Cave of Treasures'), an original Syriac work, which, according to Bezold[4] and Nöldeke[5], dates in all probability from the 6th century. It consists of an expansion of the early biblical history, somewhat after the manner of the *Book of Jubilees.* The substance of it has passed into the Ethiopic *Book of Adam*, the second and third parts of which agree with it in matter, though

[1] *B.O.*, iii. 1, 192.

[2] Of this last part is extant in Brit. Mus. Add. 14620 (Wright, *Catal.*, p. 802).

[3] See *B.O.*, iii. 1, 256, note 2; [cf. Merx, *Hist. artis gramm. ap. Syros*, p. 33 *sq.*].

[4] [*Die Schatzhöhle*, vol. i. p. x.

[5] In *Literarisches Centralblatt* for 1888, col. 234.

not verbally. The Syriac text has been edited by Bezold from four MSS.[1], and accompanied by the old Arabic version[2].]

Early in the 6th century a monk of Edessa, whose name is unknown to us, tried his hand at the composition of a tripartite historical romance[3], —a history of Constantine and his three sons; an account of Eusebius, bishop of Rome, and his sufferings at the hands of Julian the Apostate; and a history of Jovian or, as the Orientals usually call him, Jovinian, under Julian and during his own reign. The whole purports to be written by one Aplōrīs or Aplōlārīs (Apollinarius?), an official at the court of Jovian, at the request of ʿAbhdēl, abbot of Sndrūn (?) Māḥōzā, with a view to the conversion of the heathens. All three parts contain but a very small quantity of historical facts or dates, and deal in the grossest exaggerations and inventions. Yet the Syriac style is pure, and we gain from the book a good

1 Brit. Mus. Add. 25875 and 7199, Sachau MSS. 131, Cod. Vat. Syn. 164.

2 *Die Schatzhöhle*, vol. ii., Leipzig, 1888. Vol. i., published in 1882, contains a German translation from the Syriac: vol. iii., which has not yet appeared, is to furnish a general introduction. A review by Nöldeke in *Literar. Centralbl.* for 1888, coll. 233–236.]

3 Contained in Brit. Mus. Add. 14641, ff. 1–131, a MS. of the 6th century.

idea of the way in which the author's countrymen thought and spoke and acted. This romance has been published by Hoffmann[1], and Nöldeke has given a full account of it, with an abridged translation, in *Z.D.M.G.*, xxviii. p. 263 *sq.* He places the time of composition between 502 and 532. It is curious to find that this romance must have been known in an Arabic translation to the historian aṭ-Ṭabarī, who treats it as a genuine historical document[2]. From him it has passed to the *Kāmil* of Ibn al-Athīr i. 283 *sq.*, and the *Akhbār al-Bashar* of Abu 'l-Fidā (*Hist. Anteislamica*, ed. Fleischer, p. 84). Ibn Wāḍiḥ al-Ya'ḳūbī seems in his *Annals*[3] to have drawn from the same source, though independently of aṭ-Ṭabarī, and so also al-Mas'ūdī, *Murūj adh-Dhahab*, ii. 323. Bar-Hebræus has also made some use of it in his *Chronicon*, ed. Bruns and Kirsch, pp. 68–69; [ed. Bedjan, pp. 63–64]. No doubt, too, it is the work attributed by 'Abhd-īshō' to the grave ecclesiastical historian Socrates, who, as he says[4], wrote "a history of the emperors Constantine and Jovinian."

[1] *Julianos der Abtrünnige*, 1880.

[2] Aṭ-Ṭabarī, *Annales*, i. 840 *sq.*; see Nöldeke, in *Z.D.M.G.*, xxviii. 291–292, and *Geschichte der Perser und Araber zur Zeit der Sasaniden*, p. 59 *sq.*

[3] Ed. Houtsma, i. 182–183.

[4] *B.O.*, iii. 1, 41.

Another, but much inferior, romance, of which Julian is the hero, is contained in Brit. Mus. Add. 7192, a manuscript of the 7th century. It has been edited by Hoffmann, *op. cit.*, pp. 242–259, and translated by Nöldeke, *Z.D.M.G.*, xxviii. 660–674. We shall not be far wrong in assigning it likewise to the 6th century, though it is probably rather later than that just noticed.

Of real historical value, on the contrary, is the anonymous *Chronicon Edessenum*, fortunately preserved to us in the Vatican MS. clxiii.[1], and edited by Assemani in *B.O.*, i. 388–417. [It has also been edited and translated into German by Hallier in *Untersuchungen über die edessenische Chronik* (Von Gebhardt and Harnack's *Texte und Untersuchungen*, ix. 1, Leipzig, 1892).] There is an English translation of it in the *Journ. of Sacred Lit.*, 1864, vol. v. (new ser.), p. 28 *sq.* It begins with A.Gr. 180, but the entries are very sparse till we reach A.Gr. 513 (202 A.D.). The last of them refers to the year 540, about which time the little book must have been compiled. The author made use of the archives of Edessa and other documents now lost to us, as well as of the *Chronicle* of Joshua the Stylite (see above, p. 77). In religious matters he is not a violent partisan,

[1] See *Catal.*, iii. 329.

nor given to the use of harsh words, a thing to be noted in the age in which he lived.

Another writer of first-rate importance as a historian is John, bishop of Asia or Ephesus, "the teacher of the heathen," "the overseer of the heathen," and "the idol-breaker," as he loves to style himself[1]. He was a native of Āmid[2], and must have been born early in the 6th century, according to Land about 505. He was ordained deacon in the convent of St John in 529, when he must have been at least twenty years of age[3]. In 534 the terrible pestilence of the reign of Justinian broke out, and at that time John was in Palestine[4], having, doubtless, fled from Āmid to avoid the persecution of the Monophysites by Abraham bar Kīlī (?) of Tellā, bishop of Āmid (from about 520 to 546), and Ephraim bar Appian of Āmid, patriarch of Antioch (529–544), "a much worse persecutor than Paul or Euphrasius[5]." In 535 we find him at Constantinople, where in the following year, according to Bar-Hebræus[6], he

[1] See *Eccles. Hist.*, ed. Cureton, bk. ii. ch. 4, and bk. iii. ch. 36; Land, *Anecd. Syr.*, ii. 256, l. 25.

[2] *B.O.*, ii. 83; Bar-Hebræus, *Chron. Eccles.*, i. 195.

[3] *B.O.*, ii., *Dissert. de Monophysitis*, p. cxxv.; Land, *Anecd. Syr.*, 174, ll. 8, 9.

[4] *B.O.*, ii. 85–86.

[5] *E.H.*, ed. Cureton, bk. i. ch. 41, comp. *B.O.*, ii. 51.

[6] *Chron. Eccles.*, i. 195.

became bishop of the Monophysites in succession to the deposed Anthimus. Be this as it may, he was certainly received with great favour by Justinian, whose friendship and confidence he enjoyed for thirty years, and "had the administration of the entire revenues of all the congregations of the believers (*i.e.*, the Monophysites) in Constantinople and everywhere else[1]." Wishing to root out heathenism in Asia Minor, obviously for political as well as religious reasons, the emperor appointed John to be his missionary bishop[2]. In this task he had great success, to which his faithful friend and fellow-labourer for thirty-five years, Deuterius, largely contributed[3]. He interested himself, too, in the missionary efforts of Julian, Theodore, and Longinus among the Nubians and Alodæi[4]. In 546 the emperor

[1] *E.H.*, ed. Cureton, bk. v. ch. 1.

[2] *Ibid.*, bk. ii. ch. 44; bk. iii. ch. 36, 37; comp. *B.O.*, ii. 85.

[3] *E.H.*, ed. Cureton, bk. ii. ch. 44.

[4] *Ibid.*, bk. iv. ch. 6–8, 49–53; comp. Bar-Hebræus, *Chron. Eccles.*, i. 229. How just his views were as a missionary may be seen from bk. iv. ch. 50, where he says "that it was not right that to an erring and heathen people, who asked to be converted to Christianity and to learn the fear of God, there should be sent by letter, before everything that was necessary for their edification, confusion and offence and the revilings of Christians against Christians."

employed him in searching out and putting down the secret practice of idolatry in Constantinople and its neighbourhood[1]. After the death of his patron the fortunes of John soon underwent a change. Bk. i. of the third part of his *History* commences with the persecution under Justin in 571, in which he suffered imprisonment[2]. His friend Deuterius, whom he had made bishop of Caria, was also persecuted, and died at Constantinople[3]. From this time forward John's story is that of his party, and the evidently confused and disordered state of his *History* is fully explained and excused by his own words in bk. ii. 50, where he tells us[4] "that most of these histories were written at the very time when the persecution was going on, and under the difficulties caused by its pressure; and it was even necessary that friends should remove the leaves on which these chapters were inscribed, and every other particle of writing, and conceal them in various places, where they sometimes remained for two or three years. When therefore matters occurred which

[1] *B.O.*, ii. 85.

[2] *E.H.*, ed. Cureton, bk. i. ch. 17; bk. ii. ch. 4–7. Of unjust legal proceedings he complains in bk. ii. ch. 41, where he loses his προάστειον, &c.

[3] *E.H.*, ed. Cureton, bk. ii. ch. 44.

[4] Payne Smith's translation, p. 163.

the writer wished to record, it was possible that he might have partly spoken of them before, but he had no papers or notes by which to read and know whether they had been described or not. If therefore he did not remember that he had recorded them, at some subsequent time he probably again proceeded to their detail; and therefore occasionally the same subject is recorded in more chapters than one; nor afterwards did he ever find a fitting time for plainly and clearly arranging them in an orderly narrative." Some of the chapters are actually dated at various times from A.Gr. 886 (575 A.D.) to 896 (585). The time and place of his death are unknown, but he cannot have lived long after 585, being then about eighty years of age[1]. His greatest literary work is his *Ecclesiastical History* in three parts, the first two of which, as he himself tells us[2], embraced, in six books each, the period from Julius Cæsar to the seventh year of Justin II., whilst the third, also in six books, carried on the tale to the end of the author's life. The first part is entirely lost. Of the second we have copious excerpts in the *Chronicle* of Dionysius of Tell-

[1] See Land, *Joannes Bischof von Ephesos, der erste Syrische Kirchenhistoriker*, 1856. A very useful book.

[2] *E.H.*, ed. Cureton, bk. i. ch. 3.

Maḥrē[1] and in two MSS. in the British Museum[2]. The third has fortunately come down to us, though with considerable lacunæ, in Brit. Mus. Add. 14640 (of the 7th century)[3]. This book is worthy of all praise for the fulness and accuracy of its information and the evident striving of the author after impartiality. The Syriac style, however, is very awkward and involved, and abounds in Greek words and phrases. Of scarcely less value for the history of his own time is another work entitled *Biographies of Eastern Saints*, men and women, contained in Brit. Mus. Add. 14647, ff. 1–135[4]. These lives were gathered into one corpus about 569, as appears from the account of the combination of the monasteries of Āmid during the persecution of 521, which was put on paper in

[1] *B.O.*, ii. 100; comp. pp. 85–90.

[2] Add. 14647 (dated 688), ff. 136–139: Add. 14650 (dated 875), ff. 189–206. Edited by Land, *Anecd. Syr.*, ii. 289–329 and 385–391. See also a small fragment, *ibid.*, 363, from Add. 12154, f. 201 b.

[3] Edited by Cureton, 1853. There is an English translation by R. Payne Smith, 1860, and a German one by Schönfelder, 1862.

[4] Edited by Land, *Anecd. Syr.*, ii. 1–288. [These and the fragments of *E.H.* printed in *Anecd. Syr.* have also been translated into Latin by van Douwen and Land, *Commentarii de beatis orientalibus et historiae eccles. fragmenta*, Amsterdam, 1889.]

567[1], and from the history of the convent of St John, extending from its foundation in 389 to 568[2]. To these lives Land has added three more, which are ascribed in MSS. to John, but do not seem to have been included in this collection[3].

The name of Zacharias Rhetor or Scholasticus, bishop of Mitylēnē in Lesbos[4], must next be mentioned, for, though a Greek author, his work has entered into the Syriac literature as part of a compilation by a Syrian monk. The *Ecclesiastical History* of Zacharias seems to have terminated about the year 518, whereas his Syriac translator was writing as late as 569[5], and even later. The MS. in the British Museum, Add. 17202[6], cannot be younger than the beginning of the 7th century, and is clearly the compilation of a Monophysite, who used Zacharias as his chief authority in books iii.–vi.; whereas books i., ii., and vii.–xii. were

1 *Anecd. Syr.*, ii. 212, l. 17; see also p. 191, last two lines.

2 *Ibid.*, ii. 288, ll. 2, 3.

3 *Ibid.*, ii. 343–362. That of Jacob Burdĕʿānā (*ibid.*, p. 364) is not his, at least in its present shape (see above, p. 85). There is a slightly different redaction of it in the Bibl. Nation. at Paris, Anc. fonds 144 (Zotenberg, *Catal.*, p. 187).

4 See Land, *Joannes Bischof von Ephesos*, p. 35 *sq.*, and *Anecd. Syr.*, iii., Preface.

5 Land, *Anecd. Syr.*, iii. pp. xi., xii., and p. 5, l. 21 *sq.*

6 See Wright, *Catal.*, p. 1046 *sq.*

gathered from different sources, such as Moses of Aggēl (about 550–570), Simeon of Bēth Arshām (see above, p. 79 *sq.*), Mārā of Amid (see above, p. 83), the correspondence of Julian of Halicarnassus and Severus of Antioch (see above, p. 94), the history of John of Ephesus[1], &c. In a Syriac MS. in the Vatican (No. cxlv.)[2] we find a series of extracts from this Syriac work (f. 78 *sq.*) as a continuation of copious excerpts from the Greek histories of Socrates and Theodoret. The last of these, on the public buildings, statues, and other decorations of the city of Rome, has been carefully re-edited and annotated by Guidi[3]. [The Syriac version of the life of Severus of Antioch, by Zacharias Rhetor, has been edited by Spanuth from Sachau MS. 321 (Göttingen, 1893).]

[1] Not a few chapters in books vii.–x. seem to be derived, in part at any rate, from the second part of the *Ecclesiastical History*.

[2] *Catal.*, iii. 253; *B.O.*, ii. 54 *sq.*; Mai, *Scriptorum Veterum Nova Collectio*, x. pp. xi.–xiv., 332–388. The MS., which Assemani calls "pervetustus, Syriacis literis stronghylis exaratus" (p. 253), is not likely to be earlier than the middle of the 8th century, as it contains a work of the patriarch Elias, who sat from 708 to 728.

[3] *Il Testo Siriaco della Descrizione di Roma*, &c., from the *Bullettino della Commissione Archeologica di Roma*, fasc. iv. anno 1884 (Rome, 1885). It is also extant in a shorter form in Brit. Mus. Add. 12154, f. 158a (see Wright, *Catal.*, p. 984; Guidi, p. 235 *sq.*).

We turn from the historians to the ascetic writers of this century, who seem to have been more prized by their countrymen, though far less valuable to us. And first we mention the author who is commonly called John Sābhā[1] or "the Aged," placing him here on the authority of Assemani (*B.O.*, i. 433), for ʿAbhd-īshōʿ claims him as a Nestorian (*B.O.*, iii. 1, 103). His *floruit* is given as about 550. His writings consist of short sermons or tracts, exclusively intended for the training and study of monks and cœnobites, and a number of letters. ʿAbhd-īshōʿ (*loc. cit.*) says: "he composed two volumes, besides mournful epistles, on the monastic life." They were

[1] There is some uncertainty about his name. In *B.O.*, i. 434, Assemani gives ܝܘܚܢܢ ܗܘ ܕܕܠܝܬܐ, John of Dīlāitā, which, he says (p. 433), is a convent at Nineveh, on the opposite bank of the Tigris from Mosul. In vol. iii. 1, 103 he prints ܝܘܚܢܢ ܗܘ ܕܕ̈ܠܝܬܗ, which he renders Joannes Daliathensis, *i.e.*, from ad-Dāliyah, الدالية, probably meaning Dāliyat Mālik ibn Ṭauḳ, on the right bank of the Euphrates below ar-Raḳḳah and Raḥbat Mālik ibn Ṭauḳ. In the Vatican *Catalogue* he calls him Daliathensis, writing, however, in Syriac ܕܕܠܝܬܐ. But how can ܕܕ̈ܠܝܬܗ mean "of ad-Dāliyah" (ܕܠܝܐ)? Following the analogy of ܝܘܚܢܢ ܕܣܪ̈ܘܗܝ, ܡܠܟܝ ܕܟܠܒ̈ܘܗܝ, and the like, it ought rather to mean "John of the Vine-Branches," or "John with the Varicose Veins," or (as in Arabic) "John of the Buckets."

collected[1] by his brother, who has prefixed a brief apology, at the end of which the reader may find a curious example of affected humility (*B.O.*, i. 435)[2]. Two short specimens of the style of "the spiritual old man," *ash-Shaikh ar-rūḥānī*, are printed in Zingerle's *Monumenta Syr.*, i. 102–104.

A little junior to John Sābhā was the even more widely known Isaac of Nineveh[3], to whom the Nestorians also lay claim[4]. His date is fixed, as Assemani points out, by the facts of his citing Jacob of Sĕrūgh and corresponding with Simeon Stylites the younger or Thaumastorites, who died in 593. According to the Arabic biography, printed in *B.O.*, i. 444, he was a monk of the convent of Mār Matthew at Mosul, and afterwards became bishop of that city, but soon resigned his office and retired to the desert of Skētē in Egypt, where he composed his ascetic works. According to 'Abhd-īshō' (*B.O.*, iii. 1, 104), Isaac "wrote

[1] See Wright, *Catal.*, p. 863, *j*. In the *B.O.*, i. 434, Assemani gives an Arabic version of it from a Vatican MS.

[2] For a list of them in Syriac and Arabic, see *B.O.*, i. 435–444, and comp. Wright, *Catal.*, pp. 582, 584, 860, 870 (No. 16). There is also an Ethiopic version, *Aragāwī Manfasāwī*, made from the Arabic; see Zotenberg, *Catal. des MSS. Ethiopiens de la Bibl. Nation.*, No. 115, p. 134.

[3] *B.O.*, i. 444.

[4] *Ibid.*, iii. 1, 104.

seven volumes on the guidance of the Spirit, and on the Divine mysteries and judgements and dispensation." Many of his discourses and epistles have been catalogued by Assemani, *B.O.*, i. 446–460. The MS. Vat. cxxiv. contains the first half of his writings (*Catal.*, iii. 143), and similarly MSS. Brit. Mus. Add. 14632 and 14633[1]. The Arabic translation is divided into four books; the Ethiopic is naturally derived from the Arabic. A Greek version was made from the original Syriac by two monks of St Saba, near Jerusalem, named Patricius and Abraamius, on which see Assemani, *B.O.*, i. 445, and Bickell, *Conspectus*, p. 26. The only printed specimens of his discourses are two in Zingerle's *Monumenta Syr.*, i. 97–101; [and three which have been edited and translated into Latin by Chabot as an appendix to his essay *De S. Isaaci Ninivitae Vita, Scriptis et Doctrina*, Paris, 1892].

Another author of this class, but of less mark, is Abraham of Nephtar[2], who flourished towards the end of the 6th century and in the early part of the 7th[3]. Him too the Nestorians claim as

[1] Wright, *Catal.*, pp. 569, 576.

[2] Also written Nethpar and Nephrath; see Assemani, *Catal. Vat.*, iii. 138. But, as we can find no trace of any such town as Nephtar, the name of ܢܦܬܪ may have some other origin.

[3] *B.O.*, iii. 1, 191, note 1.

theirs[1]. ʿAbhd-īshōʿ speaks of "various works" of his[2], but our libraries seem to contain only eight short discourses, the titles of which are given by Assemani, *B.O.*, i. 464[3]. They have been translated into Arabic, and there was also a Persian version of them by Job the monk (*B.O.*, iii. 1, 431).

We record here the name of Moses of Aggēl as being one of those who, after Rabbūlā, undertook the translation of the writings of Cyril of Alexandria into Syriac. He made a version of the *Glaphyra*, at the request of a monk named Paphnutius, from whose letter[4] we learn that the treatise *On Worship in Spirit and in Truth* had been already translated[5], whilst from the reply of Moses, as quoted in *B.O.*, ii. 82–83, it is obvious that he was writing after the death of Philoxenus and the chorepiscopus Polycarp. Hence we may place him soon after the middle of the century, say from 550 to 570. Much later he cannot be,

[1] Compare Wright, *Catal.*, p. 187, No. 154.

[2] *B.O.*, iii. 1, 191.

[3] There seem to be ten in Cod. Vat. ccccxix.; see Mai, *Scriptt. Vet. Nova Coll.*, v. 65.

[4] Cod. Vat. cvii. (*Catal.*, iii. 53); Guidi, *Rendiconti della R. Accademia dei Lincei*, May and June, 1886, p. 399 *sq.*

[5] Brit. Mus. Add. 12166, ff. 155–258, bears date 553 (Wright, *Catal.*, p. 491).

because his translation of the History of Joseph and Āsyath (see above, p. 25) has been admitted into the Syriac compilation that passes under the name of Zacharias Rhetor (see above, p. 107)[1].

Peter of Callinīcus (ar-Raḳḳah), Jacobite patriarch of Antioch, 578–591[2], deserves mention on account of his huge controversial treatise against Damian, patriarch of Alexandria, manuscripts of parts of which, of the 7th and 8th centuries, are extant in the Vatican and the British Museum[3]. Other writings of his are an anaphora[4], a short treatise against the Tritheists[5], sundry letters[6], and a metrical homily on the Crucifixion of our Lord[7]. In the dispute between him and Damian was involved his syncellus and successor Julian, who defended Peter against an

[1] Of the Vatican MS. of the *Glaphyra* only five leaves remain (*Catal.*, iii. 54), and the MS. in the British Museum, Add. 14555, is very imperfect (Wright, *Catal.*, p. 483). As Guidi has shown, these two MSS. are merely the *disjecta membra* of one codex.

[2] *B.O.*, ii. 69, 332; Bar-Hebræus, *Chron. Eccles.*, i. 250.

[3] *B.O.*, ii. 77-82; comp. Bar-Hebræus, *Chron. Eccles.*, i. 257.

[4] *B.O.*, ii. 77.

[5] Brit. Mus. Add. 12155, f. 231 b (Wright, *Catal.*, p. 951).

[6] Wright, *Catal.*, p. 1314.

[7] Brit. Mus. Add. 14591 (Wright, *Catal.*, p. 671).

attack made upon him by Sergius the Armenian, bishop of Edessa, and his brother John[1].

Of the numerous Nestorian writers of the 6th century we unfortunately know but little more than can be learned from the catalogue of ʽAbhd-īshōʽ. Their works have either been lost, or else very few of them have as yet reached our European libraries.

The successor of Narsai (above, p. 58) in the school of Nisībis was his sister's son Abraham[2], who must have fled from Edessa with his uncle[3]. His principal writings are commentaries on Joshua, Judges, Kings, Ecclesiasticus, Isaiah, the twelve minor prophets, Daniel, and the Song of Songs[4].

To him succeeded as teacher John, also a disciple of Narsai[5]. He wrote commentaries on

[1] *B.O.*, ii. 333; Bar-Hebræus, *Chron. Eccles.*, i. 259.

[2] *B.O.*, iii. 1, 71. Assemani would seem to have confounded him with a later Abraham of Bēth Rabban; see his note, *B.O.*, iii. 1, 631.

[3] There seems to be no reason for identifying him with Abraham "the Mede," whom Simeon of Bēth Arshām nicknames "the Heater of Baths" (*B.O.*, i. 352).

[4] The hymn appended to Nestorian copies of the Psalter probably pertains to this Abraham and not to the later Abraham of Bēth Rabban (see, for example, Brit. Mus. Add. 7156, f. 157 b); comp. Bickell, *Conspectus*, p. 37, and Hoffmann, *Opusc. Nestor.*, xi., note 2.

[5] *B.O.*, iii. 1, 72. Here again Assemani seems to have mixed up this John with a later John of Bēth Rabban and

Exodus, Leviticus, and Numbers, Job, Jeremiah, Ezekiel, and Proverbs; also controversial treatises against the Magi or Persian priesthood, the Jews, and (Christian) heretics; a book of questions on the Old and New Testaments; and various hymns. If the discourses on the plague at Nisībis[1] and the death of Khosrau I. Anōsharwān be really by him, he was alive as late as 579, in the spring of which year that monarch died[2].

John was followed by Joseph Hūzāyā[3], another disciple of Narsai[4], and the first Syriac grammar-

with John Sābhā of Bēth Garmai; see his additional notes in *B.O.*, iii. 1, 631, 708.

[1] During the time of the catholics Joseph and Ezekiel, from 552 to 578; see *B.O.*, ii. 413, 433, note 2.

[2] The hymn in the Nestorian MSS. of the Psalter (mentioned in note 4, p. 114) is probably by this John and not by the later John of Bēth Rabban; comp. Hoffmann's note referred to above. The monastery of Rabban Zĕkhā-Īshō' (or Īshō'-zĕkhā) in Dāsen was not founded till about 590, and Zĕkhā-Īshō' himself did not die till the thirteenth year of Khosrau II. Parwēz, 603; see *B.O.*, iii. 1, 472.

[3] *I.e.*, of al-Ahwāz or Khūzistān. He must not be confounded with Joseph Ḥazzāyā, of whom we shall speak hereafter (see p. 128 *infra*).

[4] Bar-Hebræus, *Chron. Eccles.*, ii. 78, says that Joseph Hūzāyā was the immediate successor of Narsai; but the Nestorian writer cited by Assemani (*B.O.*, iii. 1, 64) is likely to be better informed. The passage quoted *ibid.*, p. 82, points in the same direction; comp. also *B.O.*, iii. 2, cmxxvii.

ian. Of him Bar-Hebræus observes[1] that "he changed the Edessene (or Western) mode of reading into the Eastern mode which the Nestorians employ; otherwise during the whole time of Narsai they used to read like us Westerns." He was the inventor of some of the Syriac signs of interpunction[2], and wrote a treatise on grammar[3] and another on words that are spelled with the same letters but have different meanings[4].

Of Mār-abhā[5] the Elder, catholicus from 536 to 552, we have already spoken above as a translator of the Scriptures (p. 19). He was a convert from the Zoroastrian religion, and seems to have been a man of great talent and versatility, as he mastered both the Greek and Syriac languages. Receiving baptism at Ḥērtā (al-Ḥīrah) from a teacher named Joseph, he went for the purposes of study to Nisībis, and afterwards to

[1] Bar-Hebræus, *Chron. Eccles.*, ii. 78; comp. *B.O.*, ii. 407.

[2] See Wright, *Catal.*, p. 107, col. 2. Assemani (*B.O.*, iii. 1, 64, col. 2) has mistranslated the words وهو صاحب الفحام بتسعة نقط. Comp. Hoffmann, *Opusc. Nestor.*, viii., xi.; [Merx, *Hist. artis gramm. ap. Syros*, p. 28, *sq.*].

[3] Berlin, Royal Library, Sachau 226, 4.

[4] Bar-Hebræus, *Œuvres grammaticales*, ed. Martin, ii. 77.

[5] Properly Mār(ī)-abhā, but we shall write Mār-abhā.

Edessa, where he and his teacher Thomas[1] translated into Syriac the liturgy of Nestorius[2]. They visited Constantinople together, and, escaping thence at some risk of their lives, betook themselves to Nisībis, where Mār-abhā became eminent as a teacher. On being chosen catholicus he opened a college at Seleucia and lectured there. Unluckily, he got into controversy, it is said, with the Persian monarch Khosrau I. Anōsharwān (531–579), who banished him to Ādharbāigān (Azerbijan) and destroyed the Nestorian church beside his palace at Seleucia. Mār-abhā, however, had the temerity to return to Seleucia, was thrown by the king into prison, and died there[3]. His dead body was carried by one of his disciples to Ḥērtā, where it was buried and a monastery erected over the grave. He wrote[4] commentaries on Genesis, the Psalms, and Proverbs, and the epistles of St Paul to the Romans, Corinthians, Galatians, Ephesians, Philippians,

[1] Probably the same who is mentioned among his disciples in *B.O.*, ii. 412, and some of whose writings are enumerated by 'Abhd-īshō' in *B.O.*, iii. 1, 86–7.

[2] So 'Abhd-īshō' in *B.O.*, iii. 1, 36; but in Brit. Mus. Add. 7181 the same remark is made as to the liturgy of Theodore of Mopsuestia (see Rosen, *Catal.*, p. 59).

[3] *B.O.*, ii. 411–412, iii. 1, 75, notes 1, 2; Bar-Hebræus, *Chron. Eccles.*, ii. 89–95.

[4] *B.O*, iii. 1, 75.

and Hebrews; various homilies; synodical epistles[1]; and ecclesiastical canons[2]. In these last he opposed the practice of marriage at least among the higher orders of the clergy, the bishops and catholics. What is meant by his "canones in totum Davidem" may be seen from such MSS. of the Psalter as Brit. Mus. Add. 7156[3] and Munich, cod. Syr. 4 (Orient. 147)[4]. Hymns of his are also extant[5].

Under Mār-abhā flourished Abraham of Kashkar (al-Wāsiṭ), distinguished for his acquaintance with philosophy and for his ascetic virtues. He introduced certain reforms into the Persian monasteries. After living for some time in a cave at Ḥazzah[6], he betook himself to Jerusalem and thence to Egypt. Returning to his old haunt, he led the life of a hermit for thirty years, travelling into the far north as a missionary. He died at Ḥazzah, but his body was secretly

[1] *B.O.*, iii. 1, 76, note 4.

[2] *Ibid.*, iii. 1, 81, and note 1; comp. Cod. Vat. cccvi. in Mai, *Scriptt. Vett. Nova Coll.*, v. 21.

[3] Rosen, *Catal.*, p. 12.

[4] *Verzeichniss d. orient. Handschriften d. k. Hof- u. Staats-Bibl.*, &c., p. 111.

[5] See Bickell, *Conspectus*, p. 37, and comp. Brit. Mus. Add. 17219, f. 165b (beg., *Glory to Thee, Lord; how good Thou art!*).

[6] A village near Arbēl or Irbil, in Ḥĕdhaiyabh.

removed to his native place Kashkar. He wrote a treatise on the monastic life, which was translated into Persian by his disciple Job the monk[1].

He must, it would seem, be distinguished from another Abraham of Kashkar, who lived about the same time, and with whom Assemani has confounded him[2]. This Abraham was a student at Nisībis under Abraham the nephew of Narsai. Thence he went to Ḥērtā (al-Ḥīrah), where he converted some of the heathen inhabitants, visited Egypt and Mount Sinai, and finally settled down as a hermit in a cave on Mount Īzlā, near Nisībis, where a great number of followers soon gathered about him and a large monastery was built. He introduced stricter rules than heretofore among the cœnobites[3]. His death did not take place till towards the end of the century[4].

Theodore, bishop of Marū or Merv, was appointed to this see by Mār-abhā in place of David, whom he had deposed, about 540. He seems to have been much addicted to the study of the Aristotelian dialectics, since several of the translations and treatises of Sergius of Rās'ain

1 *B.O.*, iii. 1, 155, col. 1, 431; iii. 2, dccclxxiii.

2 Comp. *B.O.*, iii. 1, 154, note 4, with Hoffmann, *Auszüge*, p. 172.

3 *B.O.*, iii. 1, 93.

4 See Hoffmann, *loc. cit.*

are dedicated to him[1]. Among his own works[2] there is mentioned "a solution of the ten questions of Sergius." He also composed a commentary on the Psalms and a metrical history of Mār Eugenius and his companions[3], who came from Klysma and introduced asceticism into Mesopotamia about the beginning of the 4th century. What may have been the contents of the "liber varii argumenti" which he wrote at the request of Mār-abhā himself it is hard to guess, in the default of any copy of it.

Theodore's brother Gabriel, bishop of Hormizdshēr[4], is stated by ʿAbhd-īshōʿ[5] to have written two controversial books against the

[1] See Brit. Mus. Add. 14658 (Wright, *Catal.*, p. 1154); Renan, *De Philosophia Peripat. ap. Syros*, p. 29.

[2] *B.O.*, iii. 1, 147.

[3] See *B.O.*, iii. 1, 147, note 4, and 633; iii. 2, dccclxii.; Bar-Hebræus, *Chron. Eccles.*, i. 85, with note 5; Hoffmann, *Auszüge*, p. 167. If the poem mentioned by Assemani (*B.O.*, iii. 1, 147, note 4) really speaks of Abraham of Kashkar and still more of Bābhai of Nisībis, it must be of later date, and Hoffmann is inclined to ascribe it to George Wardā, a writer of the 13th century (see *Auszüge*, p. 171, note 1327).

[4] A corruption of Hormizd-Ardashēr, still further shortened by the Arabs into Hormushīr. It is identical with Sūḳ al-Ahwāz, or simply al-Ahwāz, on the river Kārūn. See Nöldeke, *Gesch. d. Perser u. Araber*, p. 19, with note 5.

[5] *B.O.*, iii. 1, 147.

Manichees and the Chaldæans (astrologers), as also about 300 chapters on various passages of Scripture which needed elucidation and explanation.

The successor of Mār-abhā in the see of Seleucia was Joseph, in 552. He studied medicine in the West and practised in Nisībis, where he lived in one of the convents. Having been introduced by a Persian noble to the notice of Khosrau I., he cured that monarch of an illness, and ingratiated himself with him so much that he favoured his appointment to the office of catholicus. Of his strange pranks and cruelties as archbishop some account, doubtless highly coloured, may be read in *B.O.*, iii. 1, 432–433, and Bar-Hebræus, *Chron. Eccles.*, ii. 95–97. He was deposed after he had sat for three years, but he lived twelve years longer, during which time no successor was appointed. He promulgated twenty-three canons[1], and, according to Elias, bishop of Damascus (893)[2], after his deposition drew up a list of his predecessors in the dignity of catholicus, wherein he would seem to have paid special attention to those who had shared the

[1] *B.O.*, iii. 1, 435. Elias bar Shīnāyā cites his "synod"; see Bar-Hebræus, *Chron. Eccles.*, ii. 96, note 1.

[2] In his *Nomocanon*, quoted by Assemani, *B.O.*, iii. 1, 434.

same fate with himself. At least Bar-Hebræus[1] (perhaps not a quite trustworthy witness in this case) gives currency to the charge of his having forged the consolatory epistles of Jacob of Nisībis and Mār Ephraim to Pāpā of Seleucia on his deposition.

A little later in the century, under the sway of his successor Ezekiel (a disciple of Mār-abhā and the son-in-law of his predecessor Paul), 567–580[2], there flourished Paul the Persian[3], of Dērshar or Dērshahr[4], a courtier of Khosrau I. Anōsharwān[5]. He is said by Bar-Hebræus[6] to have been distinguished alike in ecclesiastical and philosophical lore, and to have aspired to the post of metropolitan bishop of Persis, but, being disappointed, to have gone over to the Zoroastrian religion. This may or may not be true; but it is certain that Paul thought more of knowledge than faith, for thus he speaks[7]: "Scientia enim

[1] *Chron. Eccles.*, ii. 31.

[2] See *B.O.*, iii. 1, 435–439; Bar-Hebræus, *Chron. Eccles.*, ii. 97, 103.

[3] *B.O.*, iii. 1, 439; Renan, *De Philos. Peripat. ap. Syros*, pp. 16–22.

[4] ܕܪܫܗܪ, a place not known to the present writer.

[5] See Nöldeke, *Gesch. d. Perser u. Araber*, p. 160, note 3.

[6] *Chron. Eccles.*, ii. 97.

[7] In the Preface to his *Logic*, as translated by Land (see note 3, p. 123).

agit de rebus proximis et manifestis et quæ sciri possunt, fides autem de omnibus materiis quæ remotæ sunt, neque conspiciuntur neque certa ratione cognoscuntur. Hæc quidem cum dubio est, illa autem sine dubio. Omne dubium dissensionem parit, dubii absentia autem unanimitatem. Scientia igitur potior est fide, et illam præ hac eligendum est." Bar-Hebræus speaks of Paul's "admirable introduction to the dialectics (of Aristotle)[1]," by which he no doubt means the treatise on logic extant in a single MS. in the Brit. Mus.[2] It has been edited, with a Latin translation and notes, by Land[3].

About this same time Assemani[4] places the periodeutes Bōdh, who is said to have had the charge of the Christians in the remoter districts of the Persian empire as far as India. Among his writings are specified "discourses on the faith and against the Manichees and Marcionites," as well as a book of "Greek questions," probably philosophical, bearing the strange title of *Āleph Mīgīn*[5]. All these have perished, but his name

1 *Chron. Eccles.*, ii. 97.

2 Add. 14660, f. 55b; see Wright, *Catal.*, p. 1161.

3 *Anecd. Syr.*, iv., Syr. text, pp. 1–32; transl., pp. 1–30; notes, pp. 99–113.

4 *B.O.*, iii. 1, 219.

5 Assemani, *loc. cit.*, note 1, proposes to read *Āleph Mellīn*, "the Thousand Words"; but *Āleph Mīgīn* is more

will go down to remote posterity as the translator into Syriac of the collection of Indian tales commonly called *Kalīlah and Dimnah*[1]. Of this work a single copy has come down to our time, preserved in an Oriental library. A transcript of it was first procured by Bickell[2], who, in conjunction with Benfey, edited the book (Leipsic, 1876); and since then three additional copies of the same original have been got by Sachau[3]. That Bōdh made his Syriac translation from an Indian (Sanskrit) original, as ʽAbhd-īshōʽ asserts, is wholly unlikely; he no doubt had before him a Pahlavī or Persian version[4].

Just at this period the Nestorian Church ran a great risk of disruption from an internal schism. Ḥannānā of Ḥĕdhaiyabh, the successor of Joseph Hūzāyā in the school of Nisībis [and the author of a revision of its statutes published in 590 under the metropolitan Simeon][5], who had, it is

likely to be a corruption of some Greek word. [According to Steinschneider it is τὸ ἄλφα μέγαν, *i.e.*, Book A of the *Metaphysics* of Aristotle.]

[1] The Syriac title keeps the older forms Ḳalīlagh and Damnagh.

[2] Göttingen, university library, MS. Orient. 18d.

[3] Berlin, Royal Library, Sachau 139, 149, 150.

[4] See Keith-Falconer, *Kalīlah and Dimnah*, Introd., xlii. *sq.*

[5] [See Guidi, *Scuola di Nisibi*, p. 4. Earlier writers, who had access only to an imperfect Arabic redaction of the

said, a following of 800 pupils[1], had dared to assail the doctrines and exegesis of Theodore of Mopsuestia and to follow in some points those of Chrysostom[2]. During the time of the catholicus Ezekiel (567–580)[3] he brought forward his theological views, which were condemned at a synod held under the next catholicus, Īshō'-yabh of Arzōn (581–595)[4], and at another synod presided over by his successor, Sabhr-īshō' (596–604)[5]. On the death of this latter a struggle took place between the rival factions, the orthodox Nestorians putting forward as their candidate Gregory of Tell-Besmē[6], bishop of Nisībis, whilst the others supported Gregory of Kashkar, a teacher in the school of Māḥōzē or Sĕlīḳ (Seleucia)[7]. The influence of the Persian court decided the

statutes have confused this revision with the later and final edition of the statutes published under the metropolitan Aḥā-dh'abū(hī), A.D. 602. Guidi's documents have made it necessary to omit or change a few words in this paragraph.]

1 *B.O.*, iii. 1, 81, note 2, 437.

2 *Ibid.*, iii. 1, 84, note 3.

3 *Ibid.*, ii. 413; iii. 1, 435.

4 *Ibid.*, ii. 415, iii. 1, 108; Bar-Hebræus, *Chron. Eccles.*, ii. 105, note 3.

5 *B.O.*, ii. 415; iii. 1, 82, 441.

6 Not *aromatarius*, as Assemani translates *Besmāyā*.

7 *B.O.*, ii. 416; iii. 1, 449. We need not believe the statements of Bar-Hebræus, *Chron. Eccles.*, ii. 107.

matter in favour of the latter, who was a *persona grata* in the eyes of the queen Shīrīn and her physician Gabriel of Shiggār (Sinjār)[1], a keen Monophysite, who naturally availed himself of this opportunity to harm the rival sect of Christians[2]. Gregory was not, however, a partisan of Ḥannānā, but an orthodox Nestorian, as appears from the account given of the synod over which he presided[3], by which the Nicene creed was confirmed, the commentaries of Theodore of Mopsuestia approved, and the memory and writings of Barṣaumā vindicated against his assailants. He died at the end of three years (607), and the archiepiscopal see remained vacant till after the murder of Khosrau II. Parwēz in 628, during which time of persecution Bābhai the archimandrite distinguished himself as the leader and guide of the Nestorian Church. In the overthrow of

[1] See *B.O.*, ii. 404-406, 416, 472; Bar-Hebræus, *Chron. Eccles.*, ii. 109; Nöldeke, *Gesch. d. Perser u. Araber*, p. 358, in the note; Hoffmann, *Auszüge*, pp. 118-121.

[2] [But according to the Syriac chronicle published by Guidi at the Stockholm Congress, the court favourite, who was elected catholicus, was Gregory *of Porāth* (a place near Baṣra), whereas Gregory *of Kashkar* was the unsuccessful candidate of the orthodox Nestorians. See Nöldeke, *Die von Guidi herausgegebene syrische Chronik* (Vienna, 1893), pp. 18, 19 (in *Sitzungsber. d. kaiserlichen Akad. der Wissenschaften*).]

[3] *B.O.*, iii. 1, 452.

Khosrau the oppressed Nestorians bore a part, more especially Shamṭā[1] and Ḳurṭa, the sons of the noble Yazdīn, who had been the director of the land-tax of the whole kingdom and had amassed an enormous fortune, which the king confiscated[2]. To return to Ḥannānā, his works, as enumerated by ʿAbhd-īshōʿ[3], are—commentaries on Genesis, Job, Psalms, Proverbs, Ecclesiastes, the Song of Songs, the twelve minor prophets, the Gospel of St Mark, and the epistles of St Paul; expositions of the (Nicene) creed and the liturgy; on the occasions of the celebration of Palm Sunday, Golden Friday[4], rogations[5], and the invention of the cross; a discourse on Palm Sunday; and various other writings in which he attacked the teaching of Theodore of Mopsuestia, and which the church therefore placed on its *index expurgatorius*[6].

The doctrines of Ḥannānā found a warm

[1] See *B.O.*, iii. 1, 471.

[2] See Hoffmann, *Auszüge*, pp. 115–121; Nöldeke, *Gesch. d. Perser u. Araber*, p. 383. To Yazdīn is ascribed a hymn which appears in Nestorian Psalters, *e.g.*, Wright, *Catal.*, p. 135; Zotenberg, *Catal.*, p. 9.

[3] *B.O.*, iii. 1, 83-84.

[4] The first Friday after Pentecost or Whitsunday, with reference to Acts iii. 6.

[5] See *B.O.*, ii. 413.

[6] *Ibid.*, iii. 1, 84, note 3.

champion in Joseph of Ḥazzā (Arbēl or Irbil)[1], with whom Bābhai the archimandrite entered into controversy[2]. He is said to have composed some 1900 tracts, of which 'Abhd-īshō' mentions about a dozen as "profitable," whence we may conjecture that the rest were more or less deeply tinged with heresy. The chief of them are—on theory (or speculation) and practice; the book of the treasurer, containing the solution of abstruse questions; on misfortunes and chastisements; on the reasons of the principal feasts of the church; the book of the histories of the Paradise of the Orientals, containing many notices of ecclesiastical history; an exposition of the vision of Ezekiel and of the vision of St Gregory; of the book of the merchant[3]; of (pseudo-)Dionysius (the Areopagite); and of the *capita scientiæ* or heads of knowledge (of Evagrius); besides epistles on the exalted character of the monastic life. Joseph appears to have been made a bishop in his latter

[1] *B.O.*, iii. 1, 100; Hoffmann, *Auszüge*, p. 117. Assemani confounds Joseph Ḥazzāyā with the older Joseph Hūzāyā, and translates Ḥazzāyā by "videns" instead of "Hazzæus."

[2] *E.g.*, his letters to Joseph of Ḥazzā, *B.O.*, iii. 1, 97, and the tract *De Unione*, *ib.*, 95.

[3] According to Assemani, *B.O.*, iii. 1, 102, note 4, of Isaiah of Scete, who, according to Palladius, was originally a merchant.

days, and to have taken the name of ʿAbhd-īshōʿ; at least a MS. in the India Office (No. 9) contains a tract on Zech. iv. 10 (f. 241 b), and three series of questions addressed by a pupil to his teacher, by "Mār ʿAbhd-īshōʿ, who is Joseph Ḥazzāyā" (f. 293 a)[1].

The successor of Ezekiel as catholicus of the Nestorians was Īshōʿ-yabh of Arzōn, 581–595[2]. He was a native of Bēth ʿArbāyē, educated at Nisībis under Abraham (see above, p. 114), and subsequently made bishop of Arzōn (Ἀρζανηνή). He managed to ingratiate himself with the Persian monarch Hormizd IV. (579–590), by whose influence he was raised to the archiepiscopate; and he continued to stand in favour with his son and successor Khosrau II. Parwēz, as well as with the Greek emperor Maurice. Doubtless both found the Christian archbishop a convenient ambassador and agent in public and private affairs, for Maurice had given his daughter Maria in marriage to Khosrau[3]. He was also a friend of the Arab king of Ḥērtā (al-Ḥīrah), Abū Ḳābūs Nuʿmān ibn al-Mundhir, who had been converted

[1] See Hoffmann, *Auszüge*, p. 117, note 1057.

[2] *B.O.*, ii. 415, iii. 1, 108; Bar-Hebræus, *Chron. Eccles.*, ii. 105, note 3; Nöldeke, *Gesch. d. Perser u. Araber*, p. 347, note 1.

[3] See Nöldeke, *op. cit.*, p. 283, note 2, and comp. p. 287, note 2.

to Christianity, with his sons, by Simeon, bishop of Ḥērtā, Sabhr-īshōʻ, bishop of Lāshōm, and the monk Īshōʻ-zĕkhā[1]. On a pastoral visit to this part of his diocese, the catholicus was taken ill, and died in the convent of Hind (the daughter of Nuʻmān) at al-Ḥīrah. Among his works are mentioned[2] a treatise against Eunomius, one against a heretical (Monophysite) bishop who had entered into argument with him, twenty-two questions regarding the sacraments of the church[3], an apology[4], and synodical canons and epistles.

Mĕshīḥā-zĕkhā, also called Īshōʻ-zĕkhā or Zĕkhā-īshōʻ, was a monk of Mount Īzlā[5]. When many of his brotherhood were expelled from their convent by Bābhai the archimandrite[6], he betook himself to the district of Dāsen[7], and founded there a monastery, which was henceforth known as Bēth Rabban Zĕkhā-īshōʻ or, for shortness'

[1] Bar-Hebræus (*Chron. Eccles.*, ii. 105) tries to make out that Nuʻmān was a Monophysite, and that Īshōʻ-yabh was trying to pervert him at the time of his death. But in such matters he is hardly a trustworthy witness.

[2] *B.O.*, iii. 1, 108.

[3] See a specimen in Assemani's *Catal. of the Vatican Library*, iii. 280, No. cl., v.

[4] Probably a defence of his doctrines addressed to the emperor Maurice; see *B.O.*, iii. 1, 109, in the note.

[5] *B.O.*, iii. 1, 216, note 1. See above, p. 115, note 2.

[6] *Ibid.*, iii. 1, 88–89.

[7] Hoffmann, *Auszüge*, p. 202 *sq.*

sake, Bēth Rabban simply[1]. He was the author of an ecclesiastical history, which ʿAbhd-īshōʿ praises as being "exact."

Dādh-īshōʿ was the successor of Abraham of Kashkar as abbot of the great convent on Mount Īzlā[2], apparently during the lifetime of the latter, who lived to a great age (see above, p. 119)[3]. He composed a treatise on the monastic life and another entitled *On Silence in Body and in Spirit*, a discourse on the consecration of the cell, besides funeral sermons and epistles. He also translated or edited a commentary on *The Paradise of the Western Monks* (probably meaning the *Paradise* of Palladius and Jerome), and annotated the works of Isaiah of Scete[4].

Hereabout too is the date of the monk Bar-ʿidtā[5], the founder of the convent which bears his name[6], a contemporary of Bābhai of Īzlā and Jacob of Bēth ʿĀbhē[7]. He was the author of a monastic history, which is often quoted by Thomas of Margā[8], and seems to have been a work of

[1] *B.O.*, iii. 1, 216, note 1; 255, in the note; Hoffmann, *Auszüge*, p. 206.

[2] *B.O.*, iii. 1, 98, note 1.

[3] Hoffmann, *Auszüge*, p. 173.

[4] *B.O.*, iii. 1, 99.

[5] *Ibid.*, ii. 415, col. 2. Pronounce Bar-ʿittā.

[6] *B.O.*, iii. 2, dccclxxix.; Hoffmann, *Auszüge*, p. 181.

[7] Comp. Wright, *Catal.*, p. 187, No. 152.

[8] *B.O.*, iii. 1, 453, 458, 471.

considerable value. He must be distinguished from a later Bar-ʿidtā, of the convent of Ṣĕlībhā, near the village of Hēghlā on the Tigris[1], with whom Assemani has confounded him[2].

In the *Bibl. Orient.*, iii. 1, 230, ʿAbhd-īshōʿ mentions an historian whose name is given by Assemani as Simeon Karkhāyā, with the additional information that he was bishop of Karkhā and flourished under the patriarch Timothy I. about 800. His name seems, however, to have been wrongly read, and he appears to have lived at a much earlier date. At least Elias bar Shīnāyā speaks in his *Chronicle*[3] of one Simeon Barḳāyā[4] as the author of a chronicle (in at least two books), who wrote in the reign of the Persian king Khosrau II. Parwēz, A. Gr. 902=591 A.D.

[Here may perhaps be mentioned a Syriac compilation of uncertain date, the *Kĕthābhā dhakhĕyānāyāthā* or *Liber naturalium*, which has been edited and translated into German by Ahrens[5]. It consists of a series of short chapters on land and sea animals, and on certain natural

1 See Hoffmann, *Auszüge*, p. 181, note 1414.

2 *B.O.*, iii. 1, 458.

3 See Rosen, *Catal.*, p. 88, col. 1, 2.

4 The difference in writing between ܟܪܟܝܐ and ܒܪܩܝܐ is not great. The pronunciation of the word ܒܪܩܝܐ is not quite certain.

5 [*Das "Buch der Naturgegenstände,"* Kiel, 1892.

objects. Its main contents are taken from a Syriac version of the *Physiologus*: but the author has also borrowed from Basil's Homilies on the Hexaemeron, and probably from another Syriac book on animals. As to the date of compilation we can only say that it is later than Basil and earlier than 1000 A.D.: from the style of the Syriac Nöldeke[1] is inclined to favour an approach to the earlier limit.]

The name of Sabhr-īshōʿ the catholicus carries us over into the 7th century. He was a native of Pērōz-ābādh in Bēth Garmai, became bishop of Lāshōm, and was raised to the archiepiscopate in 596 by the favour of Khosrau II. Parwēz[2]. On the murder of his father-in-law Maurice (November 602), Khosrau resolved upon war, and took the field in 604, when he besieged and captured the fortress of Dārā, the first great success in a fearful struggle of twenty-five years. Bar-Hebræus states that Sabhr-īshōʿ accompanied him and died during the siege[3]; but other authorities say, doubtless more correctly, that he died at Nisībis[4]. He is said to have been the author of an ecclesiastical history, of which a fragment,

[1] *Z.D.M.G.*, xlv., p. 695.]

[2] *B.O.*, ii. 415, iii. 1, 441 *sq.*; Baethgen, *Fragmente syr. u. arab. Historiker*, pp. 36, 119.

[3] *Chron. Eccles.*, ii. 107.

[4] *Chron. Eccles.*, *loc. cit.*, note 2; *B.O.*, iii. 1, 441, col. 1.

relating to the emperor Maurice, was supposed to be extant in Cod. Vat. clxxxiii.; but Guidi has shown that this is incorrect, and that the said fragment is merely an extract from a legendary life of Sabhr-īshōʿ by some later hand (*Z.D.M.G.*, xl., pp. 559–561)[1].

About the same time with Sabhr-īshōʿ, if Assemani be right[2], we may place Simeon of Bēth Garmai, who translated into Syriac the *Chronicle* of Eusebius. This version seems unfortunately to be entirely lost.

With the 7th century begins the slow decay of the native literature of the Syrians, to which the frightful sufferings of the people during the great war with the Persians in its first quarter largely contributed[3]. During all those years we meet with scarcely a name of any note in letters, more especially in western Syria. Paul of Tellā and Thomas of Ḥarḳel were, it is true, labouring at the revised versions of the Old and New Testaments in Alexandria[4], but even they were

[1] Assemani, *Catal.*, iii. 387.

[2] *B.O.*, iii. 1, 168, 633.

[3] See the remarks of Nöldeke in *Gesch. d. Perser u. Araber*, p. 299, note 4.

[4] See above, p. 14, *sq.* Thomas of Ḥarḳel also compiled a liturgy (*B.O.*, ii. 92, col. 1), and is said to have translated from Greek into Syriac five other liturgies (*ibid.*, col. 2), viz., those of Gregory Nazianzen, Basil,

scared by the Persian hosts, who took possession of the city in 615 or 616, shortly after the capture of Jerusalem by another army in 614[1]. A third diligent worker under the same adverse circumstances was the abbot Paul, who fled from his convent in Syria to escape the Persian invasion, and took refuge in the island of Cyprus. Here he occupied himself with rendering into Syriac the works of Gregory Nazianzen[2]. Of this version, which was completed in two volumes in 624, there are several old MSS. in the British Museum[3]. This Paul was also the translator of the *Octoëchus* of Severus, of which there is a MS. in the British Museum, Add. 17134, dated 675[4]. To this

Gregory Nyssen, Dionysius the Areopagite, and John Chrysostom.

[1] See Nöldeke, *Gesch. d. Perser u. Araber*, pp. 291–292; *Chronique de Michel le Grand*, p. 222; Bar-Hebræus, *Chron. Syr.*, p. 99.

[2] See *B.O.*, i. 171; iii. 1, 23.

[3] See the fine series of MSS. described in Wright's *Catal.*, pp. 423–435. One of these is dated 790, another 845. The other MSS. (*ibid.*, pp. 436–438) seem to contain part of the older version of the Nestorians (*B.O.*, iii. 1, 24, note 1).

[4] Wright, *Catal.*, p. 330 *sq.* The translator is wrongly described in the codex as "bishop of Edessa" (see above, p. 94, note 1). His convent was probably that of Ḳenneshrē, of which both John bar Aphtōnyā (see above, p. 84) and John Psaltēs or Calligraphus were abbots. Compare *B.O.*, ii. 54.

collection he himself contributed a hymn on the holy chrism and a translation of the "Gloria in excelsis."

The name of Mārūthā[1] is the first that deserves mention here, more, however, on account of his ecclesiastical weight and position than his literary merit. He was a native of Shurzaḳ (?), a village in the diocese of Bēth Nuhādhrē[2], was ordained priest in the convent of Nardus, lived for twenty years in the convent of Zakkāi or Zacchæus at Callinīcus (ar-Raḳḳah), and went thence to Edessa for purposes of study. On returning to the East, he resided in the convent of Mār Matthew at Mosul, where he occupied himself with remodelling its rules and orders. He sided with the Monophysite party at the Persian court, and, after the death of the physician Gabriel[3], found it advisable to retire to 'Āḳōlā (al-Kūfah)[4]. He was elevated to the dignity of metropolitan bishop of Taghrīth in 640, after the establishment of peace between the Greeks and Persians[5], and was the first real

[1] *B.O.*, ii. 416, 418.

[2] See Hoffmann, *Auszüge*, pp. 208–216, but especially p. 215.

[3] See above, p. 126.

[4] Bar-Hebræus, *Chron. Eccles.*, ii. 111; *B.O.*, ii. 416.

[5] The circumstances are given in detail by Bar-Hebræus (*Chron. Eccles.*, ii. 119 *sq.*) and Assemani (*B.O.*, ii. 419).

maphriān (maphrĕyānā) and organizer of the Jacobite Church in the East, which so rapidly increased in numbers and influence that he was called upon to ordain bishops for such remote regions as Segestān (Sīstān) and Harēw (Herāt). Mārūthā died in 649. His life was written by his successor Denḥā[1]. Mārūthā compiled a liturgy and wrote a commentary on the Gospels, both of which are sometimes wrongly assigned to the elder Mārūthā of Maiperḳaṭ[2]. He was also the author of short discourses on New (or Low) Sunday, and on the consecration of the water on the eve of the Epiphany, as well as of some hymns and sedrās[3].

Contemporary with Mārūthā, under the patriarch Athanasius Gammālā (died in 631[4]) and his successor John, flourished Severus Sēbōkht[5]

[1] See Brit. Mus. Add. 14645, f. 198 a (Wright, *Catal.*, p. 1113).

[2] See above, p. 46. From the commentary are taken the passages quoted in the *Catena* of Severus. See Assemani, *Catal.*, iii. 11 (on Exod. xv. 25), 24, and Wright, *Catal.*, p. 910.

[3] See Brit. Mus. Add. 14727, f. 140 a; 17267, f. 17 b; 17254, f. 164 a; 17128, f. 91 b.

[4] According to Bar-Hebræus, *Chron. Eccles.*, i. 275; *B.O.*, ii. 334. Dionysius of Tell-Maḥrē gives 644.

[5] On the Persian name *Sēbōkht* see Nöldeke, *Gesch. des Artachšîr i Pâpakân*, in *Beiträge z. Kunde d. indogerm. Sprachen*, iv. 49, note 4; *Gesch. d. Perser u. Araber*, p. 396, note 1.

of Nisībis[1], bishop of the convent of Ḳen-neshrē, at this time one of the chief seats of Greek learning in western Syria[2]. He devoted himself, as might be expected, to philosophical and mathematical as well as theological studies[3]. Of the first we have specimens in his treatise on the syllogisms in the *Analytica Priora* of Aristotle, his commentary on the Περὶ ἑρμηνείας, and his letters to the priest Aitīlāhā of Mosul on certain terms in the Περὶ ἑρμηνείας, and to the periodeutes Yaunān or Jonas on some points in the logic of Aristotle[4]. Of his astronomical and geographical studies there are a few examples in Brit. Mus. Add. 14538, ff. 153–155[5], such as whether the heaven surrounds the earth in the form of a wheel or sphere, on the habitable and uninhabitable portions of the earth, on the measurement of the heaven and the earth and the space between them, and on the motions of the sun and moon[6]. In the Royal Library at

[1] See Wright, *Catal.*, p. 598, col. 1.

[2] See *B.O.*, ii. 335; Bar-Hebræus, *Chron. Eccles.*, i. 275.

[3] Compare Renan, *De Philos. Peripat. ap. Syros*, pp. 29, 30.

[4] See Brit. Mus. Add. 14660 and 17156 (Wright, *Catal.*, pp. 1160–63), and the *Catal.* of the Royal Library of Berlin, Sachau 226, 6, 9.

[5] Wright, *Catal.*, p. 1008.

[6] See Sachau, *Ined. Syr.*, pp. 127–134.

Berlin there is a short treatise of his on the astrolabe[1]. More or less theological in their nature are his letter to the priest and periodeutes Basil of Cyprus, on the 14th of Nīsān, A. Gr. 976 (665 A.D.)[2], a treatise on the weeks of Daniel[3], and letters to Sergius, abbot of Shiggār (Sinjār), on two discourses of Gregory Nazianzen[4]. He is also said to have drawn up a liturgy[5].

John I., Jacobite patriarch of Antioch, was called from the convent of Eusēbhōnā at Tell-ʿAddā to the archiepiscopal throne in 631, and died in December 648[6]. Bar-Hebræus tells us that he translated the Gospels into Arabic at the command of the Arab emīr ʿAmr ibn Saʿd. He is better known as the author of numerous sedrās and other prayers, whence he is commonly called Yōḥannān dĕ-sedhrau(hī), or "John of the Sedrās." He also drew up a liturgy[7].

[To the 7th century, if we are to accept the view proposed by Nöldeke, belongs the Syriac version of Pseudo-Callisthenes's *Life of Alexander*

1 Alter Bestand 37, 2 (*Kurzes Verzeichniss*, p. 32).

2 Same MS., 3.

3 Wright, *Catal.*, p. 988, col. 2.

4 *Ibid.*, p. 432, col. 2.

5 *B.O.*, ii. 463.

6 Bar-Hebræus, *Chron. Eccles.*, i. 275; *B.O.*, ii. 335. But Dionysius of Tell-Maḥrē says 650; *B.O.*, i. 425.

7 Berlin, Sachau 185, 6.

*the Great*, which has been edited and translated into English by Budge[1]. This version was formerly believed to have been made from the Arabic, and to be a product of the 10th or 11th century. But Nöldeke has shown[2] from an examination of the language, and especially the forms of the proper names, that the Syriac must be a translation from the Pahlavī, and almost certainly not later than the 7th century.]

During the second quarter of this century, from 633 to 636, the Muḥammadan conquest of Syria took place. The petty Arab kingdoms of the Lakhmites (al-Ḥīrah), the Thaʿlabites and Kindites, and the Ghassānites, as well as the wandering tribes of Mesopotamia, were absorbed; and the Persians were beaten back into their own country, quickly to be overrun in its turn. The year 638 witnessed the last effort of the Greek empire to wrest Syria from the invaders; the Muslim yoke was no longer to be shaken off. The effects of this conquest soon begin to make themselves manifest in the literature of the country. The more the Arabic language comes into use, the more the Syriac wanes and wastes

[1] [*The History of Alexander the Great*, Cambridge, 1889.

[2] *Beiträge zur Geschichte des Alexanderromans* (in *Denkschriften der kaiserlichen Akademie der Wissenschaften*), Vienna, 1890, p. 11, *sq.*]

away; the more Muḥammadan literature flourishes, the more purely Christian literature pines and dwindles; so that from this time on it becomes necessary to compile grammars and dictionaries of the old Syriac tongue, and to note and record the correct reading and pronunciation of words in the Scriptures and other books, in order that the understanding of them may not be lost.

Among the small band of Monophysite scholars who made themselves conspicuous during the latter half of the 7th century the most famous name is that of Jacob of Edessa[1]. He was a native of 'Ēn-dēbhā (the Wolf's well), a village in the district of Gumyah (al-Jūmah), in the province of Antioch. The date of his birth is not mentioned, but it may have been about 640 or a little earlier[2]. He studied under Severus Sēbōkht at the famous convent of Ḳen-neshrē, where he learned Greek and the accurate reading of the Scriptures. Thence he went to Alexandria, but we are not told how long he remained there. After his return to Syria he was appointed bishop

[1] Bar-Hebræus, *Chron. Eccles.*, i. 289; *B.O.*, i. 468, ii. 335. Assemani tries hard in vol. i. to prove that he was not a Monophysite (p. 470 *sq.*), but in vol. ii. 337 he gives up the attempt in despair. Compare Lamy, *Dissert. de Syrorum Fide*, &c., p. 206 *sq.*

[2] The dates given in *B.O.*, i. 469, seem to be utterly wrong.

of Edessa in 679–680[1]; but Bar-Hebræus says that he was ordained by the patriarch Athanasius II., 684–687, which seems more probable, as they were intimate friends. If he was appointed in 684, the three or four years for which he held this office would terminate in 687–688, in which latter year Julian Rōmāyā (or "the Soldier")[2] was elected patriarch. Apparently Jacob was very strict in the enforcement of canonical rules, and thereby offended a portion of his clergy. He would seem to have appealed to the patriarch and his fellow-bishops, who were in favour of temporizing; whereupon Jacob burnt a copy of the rules before the gate of Julian's convent, at the same time crying aloud, "I burn with fire as superfluous and useless the canons which ye trample under foot and heed not." He then betook himself to the convent at Kaisūm, a town near Samosāta, and Ḥabbībh was appointed to Edessa in his stead. After a while the monks of Eusēbhōnā invited Jacob to their convent, and there he taught for eleven years the Psalms and the reading of the Scriptures in Greek, the study of which language had fallen into desuetude. Owing to disputes

[1] According to the calculation of Dionysius of Tell-Maḥrē, 677; see *B.O.*, i. 426.

[2] So called because he had in his younger days served along with his father in the imperial army.

with some of the brethren "who hated the Greeks," he left this house and went to the great convent at Tell-ʿAddā, where he worked for nine years more at his revised version of the Old Testament[1]. On the death of Ḥabbībh Jacob was recalled to Edessa, where he resided for four months, at the end of which time he returned to Tell-ʿAddā to fetch his library and pupils, but died there on 5th June 708[2]. In the literature of his country Jacob holds much the same place as Jerome among the Latin fathers. He was, for his time, a man of great culture and wide reading, being familiar with Greek and with older Syriac writers. Of Hebrew he probably understood very little, but he was always ready, like Aphraates, to avail himself of the aid of Jewish scholars, whose opinion he often cites. He appears before us as at once theologian, historian, philosopher, and grammarian, as a translator of various Greek works, and as the indefatigable correspondent of many students who sought his advice and assistance from far and near. As a theologian, Jacob wrote commentaries on the Old and New Testaments, which are cited

[1] See above, p. 17.

[2] According to Dionysius of Tell-Maḥrē, *B.O.*, i. 426, A.D. 710; but Elias bar Shīnāyā confirms the earlier date, See Baethgen, *Fragmente syr. u. arab. Historiker*, pp. 40, 121.

by later authors, such as Dionysius bar Ṣalībī[1] and Bar-Hebræus, as well as in the large *Catena* of the monk Severus[2], further, scholia on the whole Scriptures, of which specimens may be found in *S. Ephræmi Opera Syr.*[3] and in Phillips's *Scholia on some Passages of the Old Testament* (1864)[4]. His discourses on the six days of creation are extant at Leyden and Lyons[5] This was his latest work, being unfinished at the time of his death; it was completed by his friend George, bishop of the Arab tribes. Like many other doctors of the Syrian Church, Jacob drew up an

[1] See *Bibl. Med. Laurent. et Palat. Codd. Orientt. Catal.*, p. 85, No. xlviii.

[2] *B.O.*, i. 487–488; Cod. Vat. ciii. (*Catal.*, iii. 7); Brit. Mus. Add. 12144 (Wright, *Catal.*, p. 908). The former MS. contains a brief exposition of the Pentateuch, Job, Joshua, and Judges by Jacob, *loc. cit.*, pp. 9–11.

[3] *B.O.*, i. 489–493.

[4] See Brit. Mus. Add. 14483 and 17193, ff. 55 a, 61 a; compare Cod. Vat. v. (*Catal.*, ii. pp. 12, 13).

[5] Leyden, Cod. 66 (1) Gol. (see *Catal. Codd. Orientt.*, v. 69, and Land, *Anecd. Syr.*, i. 2–4); Lyons, No. 2 (see Neubauer in *Archives des Missions scientifiques et littéraires*, 3 ser., vol. i., p. 568, Paris, 1873). The Paris MS. is merely a partial copy of the Leyden one (Zotenberg, *Catal.*, p. 197). It is cited in Brit. Mus. Add. 14731, f. 98 b (Wright, *Catal.*, p. 854, col. 2, at the foot), and in the Bodleian *Catal.*, p. 462, No. 5. Another Paris MS. (Zotenberg, *Catal.*, p. 213) contains the punctuation and explanation of difficult words and phrases in this work.

anaphora or liturgy[1], and revised the liturgy of St James, the brother of our Lord[2]. He also composed orders of baptism[3], of the consecration of the water on the eve of the Epiphany[4], and of the solemnization of matrimony[5], with which we may connect his translation of the order of baptism of Severus[6] and the tract upon the forbidden degrees of affinity[7]. The *Book of Treasures*[8] contained expositions of the Eucharistic service, of the consecration of the water, and of the rite of baptism, probably identical with or similar to those which are found separately in MSS.[9] He likewise arranged the horologium or

[1] *B.O.*, i. 476. It is extant in many MSS.

[2] *Ibid.*; Brit. Mus. Add. 14691, f. 2 b, and elsewhere. Whether he was the translator of the anaphora of Ignatius, we are unable to affirm or deny.

[3] *B.O.*, i. 477.

[4] *Ibid.*, 486, col. 1.

[5] *E.g.*, Zotenberg, *Catal.*, pp. 66, 67.

[6] *E.g.*, Rosen, *Catal.*, p. 61, col. 2.

[7] Cod. Vat. xxxvii. (*Catal.*, ii. 244).

[8] *B.O.*, i. 487.

[9] *E.g.*, the Eucharist, Berlin, Sachau 218, 4 (addressed to the Stylite George of Sĕrūgh); Brit. Mus. Add. 14496, f. 1 a (Wright, *Catal.*, p. 224). The similar exposition edited by Assemani (*B.O.*, i. 479) is addressed to the priest Thomas; comp. Brit. Mus. Add. 17215, f. 22 b. The consecration of the water, Cod. Vat. cccv., in Mai, *Scriptt. Vett. Nova Coll.*, v. The order of baptism, Brit. Mus. 14496, f. 23 a (a mere fragment).

canonical hours of the ferial days[1], and drew up a calendar of feasts and saints' days for the whole year[2]. Of his numerous canons[3], those addressed to the priest Addai have been edited by Lamy, *Dissert. de Syrorum Fide*, &c., p. 98 *sq.*, and De Lagarde, *Reliquiæ Juris Eccles. Antiquissimæ*, p. 117 *sq.*[4] Under this head we may mention the *Scholion de Diaconissis earumque Munere* (*Catal. Vat.*, ii. 319) and the *Scholion de Foribus Ecclesiæ dum Ordinationes aut alia Sacra celebrantur occludendis* (Cod. Vat. ccciv., in Mai, *Scriptt. Vett. Nova Coll.*, v.). Jacob also composed homilies, of which a few survive in manuscript: for example—(1) that Christians are not to offer a lamb after the Jewish fashion, nor oxen and sheep, on behalf of the deceased, nor to use pure wine and unleavened bread in celebrating the Eucharist; (2) against the use of unleavened bread; (3) against the Armenians as Dyophysites, and because they offend against these doctrines[5]; (4) against certain

[1] Brit. Mus. Add. 14704, Paris, Anc. fonds 73.

[2] See *Catal. Vat.*, ii. 250–272; and comp. Berlin, Sachau 39, 4.

[3] *B.O.*, i. 477.

[4] See also [Wright's *Notulae syriacae* and] Kayser, *Die Canones Jacob's von Edessa übersetzt und erläutert, zum Theil auch zuerst im Grundtext veröffentlicht*, 1886.

[5] See *Bibl. Med. Laurent. et Palat. Codd. MSS. Orientt. Catal.*, pp. 107–108.

impious men and transgressors of the law of God, who trample under foot the canons of the church[1]. To these may be added his metrical discourses on the Trinity and the incarnation of the word[2] and on the faith against the Nestorians[3]. Whether the treatise *De Causa omnium Causarum*[4] really belongs to him can hardly be decided till it has been published. The remarks in the *Bodleian Catalogue*, p. 585, note, point to a writer of much later date. [This question has been decided in the negative since Kayser's publication of the text and translation of the work[5].] The loss of Jacob's *Chronicle* is greatly to be regretted; only a few leaves, all more or less mutilated, remain to us in Brit. Mus. Add. 14685[6]. The author's

[1] Wright, *Catal.*, pp. 984, col. 2; 996, col. 2.

[2] *Catal. Vat.*, ii. 516.

[3] *Ibid.*, iii. 353. [The text and a Latin translation of this homily, by Ugolini, are contained in the volume, *Al Sommo Pontifice Leone XIII. Ommagio Giubilare della Biblioteca Vaticana*, Rome, 1888.]

[4] See *B.O.*, i. 461–463. Besides the MS. described by Assemani, there are two in the Bodleian Library, Hunt. 123 (Payne Smith, *Catal.*, 585) and Bodl. Or. 732, and a third at Berlin, Sachau 180, with an excerpt in Sachau 203.

[5] [*Das Buch von der Erkenntniss der Wahrheit*, text published at Leipzig 1889; German translation, Strassburg 1893. Cf. Nöldeke, *Literarisches Centralblatt* for 1889, No. 30.]

[6] See Wright, *Catal.*, p. 1062.

design was to continue the *Chronicle* of Eusebius on the same plan, from the twentieth year of the reign of Constantine down to his own time. The introduction was divided into four sections, the first of which treated of the canon of Eusebius and the error of three years in his calculation; the second of the dynasties contemporary with the Roman empire, but omitted by Eusebius; the third explained what dynasties were coordinated by Jacob with the Roman empire; and the fourth contained separate chronologies of each of these dynasties. Then followed the chronological canon, beginning with Olympiad cclxxvi. The last monarchs mentioned in the mutilated MS. are Heraclius I. of Constantinople, Ardashēr III. of Persia, and the caliph Abū Bakr. This work, which was finished by the author in 692[1], has been extensively used by subsequent Syrian historians, both Jacobite and Nestorian, such as Bar-Hebræus[2], Elias bar Shīnāyā[3], &c., and it is therefore admitted by ʿAbhd-īshōʿ into his list of

[1] See Elias bar Shīnāyā in Rosen, *Catal.*, p. 88, col. 1.

[2] *B.O.*, ii. 313–314.

[3] See, for example, the notes in Abbeloos, *Bar-Hebræi Chron. Eccles.*, ii. 55, 103, 107, 123; Baethgen, *Fragmente syr. u. arab. Historiker*, extracted from Elias bar Shīnāyā, p. 3; and the anonymous epitomizer in Land, *Anecd. Syr.*, i. 2–22, transl. pp. 103–121 (Brit. Mus. Add. 14643; Wright, *Catal.*, p. 1040).

books (*B.O.*, iii. 1, 229). As a translator of Greek works Jacob deserves notice, not so much on account of any Aristotelian labours of his[1], as because of his version of the *Homiliæ Cathedrales* of Severus, a work of capital importance, which he finished in 701[2]. He also revised and corrected, with the help of Greek MSS., the abbot Paul's version of the *Octoëchus* of Severus (see above, p. 135)[3]. The statement of Bar-Hebræus[4] that Jacob translated the works of Gregory Nazianzen seems to be erroneous. He merely retouched, we believe, the version of the abbot Paul (see above, p. 135), to which he probably added notes, illustrative extracts from the writings of Severus, and Athanasius's redaction of the Συναγωγὴ καὶ ἐξήγησις ἱστοριῶν appended to the homily *In Sancta Lumina*[5]. He made the Syriac version of the history of the Rechabites as narrated by Zosimus, which he is said to have translated from

[1] Even the translation of the *Categories* in Cod. Vat. clviii. (*Catal.*, iii. 306; comp. Renan, *De Philos. Peripat. ap. Syros*, p. 34) is not by him, but by Sergius of Rās'ain (see above, p. 91).

[2] See *B.O.*, i. 494; Cod. Vat. cxli.; Brit. Mus. Add. 12159, dated 868 (Wright, *Catal.*, p. 534 *sq.*).

[3] *B.O.*, i. 487; Cod. Vat. xciv., written between 1010 and 1033; Brit. Mus. Add. 17134, dated 675 (Wright, *Catal.*, p. 330 *sq.*).

[4] *B.O.*, ii. 307, col. 2; iii. 1, 23, col. 1.

[5] See Wright, *Catal.*, pp. 423–427.

Hebrew into Greek and thence into Syriac[1]. Of philosophical writings of his we may specify the *Enchiridion,* a tract on philosophical terms[2]. The metrical composition on the same subject contained in two Vatican MSS. may perhaps also be by him[3]. As a grammarian Jacob occupies an important place in Syriac literature. Nestorian scholars, such as Narsai and his pupils, more especially Joseph Hūzāyā (see above, p. 115 *sq.*), had no doubt elaborated a system of accentuation and interpunction, which vies in minuteness with that of the Jews, and had probably begun to store up the results of their studies in Massoretic MSS. of the Bible, like those of which we have already spoken (above, p. 20 *sq.*). But Jacob was the first to give a decided impulse to these pursuits among the Western Syrians, and to induce the monks of Eusēbhōnā and Tell-ʿAddā to compile Massoretic MSS. like those of their brethren in the East, and to pay attention to minute accuracy in the matter of the diacritical points and the signs of inter-

1 See Wright, *Catal.*, p. 1128.

2 *Ibid.*, p. 984.

3 Cod. Vat. xxxvi. and xcv. (*Catal.*, ii. 243 and 516). In the latter there are three other poems ascribed to him, the first theological, the second with the title *De Philosophis et Bonis Artibus*, and the third entitled *On the Mind.* In the MSS. these poems are said to be by Jacob of Sĕrūgh, which seems altogether unlikely.

punction. Hence we usually find appended to such MSS. of the Jacobite schools the epistle of Jacob to George, bishop of Sĕrūgh, on Syrian orthography[1], and a tract by him on the pointing of verbal and nominal forms and on the signs of interpunction and accentuation, besides a tract of apparently earlier date on the same signs, with a list of their names, by Thomas the deacon[2]. Further, Jacob's acquaintance with the Greek language and Greek MSS. suggested to him a striking simplification of the system of vowel-points which was now probably beginning to be introduced among the Easterns[3]. He saw that all the vowel-sounds of the Syriac language, as spoken by the Edessenes, could be represented by

[1] See *B.O.*, i. 477 (No. 6) and p. 478 (No. 8).

[2] See, for example, *Catal. Vat.*, iii. 290; Brit. Mus., Rosen, pp. 69, 70 (Wright, p. 110); Paris, Zotenberg, *Catal.*, p. 30. The letter and tracts have been published by Phillips, *A Letter by Mār Jacob, Bishop of Edessa, on Syriac Orthography*, &c. (1869; the third Appendix, pp. 85–96, 1870), and Martin, *Jacobi epi Edesseni Epistola ad Georgium epum Sarugensem de Orthographia Syriaca* (1869). On the possible identity of Thomas the deacon with Thomas of Ḥarḳel, see Phillips, third Appendix, p. 90.

[3] In the year 899 we find the fully developed Nestorian system of vowel-points in use (Brit. Mus. Add. 12138, see the facsimile in Wright's *Catal.*, pl. xiii.). We may therefore fairly place its beginnings as early as Jacob's time.

means of the Greek vowel letters, a style of pointing which would be far clearer to the reader than a series of minute dots. Accordingly he, or his school, put ᴀ for *ă*, o for *ō* (*ā*), ε for *e*, н for *i*, oΥ for *u*; and this system has been adhered to by the Western Syrians or Jacobites since his time[1]. Jacob wished, however, to go a step farther, and sought to introduce a reform for which his countrymen were not prepared. The constant perusal of Greek MSS. had accustomed him to see the vowels placed on an equality with the consonants as an integral part of the alphabet; and, considering how much this contributed to clearness of sense and facility of reading, he

[1] The credit of inventing this vowel-system is usually given to Theophilus of Edessa, who died in 785–786 (*B.O.*, i. 64, 521), though Wiseman brought forward to our mind convincing arguments in his *Horæ Syriacæ*, pp. 181–188, in favour of the claims of Jacob. We have now, however, a MS. of Jacob's own time in which these Greek vowels are distinctly appended to Syriac words. See Brit. Mus. Add. 17134, f. 83 b, in Wright's *Catal.*, p. 337, col. 2, and pl. vi. In this plate, the handwriting of which cannot well be placed later than about 700, we find in l. 1 the vowel Υ (ypsilon) in the word ܟܘܡܬܐ, and in l. 23 the vowel O in ܩ̈ܠܡܘܢ, both in black ink, besides others in red ink in lines 6, 17, 18, 21, 22, and 31. No one can doubt, we think, that these vowels were added *a pr. manu*, especially if he compares their forms, particularly the *a*, with those of the Greek letters on the margin of pl. v.

desired to see the like done in Syriac. For this purpose he himself designed a set of vowel-signs, to be written on a line with and between the consonants[1]; and for the purpose of making this invention known to his countrymen he wrote a *Syriac Grammar*[2], in which he used them largely in the paradigms. The innovation, however, found no favour, and the work was supposed to be utterly lost, until a few fragments (partly palimpsest) were simultaneously discovered by the present writer and Dr Neubauer[3]. Finally, amid all his labours as priest and bishop, teacher and author, Jacob found time to correspond with a large number of persons in all parts of Syria; and these epistles are often among his most

[1] See Bar-Hebræus in his *Kĕthābhā dhĕ-Ṣemḥē*, as quoted by Martin, *Jacques d'Édesse et les Voyelles Syriennes* (*Journ. Asiat.*, 1869, vol. xiii. pp. 458–459), or pp. 194–195 of Martin's edition. Jacob had already before him the example of the Mandaites, from whose alphabet his figure of ܣ for *e* appears to be borrowed.

[2] *B.O.*, i. 475, 477.

[3] See Brit. Mus. Add. 17217, ff. 37, 38; 14665, f. 28; in Wright's *Catal.*, pp. 1168–73. These were reprinted, with the Oxford fragments (Bodl. 159), by Wright in *Fragments of the* ܬܘܪܨ ܡܡܠܠܐ ܢܗܪܝܐ *or Syriac Grammar of Jacob of Edessa* (1871); [and again in the Appendix to Merx's *Historia Artis Grammaticae apud Syros* (*Abhandlungen für die Kunde des Morgenlandes*, vol. ix.).]

interesting writings[1]. One of his principal correspondents was John the Stylite of the convent of Litarba (*Λίταρβα* plur., but also *Λίταργον*, *Λύταργον*; al-Athārib, near Aleppo); others were Eustathius of Dārā, Kyrīsōnā of Dārā, the priest Abraham, the deacon George, and the sculptor Thomas[2]. To the priest Addai he wrote on the orders of baptism and the consecration of the water[3], to the deacon Bar-ḥadh-bĕ-shabbā against the council of Chalcedon[4], to the priest Paul of Antioch on the Syriac alphabet, in reply to a letter about the defects of the said alphabet as compared with the Greek[5], and to George, bishop of Sĕrūgh, on Syriac orthography (see above, p. 151)[6].

After Jacob we may name his friend Athanasius of Balad, who also studied under Severus

[1] Some are metrical; see Brit. Mus. Add. 12172, ff. 65 a, 73 a; 17168, f. 154 a.

[2] See all these in Brit. Mus. Add. 12172, ff. 65–135 (Wright, *Catal.*, pp. 592–604). Three of these letters have been published, two by Wright in the *Journal of Sacred Literature*, new series, x. (1861), p. 430 *sq.*, and one by Schröter in *Z.D.M.G.*, xxiv. (1870), pp. 261—300. [Another fragment in the chrestomathy attached to Nestle's *Grammatica Syriaca.*]

[3] *B.O.*, i. 486, No. 11; Brit. Mus. Add. 14715, f. 170 a; see also Add. 12144, ff. 47 a, 52 b.

[4] Brit. Mus. Add. 14631, f. 14 b.

[5] *B.O.*, i. 477, No. 7.

[6] [A full account of Jacob's work as a grammarian in Merx, *op. cit.* chaps v. vi. vii.]

Sēbōkht at Ḳen-neshrē, and devoted himself to the translation of Greek works, philosophical and theological, in the convent of Mār Malchus in Ṭūr 'Abhdīn or at Nisībis, where he for a time officiated as priest. He was advanced to the patriarchate in 684 and sat till 687 or 688[1]. In the year 645 he translated the *Isagōgē* of Porphyry, with an introduction, which seems to be chiefly derived from the preface of the Greek commentator Ammonius[2]; and he also edited a version of an anonymous *Isagōgē*, which is found in Brit. Mus. Add. 14660[3]. At the request of Matthew, bishop of Aleppo, and Daniel, bishop of Edessa, he undertook in 669 a translation of select epistles of Severus of Antioch, and of these the sixth book survives in two MSS.[4] He also busied himself with Gregory Nazianzen, as is evidenced by a scholion introductory to the homilies[5] and the version of the Συναγωγὴ καὶ ἐξήγησις ἱστο-

[1] *B.O.*, ii. 335; Bar-Hebræus, *Chron. Eccles.*, i. 287, 293. Dionysius of Tell-Maḥrē places his death as late as 704.

[2] Cod. Vat. clviii.; Paris, Anc. fonds 161. According to Renan, *De Philos. Peripat. ap. Syros*, p. 30, note 4, the MSS. clxxxiii. and cxcvi. of the Bibl. Palat. Medic. contain this translation and not that of Ḥonain.

[3] See Wright, *Catal.*, p. 1161, and comp. Renan, *op. cit.* p. 31.

[4] Brit. Mus. Add. 12181 and 14600 (Wright, *Catal.*, pp. 558–569).

[5] Wright, *Catal.*, p. 441.

ριῶν[1]. The only other writings of his with which we are acquainted are an encyclical letter, prohibiting Christians from partaking of the sacrifices of their Muḥammadan rulers[2], and a couple of sedrās[3].

Contemporary with him, and probably an alumnus of the same school, was the translator of the poems of Gregory Nazianzen, in the year 655, whom Assemani calls Senorinus Chididatus of Āmid[4]. He has, however, misread the name. In the MS., as Professor Guidi informs us, it stands ܝܢܘܪܝ ܩܢܕܝܕܛܘܣ, not ܣܢܘܪܝ. The former part of the name seems to be Ἰανουάριος; the latter is apparently (as Guidi suggests) a corruption of Κανδίδατος. Whether the poems in Brit. Mus. Add. 18821 and 14547[5] belong to the translation of Januarius Candidatus or not, we cannot at present determine.

Another scholar of note at this time is George, bishop of the Arab tribes, the pupil and friend of Athanasius II. and Jacob[6]. He was ordained,

[1] Wright, *Catal.*, p. 425.

[2] Zotenberg, *Catal.*, p. 28, col. 2.

[3] Wright, *Catal.*, p. 218, col. 1; Zotenberg, *Catal.*, p. 47, col. 1, No. 23, d.

[4] Cod. Vat. xcvi. (*Catal.*, ii. 521); see *B.O.*, ii. cxlix., 502, col. 2; iii. 1, 23, note.

[5] Wright, *Catal.*, pp. 775, 433, col. 1.

[6] *B.O.*, i. 494; Bar-Hebræus, *Chron. Eccles.*, i. 293, 303;

it would seem, in 687 or 688, two months after the death of Athanasius, and is said to have died in the first year of Athanasius III., who was consecrated in April 724. His diocese comprised the ʿĀḳōlāyē or Arabs of ʿAḳōlā (al-Kūfah), the Ṭūʿāyē (?), the Tanūkh, the Thaʿlabites, the Taghlibites, and in general the nomad Arabs of Mesopotamia. Of his works the most important is his translation of the *Organon* of Aristotle, of which there is a volume in the British Museum, Add. 14659, comprising, in its imperfect condition, the *Categories*, Περὶ ἑρμηνείας, and the first book of the *Analytics*, divided into two parts, with introductions and commentaries[1]. Of this version a specimen has been edited by Hoffmann, *De Hermeneuticis*, &c., p. 22 *sq.*, besides small fragments at pp. 30, 38, 45, and 53. He also compiled a large collection of scholia on the homilies of Gregory Nazianzen, which exhibits a wide range of reading[2], and completed the

Hoffmann, *De Hermeneuticis apud Syros Aristoteleis*, pp. 148–151; Renan, *De Philos. Peripat. ap. Syros*, pp. 32–33.

[1] See Wright, *Catal.*, p. 1163.

[2] Brit. Mus. Add. 14725, ff. 100–215. It was evidently written after the death of Athanasius II., as shown by the remark on f. 132 a (Wright, *Catal.*, p. 443, col. 1). The commentary contained in Brit. Mus. Add. 17197, ff. 1–25 (Wright, *Catal.*, p. 441) is perhaps that of Elias, bishop of Shiggār (Sinjār), who flourished about 750, and is expressly stated (*B.O.*, ii. 339) to have compiled a commentary on

*Hexaēmeron* of Jacob of Edessa (see above, p. 144)[1]. His other writings are—a commentary, or more likely scholia, on the Scriptures, cited in the *Catena* of Severus and by Bar-Hebræus in his *Auṣar Rāzē*[2]; a short commentary on the sacraments of the church, treating of baptism, the holy Eucharist, and the consecration of the chrism[3]; a homily in twelve-syllable metre on the holy chrism in two shapes[4]; another homily on solitary monks, in heptasyllabic metre[5]; and a treatise on the *Calendar* in twelve-syllable metre[6], cited by Elias bar Shīnāyā[7]. Like Jacob of Edessa, he carried on an extensive literary correspondence, of which some specimens have luckily been preserved in Brit. Mus. Add. 12154, ff. 222–291, dated from 714 to 718. Several of them are addressed to John the Stylite of Litarba, one of whose letters to Daniel,

the first volume of Gregory Nazianzen (as translated by Paul). He followed the older exposition of Benjamin, bishop of Edessa. This Benjamin was the writer of a letter on the Eucharistic service and baptism (Wright, *Catal.*, p. 1004, col. 2).

[1] See Land, *Anecd. Syr.*, i. p. 4.

[2] *B.O.*, i. 494–495; comp. Wright, *Catal.*, p. 909, col. 2.

[3] Wright, *Catal.*, p. 985.

[4] *B.O.*, i. 332; *Catal. Vat.*, iii. 102, No. 188; Wright, *Catal.*, p. 848, No. 78.

[5] *Bodleian Catal.*, p. 425, No. 88.

[6] *B.O.*, i. 495; *Catal. Vat.*, iii. 532.

[7] Rosen, *Catal.*, p. 88, Nos. 32, 33; comp. also the "Table of the New Moons," in *Catal. Vat.*, ii. 402.

an Arab priest of the tribe of the Ṭū'āyē, is appended, f. 291. The most important of them is one written to the priest and recluse Yēshū' of Innib (near 'Azāz, north of Aleppo), part of which relates to Aphraates and his works (see above, p. 32)[1].

Contemporary with these scholars was Daniel of Ṣalaḥ (a village north-east of Midyād in Ṭūr-'Abdīn)[2], who wrote commentaries on the Psalms and Ecclesiastes[3]. The former was in three volumes, and was composed at the request of John, abbot of the convent of Eusebius at Kaphrā dhĕ-Bhārthā (Kafr al-Bārah, near Apamea)[4]. There is an abridgement of it in

[1] It has been printed by De Lagarde, *Anal. Syr.*, pp. 108–134, and partly reprinted by Wright, *The Homilies of Aphraates*, pp. 19–37. Ryssel has translated and annotated it in *Ein Brief Georgs, Bischofs der Araber, an d. Presbyter Jesus*, 1883. [Ryssel has since published a translation of a number of this bishop's poems and letters: *Georgs des Araberbischofs Gedichte und Briefe*, Leipzig, 1891; and edited the text of two poems in *Reale Accademia dei Lincei*, Rome 1892.]

[2] See Hoffmann in *Z.D.M.G.*, xxxii. 741.

[3] According to a note in Payne Smith's *Catal.*, p. 62, he was bishop of Tellā dhĕ-Mauzĕlath; but at the time when he wrote his commentary on the Psalms he was certainly only a priest and abbot of a convent (see Wright, *Catal.*, p. 605, col. 2).

[4] MSS.—part i., Pss. i.–l., Brit. Mus. Add. 17187; part ii., Pss. li.–c., Add. 14679, 14668 (only three leaves)

Brit. Mus. Add. 17125, f. 81 *sq.*[1] The commentary on Ecclesiastes is known to us only from the extracts preserved in Severus's *Catena*[2].

Regarding George, bishop of Martyropolis[3], we can add little or nothing to the scanty information collected by Assemani[4]. This scholar has, however, made a mistake in placing him so early as "circa annum Christi 580." About a century later would probably be nearer the mark. Two of his pupils were Constantine, bishop of Ḥarrān, who may have flourished during the latter part of the 7th century, and his successor Leo, who lived at the very end of it and the beginning of the 8th[5]. Constantine

(see Wright, *Catal.*, pp. 605–606); Cod. Vat. clv., Pss. i.–lxviii. (*Catal. Vat.*, iii. 297); part iii., Pss. ci.–cl., in Arabic, Berlin, Sachau 55. It is frequently cited by Bar-Hebræus in the *Auṣar Rāzē*, in Severus's *Catena*, and also by Antonius Rhetor (Wright, *Catal.*, p. 831, col. 1).

1 [Of this an extract is published in the Chrestomathy to Nestle's *Grammatica Syriaca*.]

2 *Catal. Vat.*, iii. 17; Wright, *Catal.*, p. 909.

3 *I.e.*, Maiperḳaṭ or Maiyāfāriḳīn. Assemani calls him bishop of Taghrīth or Tekrīt.

4 *B.O.*, i. 465; ii. 96. The epistles to Christopher against Probus and John Grammaticus of Alexandria, and to the monks of the convent of Mār Matthew, are also cited in Brit. Mus. Add. 17197 (Wright, *Catal.*, p. 607).

5 Assemani places Constantine as early as 630 and Leo about 640 (*B.O.*, i. 466–467). But in the *Catal. Vat.* they are more correctly described as "uterque S. Johannis Damasceni æqualis" (vol. iii. 255).

wrote several controversial works against the Monophysites, viz.,—an exposition of the creeds of the councils of Nicæa and Chalcedon, a treatise against Severus (of Antioch), an "anagnōsticon" concerning an alleged mutilation of the Trisagion[1], and a reply to a treatise of Simeon (II., Monophysite bishop of Ḥarrān)[2]. Leo's only literary effort appears to have been a letter to the Jacobite patriarch Elias, whom we have next to notice.

Elias belonged originally to the Dyophysite party in the Syrian Church, but was converted to the Monophysite sect by the study of the writings of Severus. He was a monk of the convent of Gubbā Barrāyā, and for eighteen years bishop of Apamea (or Fāmiyah), before he was raised to the patriarchate of Antioch (in 709). He died in 724[3]. The only work of his known to us is an *Apology*, addressed to Leo, bishop of Ḥarrān, in answer to a letter from him asking the reasons for Elias's change of creed[4]. It was

[1] These three are mentioned by Assemani, *B.O.*, i. 466.

[2] Wright, *Catal.*, p. 607, col. 2.

[3] *B.O.*, ii. 95, 337; Bar-Hebræus, *Chron. Eccles.*, i. 297; Baethgen, *Fragmente*, pp. 46, 123. Dionysius of Tell-Maḥrē wrongly places his death some years later, in 729.

[4] Two MSS. of this work survive, but both imperfect, the one at Rome, Cod. Vat. cxlv. (*Catal.*, iii. 253), the other in the British Museum, Add. 17197 (Wright, *Catal.*, p. 606).

probably written during the time of his episcopate. In it, besides George of Martyropolis and Constantine of Ḥarrān, he cites John of Damascus, among whose Greek works is a tract against the Jacobites, addressed to the bishop Elias in defence of Peter, archbishop of Damascus.

Lazarus of Bēth Ḳandasā is known to us only through his disciple George of Bēth Nĕḳē as the compiler of a commentary on the New Testament, of which there are two volumes in the British Museum, the one (Add. 14682) containing the Gospels of St John and St Mark, the other (Add. 14683) the third and fourth parts of the Pauline epistles from Galatians to Hebrews[1]. The commentary on the epistles is merely an abridgement of Chrysostom; in that on the Gospels use is also made of Jacob of Sĕrūgh, and occasionally of Theodore of Mopsuestia[2], Cyril of Alexandria, and Ephraim. He also quotes a passage of nine lines from the Sibylline oracles (ed. Friedlieb, viii. 287–296). At the end of part third of the Pauline epistles there is in Add. 14683 a chronological section, terminating with the accession of the ʿAbbāsī caliph al-Mahdī in 775, which probably fixes the date of the

[1] See Wright, *Catal.*, pp. 608–612.

[2] Sachau, *Theodori Mops. Fragmenta Syr.*, pp. 101 and 62.

author[1]. Much later he cannot have lived, as Add. 14683 is a MS. of the 10th century, having been presented to the convent of St Mary Deipara in Skete by the patriarch Abraham (or Ephraim), who sat from 977 to 981. In Brit. Mus. Add. 18295 there is a scholion by Lazarus explanatory of a passage in (pseudo-)Dionysius Areopagita[2].

About this time too may have lived the chronicler Daniel bar Moses the Jacobite, who is cited as an authority by Elias bar Shīnāyā in the years 122, 127, and 131 of the Hijrah, *i.e.*, from 740 to 749 A.D.[3]

Theophilus bar Thomas of Edessa[4] is stated by Bar-Hebræus[5] to have been by religious profession a Maronite. He was addicted to the study of astrology, and an anecdote is related by Bar-Hebræus of his correspondence with Ḥasanah, the concubine of the caliph al-Mahdī, which fixes the date of his death in 785. He was the author of a

[1] The words of George of Bēth Nĕḳē, *buḥḥānā dhĕdhogmā* (Wright, *Catal.*, p. 611, col. 2), probably refer to the liturgical disputes which arose among the Jacobites about this time (*B.O.*, ii. 341) and attained considerable importance a little later (p. 343). See Bar-Hebræus, *Chron. Eccles.*, i. 331.

[2] See Wright, *Catal.*, p. 1184.

[3] See Baethgen, *Fragmente*, p. 2; Bar-Hebræus, *Chron. Eccles.*, ii. 152, note 2.

[4] *B.O.*, i. 521; Cardāḥī, *Liber Thesauri*, p. 39.

[5] *Hist. Dynast.*, p. 228 (transl., p. 147).

history, which Bar-Hebræus cites[1] and commends. He also translated into Syriac "the two books of the poet Homer on the conquest of the city of Ilion[2]." This evidently means a version of the entire *Iliad* and *Odyssey*, incredible as it may appear. De Lagarde was, we believe, the first to discover citations of this work by Jacob, or Severus, bar Shakkō, bishop of Mār Matthew, who died in 1241[3]. Cardāḥī (*Liber Thesauri*, p. 40) quotes the rendering of *Iliad* ii. 204, but without saying where he found it. Theophilus is often spoken of as the first to use the Greek vowels in pointing Syriac words, but we have seen above (p. 152, note 1) instances of their occurrence in MSS. older than his time. Perhaps, however, he may have finally settled some details of the system and assisted in bringing it into more general use[4].

George of Bĕʿelthān, a village near Ḥimṣ, was educated at the convent of Ḳen-neshrē, and became the syncellus of Theodore, bishop of

[1] *Op. cit.*, p. 98 (transl., p. 63).

[2] *Op. cit.*, p. 228 (transl., p. 148). Also at p. 40 (transl., p. 26) Bar-Hebræus says that "the poet Homer bewailed her (fall) in two books, which Theophilus the astrologer of Edessa translated from Greek into Syriac."

[3] *E.g.*, *Iliad*, i. 225, 226; vi. 325; xvi. 745; *Odyssey*, xviii. 26; see *The Academy* for October 1, 1871, p. 467.

[4] Compare *B.O.*, i. 64.

Samosāta, who prophesied great things of him. On the death of Athanasius III. a synod was held at Mabbōgh, at the close of 758, when a large majority of those present raised George, who was only a deacon, to the see of Antioch[1]. At the instigation of the anti-patriarch David, the caliph al-Manṣūr scourged him and threw him into prison, where he remained for nine years, till he was set free by his son and successor al-Mahdī. He was taken ill during one of his diocesan journeys at Ḳalaudiyah (Claudia), in the far north of Mesopotamia, and died in the convent of Bar-ṣaumā near Melitēne (Malaṭyah), in 790[2]. During his long imprisonment George is said to have composed many discourses and metrical homilies. He was also the author of a commentary on the Gospel of St Matthew, the unique but imperfect MS. of which has been described by Assemani in *Catal. Vat.*, iii. 293.

Cyriacus, a man of Taghrītan family[3] and a monk of the convent of Bīzōnā, otherwise called the convent of the Pillar, near Callinīcus, was

1 The minority appointed as anti-patriarch John of Callinīcus (ar-Raḳḳah), who held office for four years (*B.O.*, ii. 340, col. 2) and was succeeded by David, bishop of Dārā (*ibid.*).

2 *B.O.*, ii. 340; Baethgen, *Fragmente*, pp. 57, 128; Bar-Hebræus, *Chron. Eccles.*, i. 319 *sq.*, ii. 175.

3 Bar-Hebræus, *Chron. Eccles.*, i. 343.

ordained patriarch of the Jacobites in 793, and died at Mosul in 817. The record of his troubled life may be read in Bar-Hebræus's *Chron. Eccles.*, i. 329 *sq.*; *B.O.*, ii. 116, 341–344. In the year 798 he endeavoured to effect a union with the Julianists, whose patriarch was Gabriel, and a creed was drawn up and signed by them and sundry other bishops, which has been preserved in Brit. Mus. Add. 17145, f. 27 b[1]. Besides an anaphora[2] and canons[3], he wrote a homily on the parable of the vineyard[4] and a synodical epistle on the Trinity and the Incarnation addressed to Mark, patriarch of Alexandria, which is extant only in Arabic[5].

The number of Nestorian writers during the 7th and 8th centuries is relatively much larger than that of Jacobite, and the loss of many of their writings is much to be regretted, especially those bearing on ecclesiastical and political history. Want of space compels us, however, to omit many names which we would otherwise gladly have noticed.

1 See Bar-Hebræus, *Chron. Eccles.*, i. 335.

2 Wright, *Catal.*, pp. 206, 210.

3 Wright, *Catal.*, p. 222, col. 2; Zotenberg, *Catal.*, p. 28, No. 54.

4 Brit. Mus. Add. 14727, f. 110 a (Wright, *Catal.*, p. 887).

5 *B.O.*, ii. 117.

Our list begins with the name of Bābhai the archimandrite[1], called Bābhai the Elder, to distinguish him from the later Bābhai bar Nĕṣībhnāyē. He was a native of the village of Bēth 'Aināthā or Bā-'aināthā in Bēth Zabhdai, and succeeded Mār Dādh-īshō' (see above, p. 131) as abbot of the great convent on Mount Īzlā. On the death of the catholicus Gregory of Kashkar in 607 (see above, p. 126) a time of persecution followed, during which the Nestorian Church was ruled by Bābhai with a firm and skilful hand. The bishops of Nisībis, Ḥĕdhaiyabh, and Karkhā dhĕ-Bēth Sĕlōkh (or Bēth Garmai) entrusted him with the duties of inspector of convents, with the express object of rooting out all who held the doctrines of the *Mĕṣallĕyānē*[2], as well as the followers of Ḥannānā of Ḥĕdhaiyabh and Joseph of Ḥazzā[3]. So well did he acquit himself in this post[4] that, after the murder of Khosrau II. in 628, when his successor Ḳawādh II. Shērōē permitted a synod to be held, he would have been unanimously elected to the dignity of catholicus, had he only given his consent, in default of which the choice

[1] See *B.O.*, iii. 1, 88 *sq.*, 472; Hoffmann, *Auszüge*, pp. 121, 161, 173.

[2] See *B.O.*, iii. 1, 101; Bar-Hebræus, *Chron. Eccles.*, i. 573.

[3] See above, pp. 124–128.

[4] See *B.O.*, iii. 1, 88, 89, 473.

fell upon Īshō'-yabh of Gĕdhālā (628–644). As a writer Bābhai would seem to have been very prolific, for no less than eighty-three or eighty-four works are set down to his account[1]. The principal of these, as enumerated by 'Abhd-īshō', are—a commentary on the whole text of Scripture; on the commemorations of the Blessed Virgin Mary and St John, and other commemorations and feasts throughout the year; on the reasons of the celebration of Palm Sunday and of the festival of the holy cross[2]; a discourse on the union (of the two natures in our Lord, against the Monophysites)[3]; exposition of the *Centuries* of Evagrius[4]; exposition of the discourses of Mark the monk (on the spiritual law)[5]; rules for novices; canons for monks; (controversial) letters to Joseph Ḥazzāyā; history of Diodore of Tarsus and his followers; on Matthew the wanderer, Abraham of Nisībis, and Gabriel Ḳaṭrāyā[6]. To these must be added an account of the life and martyrdom of his contemporary George, a convert from Zoroastrianism, whose heathen name was

1 *B.O.*, iii. 1, 94, and note 1.

2 See next paragraph.

3 See *Catal. Vat.*, iii. 372.

4 *Ibid.*, iii. 367 *sq.*

5 Brit. Mus. Add. 17270 (Wright, *Catal.*, p. 482).

6 That is, of Ḳatar, on the coast of al-Baḥrein.

Mihrāmgushnasp[1], and a few hymns, contained in Nestorian psalters[2].

The successor of Bābhai was, as we have just mentioned, Īshōʿ-yabh II. of Gĕdhālā[3], who was elected in 628 and sat till 644[4]. He studied at Nisībis, and was bishop of Balad at the time of his elevation to the patriarchate. He was sent in 630 by Bōrān, the daughter of Khosrau II., on an embassy to Heraclius, the emperor of Constantinople, whom he met at Aleppo, and to whom, we are told, he restored the holy cross, which had been carried off by the Persians when they captured Jerusalem in 614[5]. Foreseeing the downfall of the enfeebled Persian monarchy, Īshōʿ-yabh prudently made conditions on behalf of his flock with the Muḥammadan ruler, it is said through the intervention of a Christian chief at Najrān and of

[1] Brit. Mus. Add. 7200, f. 14; Hoffmann, *Auszüge*, pp. 91 *sq.*, 173.

[2] *E.g.*, Brit. Mus. Add. 7156, 17219; see Bickell, *Conspectus*, pp. 37, 38.

[3] Judāl, near Mosul.

[4] *B.O.*, ii. 416–418, iii. I, 105, 475; Bar-Hebræus, *Chron. Eccles.*, iii. 113 and note 1, 127 and note 3; Baethgen, *Fragmente*, pp. 13, 19, 108, 111.

[5] This, however, seems to have been given back by Ardashēr III. in 628–629, as the festival to celebrate its restoration took place at Jerusalem in 629; see Bar-Hebræus, *Chron. Eccles.*, ii. 113; *B.O.*, iii. 1, 96, note 3, 105–106; Nöldeke, *Gesch. d. Perser u. Araber*, pp. 391–392.

Yēshū' (or Īshō'), bishop of that place[1]. The deed or ordinance containing the terms of agreement was renewed and confirmed by 'Omar ibn al-Khaṭṭāb[2]. According to 'Abhd-īshō', the principal writings of Īshō'-yabh were a commentary on the Psalms and sundry epistles, histories, and homilies. A hymn of his occurs in the Nestorian psalter Brit. Mus. Add. 14675[3].

Sāhdōnā of Halamūn, a village in Bēth Nuhādhrē[4], was educated at Nisībis, and became a monk under Mār Jacob, the founder of the famous convent of Bēth 'Ābhē[5]. Here he composed a treatise in two volumes on the monastic life, besides a history of his master, and a funeral sermon on him[6]. He became bishop of Māḥōzē dh'Arēwān in Bēth Garmai[7], and was one of the Nestorian clergy who accompanied Īshō'-yabh of Gĕdhālā on his embassy to Heraclius. Whilst halting at Apamea, Īshō'-yabh, John the Nestorian bishop of Damascus, and Sāhdōnā tried their hand

[1] *B.O.*, ii. 418, iii. 1, 108, col. 1; Bar-Hebræus, *Chron. Eccles.*, ii. 115. Bar-Hebræus names Muḥammad himself, but it was more likely Abū Bakr (632–633).

[2] See *B.O.*, iii. 1, 108, col. 1.

[3] Wright, *Catal.*, p. 130, col. 2.

[4] Hoffmann, *Auszüge*, p. 215.

[5] *Ibid.*, p. 226.

[6] *B.O.*, iii. 1, 453, 462.

[7] See *B.O.*, iii. 1, 116, col. 1, at the foot. Assemani pronounces the name Aryūn, but Arēwān is more likely to be correct. See Hoffmann, *Auszüge*, p. 277.

at converting the monks of a neighbouring (Jacobite) convent, the result of which was that Sāhdōnā himself was converted[1], and afterwards wrote several heterodox works. This incident caused much scandal in the East, as may be seen from the numerous letters which Īshō'-yabh of Ḥĕdhaiyabh, another member of the embassy, found it necessary to write upon the subject[2].

This Īshō'-yabh was the son of a wealthy Persian Christian named Bas-ṭuhmag, of Kuphlānā in Ḥĕdhaiyabh or Adiabēnē, who used often to visit the convent of Bēth-'Ābhē[3]. He was educated at the school of Nisībis, became bishop of Mosul, and afterwards metropolitan of Ḥazzā (Arbēl or Irbil) and Mosul. The chief event of his rule at Mosul seems to have been that he hindered the Jacobites from building a church in that city[4], notwithstanding that they were supported by all the weight and influence of the

[1] We cannot see that Assemani has any ground for asserting that Sāhdōnā was converted "ab erroribus Nestorianis ad Catholicam veritatem" (*B.O.*, iii. 1, 107, col. 1; comp. col. 2, ll. 10–12, and p. 120, col. 2, ll. 11–13).

[2] *B.O.*, iii. 1, 116–123. Bar-Hebræus (*Chron. Eccles.*, ii. 113) spitefully improves the occasion by making out that the catholicus Īshō'-yabh of Gĕdhālā himself was the pervert.

[3] *B.O.*, iii. 1, 472; Hoffmann, *Auszüge*, p. 226.

[4] *B.O.*, iii. 1, 114–115.

Taghrītans[1]. Bar-Hebræus declares that he bribed right and left to effect this[2]. He was one of those who accompanied Īshō'-yabh of Gĕdhālā on his embassy to Heraclius[3], and stole a very costly and beautiful casket, containing relics of the Apostles, from a church at Antioch, the which he conveyed (apparently quite openly and shamelessly) to the convent of Bēth 'Ābhē[4]. On the death of Mār-emmēh[5] (who sat 644–647)[6] he was elevated to the dignity of catholicus[7], which he held till 657–658[8]. In his desire to do something for the promotion of learning he wished to found a school in the convent of Bēth 'Ābhē, where he had built a magnificent church, but the abbot Ḳām-īshō' and

[1] Taghrīth was always strongly Jacobite, and the Nestorians had no church there till 767 (see *B.O.*, iii. 1, 111, note 4; Hoffmann, *Auszüge*, pp. 190–191; Bar-Hebræus, *Chron. Eccles.*, ii. 155–157).

[2] *Chron. Eccles.*, ii. 127.

[3] *B.O.*, iii. 1, 106, col. 1.

[4] There is no reason to doubt the circumstantial recital of a Nestorian writer, *B.O.*, iii. 1, 106, col. 2, 475. Strange to say, Assemani does not improve this occasion!

[5] Properly Mār(ī)-emmēh (see *B.O.*, ii. 389, col. 2, No. 29).

[6] According to others, 647–650; *B.O.*, ii. 420, iii. 1, 113, 615.

[7] In 647 or 648.

[8] Or, according to the other reckoning, till 660, *B.O.*, *locc. citt.* He predeceased the maphriān Denḥā, who died in 660 (Bar-Hebræus, *Chron. Eccles.*, ii. 129, 131).

the rest of the lazy brotherhood would have none of this, and preferred to quit the convent and withdraw to the neighbouring village of Ḥerpā in Saphsāphā[1]. Hereupon the catholicus gave up this part of his plan and built his college in his father's village of Kuphlānā (or Kulpānā)[2]. Soon afterwards he found himself involved in another and more serious dispute with Simeon, the metropolitan of Rēv-Ardashēr[3] in Persis and of the Ḳaṭrāyē[4], who refused obedience to him as his diocesan; and this led to a lengthy correspondence, regarding which see *B.O.*, iii. 1, 127–136. His works, as enumerated by ʿAbhd-īshōʿ, are—*Hup-pākh Ḥushshābhē* or "Refutation of (Heretical) Opinions[5]," written for John, metropolitan of Bēth Lāpāt[6], and other controversial tracts, consolatory and other discourses, various hymns[7], and an

[1] See Hoffmann, *Auszüge*, pp. 223, 227.

[2] *B.O.*, iii. 1, 124–125.

[3] Or Rēshahr (Yāḳūt); see Nöldeke, *Gesch. d. Perser u. Araber*, p. 19, note 4.

[4] Or Arabs of Ḳaṭar, on the Persian Gulf, and the adjacent districts. See *B.O.*, iii. 1, 136.

[5] *B.O.*, iii. 1, 137, note 1.

[6] *B.O.*, iii. 1, 138, col. 1; Nöldeke, *Gesch. d. Perser u. Araber*, p. 41, note 2; Hoffmann, *Auszüge*, p. 41, note 351.

[7] The composition on the martyr George quoted by Cardāḥī (*Liber Thes.*, pp. 124–125) is probably of much later date. At least we should not expect such artificial riming in the 7th century.

exhortation to certain novices. He arranged the Ḥudhrā[1] or service-book for the Sundays of the whole year, for Lent, and for the fast of Nineveh[2], and drew up offices of baptism[3], absolution[4], and consecration[5]. He also wrote a history of the monk Īshō'-sabhran, a convert from the religion of Zoroaster and a Christian martyr[6]. A large collection of his letters is extant in Cod. Vat. clvii. (*Catal.*, iii. 299), a judicious selection from which would be worth printing[7].

'Ănān-īshō'[8] of Ḥĕdhaiyabh and his brother Īshō'-yabh were fellow-students at Nisībis with Īshō'-yabh III., and afterwards entered the great convent on Mount Īzlā. Īshō'-yabh subsequently became bishop of Ḳārdāliyābhādh[9]; but 'Ănān-

[1] *B.O.*, iii. 1, 139, 144, col. 2.

[2] See Badger, *The Nestorians*, ii. p. 22.

[3] Brit. Mus. Add. 7181 (Rosen, *Catal.*, p. 59).

[4] *E.g.*, of apostates and heretics, *Catal. Vat.*, ii. 307, 367; of public penitents, *ibid.*, 291, Brit. Mus. Add. 7181 (Rosen, *Catal.*, p. 59).

[5] *E.g.*, the consecration of an altar with the chrism, *Catal. Vat.*, ii. 302, 368; see also *ibid.*, 294, where canons of his are given, and Cod. Vat. ccxci., in Mai, *Scriptt. Vett. Nova Coll.*, v.

[6] *Catal. Vat.*, iii. 328; *B.O.*, iii. 1, 285, note 2, and p. 633.

[7] *B.O.*, iii. 1, 140–143.

[8] Properly 'Ănā-n(ī)-īshō'; see *B.O.*, iii. 1, 144–146; Hoffmann, *Opusc. Nestor.*, p. iv.

[9] The older name of Shennā dhĕ-Bhēth Remmān, in

Īshō' was seized with a fit of wandering, and visited Jerusalem, whence he went on to the desert of Skete in Egypt, and made himself thoroughly acquainted with the lives and habits of its monks, regarding whom he had read so much in the *Paradise* of Palladius. On his return he soon forsook the great convent, because of dissensions that had arisen in it, and betook himself with his brother to the convent of Bēth 'Ābhē, where he devoted himself to study, and so distinguished himself that he was employed by Īshō'-yabh III. to assist in arranging the Ḥudhrā (see above). 'Ănān-īshō' wrote a volume of philosophical divisions and definitions, with a copious commentary, dedicated to his brother[1], and compiled a work on the correct reading and pronunciation of difficult words in the writings of the fathers[2], thus following in the footsteps of Joseph Hūzāyā (see above, p. 116), and anticipating Jacob of Edessa and the monks of the convent of Ḳarḳaphĕthā (see above, p. 20 *sq.*). He was also the author of a treatise entitled *Liber Canonum de Æquilitteris, i.e.*, on the different pronunciation and signification of words that are spelt with the

Arabic Sinn Bā-rimmā, or simply as-Sinn ; see Hoffmann *Auszüge*, pp. 189, 253.

[1] *B.O.*, iii. 1, 144, col. 2, near the foot.

[2] *Ibid.*, iii. 1, 144.

same letters. This has been published, with the additions of Ḥonain ibn Isḥāḳ of al-Ḥīrah (died in 873) and another compiler, by Hoffmann, *Opuscula Nestoriana*, pp. 2–49[1]. His greatest work, however, was a new recension or redaction, in two volumes, of the *Paradise* of Palladius and Jerome, with additions collected by himself from other sources and from his own experience[2]. This he compiled at the request of the patriarch George, and it became the standard work on the subject in the Nestorian convents[3].

John of Bēth Garmai (Garmĕḳāyā), called John the Elder, was a disciple of Jacob of Bēth 'Ābhē, and his successor as abbot of that convent. After a few months, however, he secretly fled from Bēth 'Ābhē and betook himself to a hill near Dāḳūḳā[4] in Bēth Garmai, where the monastery of Ezekiel[5] was soon afterwards built, in

[1] From a MS. in the India Office library, London. There is another copy in the collection of the S.P.C.K., now at Cambridge.

[2] See *B.O.*, ii. 493; iii. 1, 49, 145, col. 2, 151, col. 1, middle.

[3] The *Illustrations of the Book of the Paradise* in Brit. Mus. Add. 17263, 17264 (Wright, *Catal.*, pp. 1078–80) and Orient. 2311 seems to be a different work. The author of it is said to have been a Ḳaṭrāyā, "a native of Ḳaṭar," which 'Ănān-īshō' was not.

[4] Hoffmann, *Auszüge*, p. 273.

[5] So called from its founder; see Hoffmann, *op. cit.*, p. 274, note 2154.

which he ended his days[1]. His works, according to ʿAbhd-īshōʿ[2], are—a collection of heads of knowledge or maxims, rules for novices, a brief chronicle, histories of Abraham, abbot of the great convent on Mount Īzlā, of the monk Bar-ʿidtā[3], and of Mār Khodhāhwai, the founder of the convent of Bēth Ḥālē (near al-Ḥadīthah, by Mosul), with a discourse and hymns on the last named.

Sabhr-īshōʿ Rusṭam[4] was a native of a village called Ḥĕrem, in Ḥĕdhaiyabh, and entered the great convent on Mount Īzlā under the abbot Narsai, the successor of Bābhai. Here, at the request of the monks, he wrote a tract on the occasion of the celebration of Golden Friday, and also a large volume of disputations against heresies and other theological questions. He migrated thence, perhaps along with Narsai, to Bēth ʿĀbhē, where, however, he resided only for a short time, being invited by the monks of Bēth Ḳūḳā[5] to become their prior. Here he composed

[1] *B.O.*, iii. 1, 203–204, 474. But he must have lived till after 661, for Mār Khodhāhwai was still alive in that year (*B.O.*, iii. 1, 151, near the top).

[2] *B.O.*, iii. 1, 204.

[3] *Ibid.*, iii. 1, 467, col. 2, ch. 4.

[4] *Ibid.*, iii. 1, 454–455.

[5] On the Great Zāb, in Ḥĕdhaiyabh, see Hoffmann, *Auszüge*, p. 215, note 1715.

eight discourses on the dispensation of our Lord, the conversion of the various countries by the Apostles, and on continence and the monastic life. Further, at the request of Mār Ḳardagh, the syncellus of Īshō'-yabh III., he wrote lives of Īshō'-Zĕkhā (of the convent of Gaṣṣā), of Īshō'-yabh III., of Abraham abbot of Bēth 'Ābhē, who came thither from the convent of Zĕkhā-īshō'[1], of Ḳām-īshō' abbot of Bēth 'Ābhē[2], of Abraham of Nethpar, of Rabban Īyōbh (or Job) the Persian, and of the elder Sabhr-īshō', the founder of the convent of Bēth Ḳūḳā[3], to which may be added the lives of the brothers Joseph and Abraham[4].

George, the pupil and successor of Īshō'-yabh III., was a native of Kaphrā in Bēth Gĕwāyā, a district of Bēth Garmai[5]. His parents were wealthy, and owned two farms in the neighbourhood of the convent of Bēth 'Ābhē. Being sent to take charge of these, he got acquainted with the monks and ultimately joined their body. When Īshō'-yabh was promoted to the patriarchate, he appointed George to be metropolitan of

[1] *B.O.*, iii. 1, 468, col. 1, at the top.

[2] Who died in 652; see Baethgen, *Fragmente*, pp. 21, 112.

[3] *B.O.*, ii. 418, col. 2.

[4] *Ibid.*, iii. 1, 228, col. 1, near the foot.

[5] *Ibid.*, ii. 421, iii. 1, 149; Bar-Hebræus, *Chron. Eccles.*, ii. 131, 133; Hoffmann, *Auszüge*, p. 277.

Ḥĕdhaiyabh in his stead[1]; and, on the death of his friend, George succeeded to the patriarchate in 661, and sat till 680. As an author he is not of much account, having written merely a few homilies, with hymns and prayers for certain occasions, and published nineteen canons[2]. His too in all probability is the "epistola dogmatica" contained in Cod. Vat. cccclvii., p. 360[3].

Elias, bishop of Marū or Merv, was one of those who were present at the death of Īshō'-yabh III. and elected George as his successor[4]. He compiled a *Catena patrum* (*Mallĕphānūthā dhĕ-Ḳadhmāyē*) on the four Gospels, and wrote commentaries on Genesis, Psalms, Proverbs, Ecclesiastes, the Song of Songs, Ecclesiasticus, Isaiah, the twelve minor Prophets, and the epistles of St Paul. His letters would probably be of some interest to us, and the loss of his

[1] He must be distinguished from two other Georges, Persians by race, also disciples of Īshō'-yabh, viz., George, bishop of Pĕrath dĕ-Maishān or al-Baṣrah, and George, bishop of Nisībis, the latter of whom is the author of a well-known hymn (see *B.O.*, iii. 1, 456; Bickell, *Conspectus*, p. 38), often found in Nestorian psalters, *e.g.*, Rosen, *Catal.*, p. 14, w; Wright, *Catal.*, p. 131, col. 1; Munich *Catal.*, Cod. Syr. 4, p. 112.

[2] *B.O.*, iii. 1, 153.

[3] Mai, *Scriptt. Vett. Nova Coll.*, v.

[4] *B.O.*, ii. 420.

ecclesiastical history, to which ʿAbhd-īshōʿ applies the epithet of "trustworthy" is to be regretted[1].

Of Daniel bar Maryam we can only say that he flourished under Īshōʿ-yabh III. of Ḥĕdhaiyabh, about 650[2]. He wrote an ecclesiastical history in four volumes, and an explanation of the calendar. The history is cited by George of Arbēl in the 10th century for the date of the destruction of Jerusalem[3].

Gabriel, surnamed Taurĕthā, was a native of the province of Siarzūr or Shahrazūr[4]. He studied at Nisībis, and then entered the great convent on Mount Īzlā, where he took part in a controversy with the Monophysite monks of the convent of Ḳartamīn (near Mārdīn) and against Sāhdōnā. He afterwards migrated to Bēth ʿĀbhē, where he wrote a life of Mār Narsai the abbot, an account of the martyrs of Ṭūr Bĕrā'īn or Ṭūr Bĕrēn (Ādhurparwā, Mihrnarsai, and their sister Māhdokht, in the ninth year of Sapor II.), a homily for the washing of the feet, &c.[5] He became abbot of

[1] *B.O.*, iii. 1, 148.

[2] *Ibid.*, ii. 420; iii. 1, 231.

[3] *Ibid.*, iii. 1, 521.

[4] See Hoffmann, *Auszüge*, p. 43, notes 364, 365, p. 254 *sq.*

[5] *B.O.*, iii. 1, 456–458; Hoffmann, *Auszüge*, pp. 9–16, from Brit. Mus. Add. 12174 (Wright, *Catal.*, p. 1133).

Bēth ʿĀbhē under the catholicus Ḥĕnān-īshōʿ I. (686–701)[1].

Ḥĕnān-īshōʿ I., called the Elder or the Lame (*ḥĕghīrā*), was appointed catholicus in 686[2], in succession to John bar Mārtā[3], the follower of George. He was opposed by Īshōʿ-yabh of al-Baṣrah, whom he threw into prison, but afterwards released on his making his submission. A more serious rival was John of Dāsen, bishop of Nisībis, surnamed the Leper, who curried favour with the caliph ʿAbd al-Malik ibn Marwān and procured the deposition of Ḥĕnān-īshōʿ, whose place he occupied for nearly two years[4]. Bar-Hebræus adds[5] that John put him for some days into prison, and then sent him off to a convent among the mountains in charge of two of his disciples, who threw the luckless catholicus down a precipice and left him there for dead. Luckily he was found by some shepherds, who took good care of him, though he seems to have been lame ever after. On his recovery he withdrew to the

[1] Bar-ṣaumā was abbot at the beginning of Ḥĕnān-īshōʿ's patriarchate; see *B.O.*, iii. 1, 457, col. 1.

[2] Bar-Hebræus, *Chron. Eccles.*, ii. 135; Baethgen, *Fragmente*, pp. 32, 117; *B.O.*, ii. 423.

[3] He sat 680–682; *B.O.*, ii. 422, iii. 1, 615; Bar-Hebræus, *Chron. Eccles.*, ii. 133.

[4] Baethgen, *Fragmente*, pp. 34, 35, 118, 119.

[5] *Chron. Eccles.*, ii. 135 *sq.*; *B.O.*, ii. 423.

convent of Yaunān (or Jonah)[1] near Mosul, where he stayed till the death of his rival. He continued to rule the Nestorian Church till 701[2], and was buried in the convent of Jonah[3]. Besides composing homilies, sermons, and epistles, he was the author of a life of Sergius Dĕwādhā[4] of Daraukạrah or Daukạrah, near Kashkar, who was a contemporary of his. He also wrote a treatise *On the Twofold Use of the School* or university as a place of moral and religious training as well as of instruction in letters, and a commentary on the *Analytics* of Aristotle[5].

Presumably to this century belong two ecclesiastical historians who are known to us only from the *Chronicle* of Elias bar Shīnāyā. Alāhā-zĕkhā is quoted by him in regard to events that took place in 594–596 and 606[6]. Perhaps he is identical with that Alāhā-zĕkhā to whom we find

[1] *B.O.*, ii. 424, note 3. Bar-Hebræus calls it "the convent of John."

[2] According to Elias bar Shīnāyā in Baethgen, *Fragmente*, pp. 38, 120. Others say 699.

[3] His Arab biographer and co-religionist adds that his grave was opened 650 years afterwards, and his body found undecayed and looking as if he slept.

[4] Not Dūdhā. The word means "liable to fits," "epileptic," "crazy."

[5] *B.O.*, iii. 1, 154.

[6] See Bar-Hebræus, *Chron. Eccles.*, ii. 106, note 3, 107, note 3.

Īshō'-yabh III. writing a letter whilst he was yet bishop, consequently in the earlier part of the century[1]. Mīkhā or Micah is cited by Elias as an authority for the years 594–596 and 605[2].

[Here also may be mentioned the anonymous chronicle, of Nestorian origin, published by Guidi in the transactions of the Stockholm Congress[3] It extends from the death of Hormizd IV. to the fall of the Sassanian empire, and the final redaction is assigned by Nöldeke with much probability to *circa* A.D. 670–680.]

Passing over into the 8th century, we may mention David of Bēth Rabban, that is, of the convent of Zĕkhā-īshō', afterwards of Bēth 'Ābhē, who was the author of a monastic history, called *The Little Paradise*, which is frequently cited by Thomas of Margā. Its first chapter contained anecdotes relative to George Neshrāyā, Nathaniel, and other monks of Bēth 'Ābhē, who lived under Ḥĕnān-īshō' I., towards the end of the 7th century[4]. David attained episcopal dignity,

1 *B.O.*, iii. 1, 141, No. 35.

2 See Bar-Hebræus, *Chron. Eccles.*, ii. 106, note 3, 107, note 2.

3 [Also separately under the title *Un nuovo testo siriaco sulla storia degli ultimi Sassanidi* (Leyden, Brill, 1891). German translation and commentary by Nöldeke in *Sitzungsberichte* of the Vienna Academy, 1893.]

4 *B.O.*, iii. 1, 217, col. 2, 218, col. 1 ; see also pp. 49, note 1, 184, col. 1, l. 1.

though we do not know the name of his see. He wrote also a geographical treatise *Upon the Limits of Climates or Countries, and the Variations of the Days and Nights*[1].

Bābhai bar Nĕṣībhnāyē (so called because his parents were of Nisībis) flourished under the catholicus Ṣĕlībhā-zĕkhā (713–729), the successor of Ḥĕnān-īshō'[2]. He was a native of Gĕbhīltā or Jabiltā in Ṭīrhān[3], and is described by Thomas of Margā as being a tall, powerful man, with a magnificent voice, gentle and modest, and learned withal. He devoted himself to the reformation of the musical services of the Nestorian Church, which had fallen into sad confusion, and founded many schools, more particularly in the dioceses of Ḥĕdhaiyabh and Margā, with the special object of promoting the study of church music. The most important of these were at Kĕphar-'Uzzēl[4]

[1] *B.O.*, iii. 1, 255. The poems referred to by Assemani in note 1 are no doubt of much later date. The first of them is edited by Cardāḥī in his *Liber Thesauri*, pp. 41–46. Cardāḥī places David's death "in the year 800." Twenty-two very artificial poems "on the love of wisdom," ascribed to him, are printed in the *Directorium Spirituale* of John of Mosul, edited by the bishop Elias John Millos, 1868, pp. 172–214.

[2] According to Elias bar Shīnāyā, in Baethgen, *Fragmente*, pp. 42, 47, 122, 124. Assemani (*B.O.*, ii. 430) gives 714–728.

[3] Hoffmann, *Auszüge*, p. 188. [4] *Ibid.*, p. 236 *sq.*

in Ḥĕdhaiyabh and Bāshūsh in the district of Saphsāphā in Margā[1]. At the former he took up his residence, but used to visit and inspect the others once a year. In his latter years he returned to Gĕbhīltā and died there. He wrote discourses and homilies of different kinds, numerous hymns for various occasions, histories (of holy men), and letters[2].

Bar-Sāhdĕ of Karkhā dhĕ-Bhēth Sĕlōkh flourished, according to Assemani, under the catholicus Pethiōn (731–740)[3]. ʽAbhd-īshōʽ states that he wrote an ecclesiastical history[4] and a treatise against the Zoroastrian religion.

When Bābhai the Nisibene was residing at Kĕphar-ʽUzzēl (see above), a woman from the village of Bēth Ṣaiyādhē brought to him her crippled son, whom she called "only half a man," and begged him to bless him. "This is no half man," was the gentle monk's reply; "this shall be a father of fathers and a chief of teachers; his

1 Hoffmann, *Auszüge*, p. 223.

2 See *B.O.*, iii. 1, 117–181. Of his hymns a few are still extant; see Bickell, *Conspectus*, p. 38; Brit. Mus. Add. 7156 (Rosen, *Catal.*, p. 14, v, x, y, z), Add. 14675 (Wright, *Catal.*, p. 131, col. 1), 17219 (*ibid.*, p. 136, col. 1); Paris, Suppl. 56 (Zotenberg, *Catal.*, p. 9, col. 1, t); Munich, Cod. Syr. 4 (Orient. 147).

3 *B.O.*, ii. 430; Baethgen, *Fragmente*, pp. 49, 125.

4 Cited by Elias bar Shīnāyā; see Bar-Hebræus, *Chron. Eccles.*, ii. 65, note 1.

name and his teaching shall be famous throughout the whole East[1]." This was Abraham bar Dāshandādh "the Lame," whose works are enumerated by ʿAbhd-īshōʿ as follows[2]—a book of exhortation, discourses on repentance[3], letters, the book of the king's way, a disputation with the Jews, and a commentary on the discourses of Mark the monk[4]. He was teacher at the school of Bāshūsh in Saphsāphā, where the future catholicus Timothy I. received his early education, as well as his successor Īshōʿ bar Nōn and Abū Nūḥ al-Anbārī[5].

Mār-abhā, the son of Bĕrīkh-ṣebhyānēh, was a native of Kashkar[6], and became bishop of that town. From this see he was promoted in 741 to the dignity of catholicus[7]. At first he had some difficulties with the emīr Yūsuf ibn ʿOmar ath-Thaḳafī, but these were settled by a visit to

[1] *B.O.*, iii. 1, 179.

[2] *Ibid.*, iii. 1, 194.

[3] According to another reading *on desire* or *cupidity*.

[4] See Brit. Mus. Add. 17270 (Wright, *Catal.*, p. 482).

[5] Assemani (*B.O.*, iii. 1, 196, note 4) says that Timothy I. was a pupil of Abraham bar Līphah, but Īshōʿ bar Nōn and Abū Nūḥ are expressly stated to have been pupils of Abraham "the Lame," *ibid.*, p. 165, note 4, and p. 212, note 2; see also p. 486, col. 1.

[6] Others say of Dauḳarah, in the neighbourhood of Kashkar, *B.O.*, ii. 431.

[7] Baethgen, *Fragmente*, pp. 50, 125; Bar-Hebræus, *Chron. Eccles.*, ii. 153; *B.O.*, ii. 431, iii. 1, 157.

al-Kūfah, which gave him an opportunity of going also to al-Ḥīrah, where he was received with great honour by the aged bishop John Azraḳ. He shortened his name to Abhā, the better to distinguish himself from his predecessor Mār-abhā I. (see above, p. 116 *sq.*). In the sixth year of his patriarchate he got into a dispute with his clergy about the management of the school at Seleucia, and withdrew to Kashkar, but returned to Seleucia before his death, which took place in 751, at the age, it is said, of 110 years. According to Bar-Hebræus, "he was learned in ecclesiastical works and in dialectics, and composed a commentary on Theologus (*i.e.*, Gregory Nazianzen)[1], and all his time he was occupied in reading books." ʿAbhd-īshōʿ mentions him in two places, as Abhā of Kashkar[2] in *B.O.*, iii. 1, 154, and as Abhā bar Bĕrīkh-ṣebhyānēh at p. 157. In the former place he ascribes to him expositions, letters, and a commentary on the whole *Dialectics* of Aristotle[3], and in the latter, *The Book of the Generals,* or *Military Governors*[4], and other works.

[1] See *B.O.*, iii. 1, 157, col. 2.

[2] Whom Assemani takes for Abraham of Kashkar (see above, p. 118); for what reason we cannot see.

[3] See *B.O.*, iii. 1, 157, col. 2.

[4] Perhaps a chronicle of the Muḥammadan governors of al-ʿIrāḳ.

Simeon bar Ṭabbākhē (the Butcher) of Kashkar held the important post of chief officer of the treasury under the caliph al-Manṣūr[1], about the same time that his co-religionist George bar Bōkht-īshō' of Gundē-Shābhōr or Bēth Lāpāṭ[2], in Khūzistān, was court physician[3]. The only work of his mentioned by 'Abhd-īshō' is an ecclesiastical history, which from his position at Baghdādh doubtless contained much valuable information.

Sūrēn or Sūrīn[4], bishop of Nisībis and afterwards of Ḥalaḥ or Ḥolwān in Bēth Mādhāyē[5], was raised to the patriarchate in 754, by the orders of Abān, the Muḥammadan emīr of al-Madāïn (Seleucia). The bishops appealed to the caliph 'Abdallāh as-Saffāḥ[6], and not in vain. The election was cancelled, and Jacob, bishop of Gundē-Shābhōr, was chosen in his place (who sat till 773). Their continued squabbles, however, so irritated al-Manṣūr that he gave orders to throw them both into prison. Sūrēn made his escape in

[1] *B.O.*, iii. 1, 206, col. 1, ll. 4, 5.

[2] Nöldeke, *Gesch. d. Perser u. Araber*, p. 41, note 2.

[3] *B.O.*, iii. 1, 205, col. 2, note 4; Baethgen, *Fragmente*, pp. 59, 60, 129; Bar-Hebræus, *Hist. Dynast.*, 221; Wüstenfeld, *Gesch. d. arab. Aerzte*, No. 26.

[4] On the name see Nöldeke, *Gesch. d. Perser u. Araber*, p. 438, note 4.

[5] See Hoffmann, *Auszüge*, p. 120.

[6] He died in June of this same year.

time, but Jacob was caught and spent the next nine years under strict ward, during which time "the second Judas," 'Īsā ibn Shahlāthā or Shahlāfā[1], deacon and physician, trampled the rights of the bishops under foot. On his release, he sent Sūrēn as bishop to al-Baṣrah, at the request of some of the Christian citizens, but others would not receive him, and their quarrels once more attracted the caliph's attention. Sūrēn, warned by 'Īsā, again made his escape, but was captured by the emīr of al-Madāïn and died in prison[2]. The epithet of *Mĕphashshĕḳānā*, given to him by 'Abhd-īshō'[3], implies that he was either a commentator on Scripture or a translator of Greek works into Syriac. He composed a treatise against heretics, but the remainder of 'Abhd-īshō''s text is not clear in Assemani's edition[4].

Cyprian, bishop of Nisībis, was appointed to that see in 741[5]. The great event of his life was the building of the first Nestorian church in the Jacobite city of Taghrīth, just outside of the walls, on the banks of the Tigris. The idea

[1] See Bar-Hebræus, *Hist. Dynast.*, p. 221; Wüstenfeld, *Gesch. d. arab. Aerzte*, No. 26.

[2] *B.O.*, ii. 431; iii. 1, 168, 205–206.

[3] *Ibid.*, iii. 1, 168.

[4] *Ibid.*, iii. 1, 169.

[5] Baethgen, *Fragmente*, pp. 50, 125; Bar-Hebræus, *Chron. Eccles.*, ii. 154, note 1.

originated with Ṣĕlībhā-zĕkhā, bishop of Ṭīrhān, but would never have been realized, had not Cyprian allowed the Jacobites to resume possession of the church of Mār Domitius at Nisībis. The building of the church at Taghrīth was commenced in 767[1]. Cyprian also erected a magnificent church at Nisībis, on which he expended the sum of 56,000 dīnārs, in 758–759[2]. After this time it so happened that the patriarchs of the three Christian sects, Theodoret the Malkite, George the Jacobite, and Jacob the Nestorian, were all in prison at once at Baghdādh. 'Īsā the physician, thinking to improve the occasion to his own advantage, wrote to Cyprian that the caliph al-Manṣūr coveted some of the golden and silver vessels of the church of Nisībis, hinting at the same time in pretty plain language that a handsome present to himself might be of some avail at this juncture. Cyprian had the courage to go straight to Baghdādh with the letter and show it to the caliph, who disgraced 'Īsā and confiscated his property[3], releasing the three patriarchs at the same time[4]. Cyprian died in 767[5]. Ac-

[1] Bar-Hebræus, *Chron. Eccles.*, ii. 155–157.

[2] Baethgen, *Fragmente*, pp. 57, 128.

[3] Bar-Hebræus, *Hist. Dynast.*, p. 224.

[4] Bar-Hebræus, *Chron. Eccles.*, ii. 161–163; *B.O.*, iii. 1, 111–112.

[5] Baethgen, *Fragmente*, pp. 60, 129.

cording to ʿAbhd-īshōʿ, he wrote a commentary on the theological discourses of Gregory Nazianzen and various forms of ordination[1].

Timothy I. was a native of Ḥazzā in Ḥĕdhaiyabh, and had been a pupil of Abraham bar Dāshandādh (see above, p. 186) at the school of Bāshūsh in Saphsāphā. He became bishop of Bēth Bāghēsh[2], and stood well with the Muḥammadan governor of Mosul, Abū Mūsā ibn Musʿab, and his Christian secretary Abū Nūḥ al-Anbārī[3]. On the death of Ḥĕnān-īshōʿ II. in 779[4], several persons presented themselves as candidates for the dignity of catholicus. Timothy got rid of Īshōʿ-yabh, abbot of Bēth ʿĀbhē, by pointing out to him that he was an old man, unfit to withstand

[1] *B.O.*, iii. 1, 111–113. By the "theology" of Gregory Nazianzen are probably meant the discourses bearing the title *Theologica Prima*, &c.; see, for example, Wright, *Catal.*, p. 425, Nos. 22–25.

[2] Hoffmann, *Auszüge*, p. 227 *sq.*

[3] Also a pupil of Abraham bar Dāshandādh (*B.O.*, iii. 1, 212, note 2, 159, col. 1). He is mentioned in commendatory terms by Timothy in his encyclical letters of 790 and 805 (*B.O.*, iii. 1, 82, col. 1, 164, col. 1; ʿAbhd-īshōʿ, *Collectio Canonum Synodicorum*, ix. 6, in Mai, *Scriptt. Vett. Nova Coll.*, x. pp. 167, col. 1, 329, col. 1). He was the author of a refutation of the Ḳor'ān, a disputation against heretics, and other useful works (*B.O.*, iii. 1, 212), among which may be mentioned a life of the missionary John of Dailam (*B.O.*, iii. 1, 183, col. 2).

[4] Or, according to others, 777.

his younger rivals, and by promising, if he himself were successful, to make him metropolitan of Ḥĕdhaiyabh, which he afterwards did. Meantime Thomas of Kashkar and other bishops held a synod at the convent of Mār Pethiōn in Baghdādh, and elected the monk George, who had the support of ʿĪsā the court physician; but this formidable opponent died suddenly. Having by a mean trick obtained the support of the archdeacon Bērōë and the heads of the various colleges, Timothy managed at last to get himself appointed catholicus, about eight months after the death of his predecessor. He still, however, encountered strong opposition. Ephraim metropolitan of Gundē-Shābhōr, Solomon bishop of al-Ḥadīthah, Joseph metropolitan of Marū or Merv, Sergius bishop of Maʿallĕthāyā, and others held a synod at the convent of Bēth Ḥālē, in which they made Rusṭam, bishop of Ḥĕnāithā[1], metropolitan of Ḥĕdhaiyabh in place of Īshōʿ-yabh[2], and excommunicated Timothy, who retorted with the same weapon and deposed Joseph of Merv. Joseph brought the matter before the caliph al-Mahdī, but, failing to gain any redress, in an evil hour for himself became a Muḥammadan[3]. Once more

[1] Hoffmann, *Auszüge*, p. 216 *sq.* [2] *B.O.*, iii. 1, 207.

[3] We need not believe all the evil that Bar-Hebræus tells us of this unhappy man, *Chron. Eccles.*, ii. 171 *sq.*

Ephraim summoned his bishops to Baghdādh and excommunicated Timothy for the second time, with no other result than a counter-excommunication and some disgraceful rioting, which led to the interference of ʿĪsā and the restoration of peace[1]. Timothy was duly installed in May 780[2]. He made the bishops of Persia subject to the see of Seleucia, and appointed over them one Simeon as metropolitan with orders to enforce a stricter rule than heretofore[3]. In his days Christianity spread among the Turks, and the khāḳān himself is said to have become a convert[4]. Timothy's disgraceful response to the caliph ar-Rashīd in the matter of the divorce of Zubaidah may be seen in *B.O.*, iii. 1, 161. He is said to have died in 204 A.H. = 819–820 A.D., or 205 = 820–821; but, if he was catholicus for forty-three years, his death

[1] See the whole miserable story told in full in *B.O.*, ii. 433, iii. 1, 158–160; Bar-Hebræus, *Chron. Eccles.*, ii. 165–169.

[2] Baethgen, *Fragmente*, pp. 64, 131.

[3] Bar-Hebræus, *Chron. Eccles.*, ii. 169; *B.O.*, ii. 433.

[4] *B.O.*, iii. 1, 160. Compare Chwolson's interesting memoir "Syrische Grabinschriften aus Semirjetschie" (west of the Chinese province of Kuldja, more correctly Kulja), in *Mém. de l'Acad. Imp. des Sc. de St. Pétersb.*, 7th ser., vol. xxxiv., No. 4. The oldest of these tombstones is dated A. Gr. 1169 = 858 A.D., and marked "the grave of Mengkū-ṭenesh the believer" (p. 7); but most of them belong to the 13th and 14th centuries.

cannot have taken place till 823[1]. ʿAbhd-īshōʿ informs us that Timothy wrote synodical epistles, a volume on questions of ecclesiastical law, another on questions of various sorts, a third containing disputations with a heretic, viz., the Jacobite patriarch George, about 200 letters in two volumes, a disputation with the caliph al-Mahdī or his successor al-Hādī (on matters of religion), and an astronomical work on the stars[2]. Bar-Hebræus adds hymns for the dominical feasts of the whole year and a commentary on Theologus (Gregory Nazianzen)[3].

In this century too we may place the two following historical writers, whose names and works are unfortunately known to us only through the mention made of them by a later annalist. (1) An anonymous author, the abbot of the great convent (of Abraham on Mount Īzlā), cited by Elias bar Shīnāyā in his *Chronicle* under the years 740–741[4]. (2) An ecclesiastical historian

[1] See *B.O.*, ii. 434; iii. 1, 160.

[2] *B.O.*, iii. 1, 162–163.

[3] *Chron. Eccles.*, ii. 179. He is probably the author of the hymn in Brit. Mus. Add. 7156 (Rosen, *Catal.*, p. 13, col. 1, l) and Paris, Suppl. 56 (Zotenberg, *Catal.*, p. 9, col. 1, i).

[4] See Baethgen, *Fragmente*, p. 2, No. 3; Bar-Hebræus, *Chron. Eccles.*, ii. 152, note 2, 154, note 1 (Abbeloos writes "the abbots of the great convent").

called Pethiōn, identified by Baethgen (*Fragmente*, p. 2, No. 6) with the catholicus of that name. This is, however, impossible, because the catholicus died in 740, whereas the *Ecclesiastical History of Pethiōn* is cited by Elias bar Shīnāyā under the years 765 and 768.

We conclude our enumeration of the Nestorian writers of this century with the name of another historian. In the *Bibl. Orient.*, iii. 1, 195, the text of ʿAbhd-īshōʿ, as edited by Assemani, speaks of a writer named Īshōʿ-dĕnaḥ, bishop of Ḳaṣrā. Other MSS., however, read Baṣrā (al-Baṣrah), which is confirmed by Elias bar Shīnāyā in Baethgen's *Fragmente*, p. 2. The variation Dĕnaḥ-īshōʿ in Bar-Hebræus (*Chron. Eccles.*, i. 334) is of no consequence, and even there the MSS. differ. Besides the usual homilies and some metrical discourses, he wrote an introduction to logic, a work entitled *The Book of Chastity*, in which he collected lives and anecdotes of holy men and founders of monasteries, and an ecclesiastical history in three volumes[1]. This valuable work is known to us only by a few citations in Bar-Hebræus and Elias bar Shīnāyā. Those in Bar Shīnāyā[2] range from 624 to 714, but the extract in Bar-Hebræus[3] brings us down to 793.

[1] *B.O.*, iii. 1, 195. [2] Baethgen, *Fragmente*, p. 2.
[3] *Chron. Eccles.*, i. 333; *B.O.*, iii. 1, 195, note 4 (where

Reverting now to the Jacobite Church, we shall find that the number of its literary men in the 9th century is not large, though some of them are of real importance as theologians and historians.

Dionysius Tell-Maḥrāyā was, as his surname implies, a native of Tell-Maḥrē, a village situated between ar-Raḳḳah and Ḥiṣn Maslamah, near the river Balīkh[1]. He was a student in the convent of Ḳen-neshrē[2], and on its destruction by fire[3] and the consequent dispersion of the monks, he went to the convent of Mār Jacob at Kaisūm, in the district of Samosāta[4]. He devoted himself entirely to historical studies[5], which he seems to have carried on in peace and quiet till 818. The patriarch Cyriacus (see above, p. 165) had got

695 is a mistake for 793). See also Bar-Hebræus, *Chron. Eccles.*, ii. 42, note 2, 114, note 1, 122, note 1, 127, note 3, 138, notes 1, 2, 140, note 1.

[1] See Hoffmann in *Z.D.M.G.*, xxxii. (1878), p. 742, note 2.

[2] Bar-Hebræus, *Chron. Eccles.*, i. 347–349.

[3] *B.O.*, ii. 345, col. 1, where the rebuilding of it by Dionysius is mentioned; Bar-Hebræus, *Chron. Eccles.*, i. 355, at the top.

[4] Bar-Hebræus, *Chron. Eccles.*, i. 347–349. A previous residence at the convent of Zuḳnīn near Āmid (*B.O.*, ii. 98, col. 2) is uncertain, as the words *dairā dhīlan* probably mean no more than "the convent of us Jacobites."

[5] Bar-Hebræus, *Chron. Eccles.*, i. 347, last line.

entangled in a controversy with the monks of Cyrrhus and Gubbā Bạrrāyā about the words *laḥmā shĕmaiyānā* ("the heavenly bread"), &c., in the Eucharistic service, which ended in the malcontents setting up as anti-patriarch Abraham, a monk of the convent of Ḳartamīn. After the death of Cyriacus in 817, a synod was held in June 818 at Callinīcus (ar-Raḳḳah), in which, after considerable discussion, Theodore, bishop of Kaisūm, proposed the election of Dionysius, which was approved by most of those present, including Basil I., maphriān of Taghrīth[1]. The poor monk was accordingly fetched to Callinīcus, received deacon's orders on Friday in the convent of Estūnā or the Pillar, priest's orders on Saturday in the convent of Mār Zakkāi or Zacchæus, and was raised to the patriarchate in the cathedral on Sunday the first of Ābh, 818, the officiating bishop being Theodosius of Callinīcus. Abraham and his partisans, seeing their hopes disappointed, maintained their hostile attitude, which led afterwards to the usual scandalous scenes before the Muslim authorities[2]. Immediately after his installation, Dionysius commenced a visitation of his vast

[1] Bar-Hebræus, *Chron. Eccles.*, i. 347.

[2] *Ibid.*, i. 355–357; *B.O.*, ii. 345. Abraham died in 837, and was succeeded by his brother Simeon as anti-patriarch.

diocese, going first northwards to Cyrrhus, thence to Antioch, Kirkēsion (Ḳirḳīsiyā), the district of the Khābhūr, Nisībis, Dārā and Kĕphar-tūthā, and so back to Callinīcus, where he enjoyed the protection of ʿAbdallāh ibn Ṭāhir against his rival Abraham. He did not on this occasion visit Mosul and Taghrīth, because the maphriān Basil thought the times unfavourable[1]. In 825 ʿAbdallāh ibn Ṭāhir was sent to Egypt to put down the rebellion of ʿObaidallāh ibn as-Sarī, where he remained as governor till 827[2]. His brother Muḥammad ibn Ṭāhir was by no means so well disposed towards the Christians, and destroyed all that they had been allowed to build in Edessa[3]. Wherefore the patriarch went down into Egypt to beg the emīr ʿAbdallāh to write to his brother and bid him moderate his zeal against the Church, which he accordingly did[4]. On his return from Egypt the patriarch had troubles with Philoxenus, bishop of Nisībis, who espoused the cause of the anti-patriarch Abraham[5]; and he then went to Baghdādh in 829 to confer with the caliph al-Ma'mūn as to an edict that he had issued on the occasion

[1] Bar-Hebræus, *Chron. Eccles.*, i. 353.

[2] Wüstenfeld, *Die Statthalter von Aegypten*, 1te Abth., p. 32 *sq.*; De Sacy, *Relation de l'Égypte par Abd-allatif*, pp. 501–508 and 552–557.

[3] Bar-Hebræus, *Chron. Eccles.*, i. 359.

[4] *Ibid.*, i. 369.

[5] *Ibid.*, i. 363.

of dissensions between the Palestinian and Babylonian Jews regarding the appointment of an exiliarch[1]. During his stay in the capital disputes took place among the Christians, which ended in a reference to the caliph and in the deposition of the bishop Lazarus bar Sābhĕthā[2]. From Baghdādh Dionysius proceeded to Taghrīth and Mosul, and nominated Daniel as maphriān in place of the deceased Basil. In 830 al-Ma'mūn made an attack on the Greek territory, and the patriarch tried to see him on his return at Kaisūm, but the caliph had hurried on to Damascus, whither Dionysius followed him and accompanied him to Egypt on a mission to the Bashmuric Copts, who were then in rebellion. Any efforts of his and of the Egyptian patriarch were, however, of no avail, and the unfortunate rebels suffered the last horrors of war at the hands of al-Ma'mūn and his general Afshin[3]. On this journey Dionysius saw and examined the obelisks of Heliopolis, the pyramids, and the Nilometer[4]. In 835 he revisited Taghrīth to settle some disputes between the Taghrītans and the monks of Mār Matthew at Mosul, and to

[1] Bar-Hebræus, *Chron. Eccles.*, i. 365.

[2] *Ibid.*, i. 365–371.

[3] Bar-Hebræus, *Chron. Eccles.*, i. 373; Weil, *Gesch. d. Khalifen*, ii. 246; Wüstenfeld, *Die Statthalter von Aegypten*, 1te Abth., pp. 40–43.

[4] Bar-Hebræus, *Chron. Eccles.*, i. 377–381.

ordain Thomas as maphriān in place of the deceased Daniel[1]. In the same year he went once more to Baghdādh to salute al-Ma'mūn's successor al-Muʿtaṣim, and met there the son of the king of Nubia, who had come on the same errand[1]. The latter years of Dionysius were embittered by the oppressions and afflictions which the Christians had to endure at the hands of the Muḥammadans. He died on 22d August 845, and was buried in the convent of Ḳen-neshrē[2]. He left behind him one great work, his *Annals*, covering the whole period of the world's history from the creation down to his own time. Of this there were two recensions, a longer and a shorter. The longer redaction was dedicated to John, bishop of Dārā, and came down at all events to the year 837, or perhaps a little later[3]. Assemani has published an extract from it, which he was fortunate enough to find in Cod. Vat. cxliv., f. 89, in the *B.O.*, ii. 72–77[4]. It would seem to have been written, after the manner of John of Asia, in a series of chapters dealing with particular topics. The shorter redaction is extant in a single imperfect MS., Cod. Vat. clxii.[5], and is dedicated

[1] Bar-Hebræus, *Chron. Eccles.*, i. 381.

[2] *Ibid.*, 385.

[3] *Ibid.*, 383–385.

[4] See *Catal. Vat.*, iii. 253.

[5] See *Catal. Vat.*, iii. 328. Assemani's account of this MS. is not so clear as could have been wished. In the

to George, chorepiscopus of Āmid, Euthalius the abbot (of Zuḳnīn ?), Lazarus the periodeutes, the monk Anastasius, and the rest of the brotherhood. It is arranged by successive years, and ended with the year of the Greeks 1087 = 776 A.D.[1] The author has adopted a division into four parts. Part first extends from the creation to the reign of Constantine. Here the chief authority is the *Chronicorum Canonum Liber* of Eusebius, supplemented by some extracts from other Greek sources, such as Eusebius's *Ecclesiastical History* and the *Chronographia* of Julius Africanus. With these Dionysius has incorporated matter derived from sundry other works, *e.g.*, the *Chronicle of Edessa* (see above, p. 101), the *Mĕʿarrath Gazzē* or "Cave of Treasures[2]," Pseudo-Callisthenes's *Life of Alexander the Great*, the story of the seven sleepers[3],

*Catal. Vat.*, iii. 329, he says that it is "unus ex iis codicibus, quos Moses Nisibenus cœnobiarcha e Mesopotamia in Scetense S. Mariæ Syrorum monasterium intulit" (viz., in 932); but there is now no note whatever in the MS. to show that this was the case.

1 *B.O.*, ii. 99. At present the MS. ends in the year 775, a few leaves being wanting at the end.

2 Translated into German by Bezold, *Die Schatzhöhle* (1883). [The Syriac text appeared in 1888; see above, p. 98 *sq.*]

3 Guidi, *Testi Orientali inediti sopra i Sette Dormienti di Efeso* (Reale Accad. dei Lincei), 1885; see in particular p. 34, note 3.

and Josephus's *Jewish War*[1]. The second part of Dionysius's *Chronicle* reaches from Constantine to Theodosius II., and here he principally followed the *Ecclesiastical History* of Socrates (compare Cod. Vat. cxlv.). The third part extends from Theodosius II. to Justin II. Here Dionysius acknowledges himself chiefly indebted to his countryman John of Asia (see above, p. 105 *sq.*), but has also incorporated the short *Chronicle* of Joshua the Stylite (see above, p. 77 *sq.*) and the epistle of Simeon of Bēth Arshām on the Ḥimyarite Christians (see above, p. 81). The fourth part, coming down to 158 A.H. = 774–775 A.D., is his own compilation, partly from such written documents as he could find, partly from the oral statements of aged men, and partly from his own observation. Assemani has given an account of the whole work, with an abridgement or excerpt

[1] The Syriac text of this first part was edited by Tullberg, *Dionysii Telmaharensis Chronici liber primus*, 1850 (compare Land, *Joannes Bischof von Ephesos*, pp. 39–41). The Eusebian extracts have been translated and compared with the Greek original (so far as possible), the Latin version of Jerome, and the Armenian version, by Siegfried and Gelzer, *Eusebii Canonum Epitome ex Dionysii Telmaharensis Chronico petita* (1884). On this work see Gutschmid, *Untersuchungen über d. syrische Epitome der Eusebischen Canones* (1886). The editors have not always correctly rendered the text of their "blatero Syrius"; see a flagrant example on p. 79, last paragraph.

of the fourth part, in the *Bibl. Orient.*, ii. 98–116; but the labours of Dionysius of Tell-Maḥrē will never be appreciated as they deserve till the appearance of the edition which is now being prepared by Guidi.

Under Dionysius flourished his brother Theodosius, bishop of Edessa, also a student of Greek at Ḳen-neshrē. Bar-Hebræus makes mention of him as accompanying Dionysius to Egypt in 825–826 to complain to ʿAbdallāh ibn Ṭāhir of the wrongs of the Christians[1]. At an earlier period (802–803), when only a priest, he translated the homily of Gregory Nazianzen on the miracles of the prophet Elijah[2], and Bar-Hebræus says that he also rendered into Syriac the poems of the same author[3].

A friend of his was Antonius, a monk of Taghrīth, surnamed "the Rhetorician[4]." He was the author of a treatise on rhetoric in seven chapters[5], of a work on the good providence of

[1] Bar-Hebræus, *Chron. Eccles.*, i. 361; *B.O.*, ii. 345.

[2] Cod. Vat. xcvi., *Catal. Vat.*, ii. 521; *B.O.*, ii. p. cxlix, No. 17.

[3] Bar-Hebræus, *Chron. Eccles.*, i. 363; *B.O.*, ii. 345. To this version perhaps belong the poems contained in Brit. Mus. Add. 14547 (Wright, *Catal.*, p. 433) and 18821 (*ibid.*, p. 775).

[4] Bar-Hebræus, *Chron. Eccles.*, i. 363; *B.O.*, ii. cl and 345.

[5] Brit. Mus. Add. 17208 (Wright, *Catal.*, p. 614).

God in four discourses[1], and of various encomia, thanksgivings, consolatory epistles[2], and prayers[3], in many of which he makes use not merely of metre but also of rime[4].

Lazarus bar Sābhĕthā, called as bishop Philoxenus and Basil[5], ruled the see of Baghdādh in the earlier part of the 9th century. As mentioned above, he was deposed by Dionysius in 829. He compiled an anaphora or liturgy[6], and wrote an exposition of the office of baptism[7]. The latter may be only part of a larger work on the offices of the church, from which Bar-Hebræus may have derived the information regarding the musical services quoted by Assemani, *B.O.*, i. 166.

Contemporary with these was John, bishop of Dārā, to whom Dionysius dedicated the larger recension of his history (see above). He compiled a liturgy[8], and was the author of the following works—a commentary on the two books of Pseudo-Dionysius Areopagita *De Hierarchia*

[1] Brit. Mus. Add. 14726 (Wright, *Catal.*, p. 617).

[2] Brit. Mus. Add. 17208.

[3] Brit. Mus. Add. 14726.

[4] See a specimen in Rödiger's *Chrestom. Syr.*, 2d ed., pp. 110–111.

[5] See Wright., *Catal.*, p. 496, col. 2.

[6] See Renaudot, ii. 399.

[7] Cod. Vat. cxlvii., *Catal.*, iii. 276.

[8] *B.O.*, ii. 123.

*Cœlesti et Ecclesiastica*[1], four books on the priesthood[2], four books on the resurrection of the dead[3], and a treatise on the soul[4].

Nonnus was an archdeacon of the Jacobite Church at Nisībis during the first half of this century, the Nestorian bishop Cyprian having allowed the Monophysites to resume possession of the church of St Domitius in 767 (see above, p. 190). He is mentioned by Bar-Hebræus as bringing charges against the bishop Philoxenus, who had sided with the anti-patriarch Abraham, and was therefore deposed by a synod held at Rās'ain in 827 or 828[5]. We know also that he was in prison at Nisībis when he wrote his work against Thomas bishop of Margā and metropolitan

[1] *B.O.*, ii. 120–121; Cod. Vat. c. (*Catal.*, ii. 539), ccclxiii. (Mai, *Scriptt. Vett. Nova Coll.*, v.); Bodl. Or. 264 (Payne Smith, *Catal.*, pp. 487–492). There is an extract in Cod. Vat. ccccxi. p. 1 (Mai, *op. cit.*).

[2] *B.O.*, ii. 121; Cod. Vat. c. (*Catal.*, ii. 542), ccclxiii. (Mai, *op. cit.*); Bodl. Or. 264 (P. Smith, pp. 492–496). Extracts from bks. ii. and iv. in Zingerle, *Monum. Syr.*, i. 105–110; from bk. iv. in Overbeck, *S. Ephraemi*, &c., *Opp. Sel.*, pp. 409–413; see Bar-Hebræus, *Chron. Eccles.*, ii. 394, note 1, No. 13.

[3] *B.O.*, ii. 119; Cod. Vat. c. (*Catal.*, ii. 531), ccclxii. (Mai, *op. cit.*).

[4] *B.O.*, ii. 219, note 1. From it there are extracts in Cod. Vat. cxlvii. (*Catal.*, iii. 276).

[5] Bar-Hebræus, *Chron. Eccles.*, i. 363; *B.O.*, ii. 346, col. 1.

of Bēth Garmai, who flourished under the Nestorian catholici Abraham (837–850) and Theodosius (852–858). Besides this controversial treatise in four discourses, Nonnus was the writer of sundry letters of a similar character[1].

Romanus the physician, a monk of the convent of Ḳartamīn, was elected patriarch at Amid in 887, and took the name of Theodosius[2]. He died in 896. He was the author of a medical syntagma (*kunnāshā*) of some repute[3]. He wrote a commentary on Pseudo-Hierotheus, *On the Hidden Mysteries of the House of God*[4], and dedicated it to Lazarus, bishop of Cyrrhus[5]. The work is divided into five books, the first and second of which he finished at Āmid, before going down to the East, and the third at Samosāta. He also compiled a collection of 112 Pythagorean maxims and proverbs, with brief explanations in

[1] These writings are all contained in Brit. Mus. Add. 14594 (Wright, *Catal.*, pp. 618–620).

[2] Bar-Hebræus, *Chron. Eccles.*, i. 391; ii. 213.

[3] *Ibid.*, i. 391. Assemani suggests that it may be the work contained in Cod. Vat. cxcii. (*Catal.*, iii. 409). Compare Frothingham, *Stephen bar Sudaili the Syrian Mystic and the Book of Hierotheos*, 1886, p. 84 *sq.*

[4] A forgery of Stephen bar Ṣūdh-ailē; see above, p. 76.

[5] Brit. Mus. Add. 7189 (Rosen, *Catal.*, p. 74). This is the very copy which was procured with some difficulty for the use of Gregory Bar-Hebræus (Wright, *Catal.*, p. 1205).

Syriac and Arabic, addressed to one George[1]. A synodical epistle of his is extant in Arabic, written to the Egyptian patriarch Michael III.[2], and a Lenten homily in Arabic[3].

Moses bar Kēphā was the son of Simeon Kēphā (or Peter) and his wife Maryam. The father was from the village of Mashhad al-Koḥail, on the Tigris opposite al-Ḥadīthah[4], the mother a native of Balad, in which town their son was born somewhere about 813. He was taught from his early youth by Rabban Cyriacus, abbot of the convent of Mār Sergius on the Ṭūrā Ṣahyā, or Dry Mountain, near Balad, and there assumed the monastic garb. He was elected bishop of Bēth Remmān (Bārimmā)[5], Bēth Kiyōnāyā[6], and Mosul[7], about 863, and took the name of Severus. He was also for ten years periodeutes or visitor of the

[1] Paris, Ancien fonds 118, 157 (Zotenberg, *Catal.*, p. 147, col. 1, 166, col. 1); Bodl. Marsh. 201, f. 58 (Payne Smith, *Catal.*, p. 507); *B.O.*, ii. 125. It is admirably edited by Zotenberg in the *Journ. Asiat.*, 1876, pp. 426-476.

[2] *B.O.*, ii. 124.

[3] Brit. Mus. Add. 7206, f. 73 (Rosen, *Catal.*, p. 103).

[4] See Hoffmann, *Auszüge*, p. 190.

[5] *Ibid.*, p. 190.

[6] *B.O.*, ii. 218, note 1, col. 2; Hoffmann, *Auszüge*, p. 30, note 243. In Wright's *Catal.*, p. 620, col. 2, the name is written Bēth Kiyōnā; in *B.O.*, ii. 127, Bēth Kēnā.

[7] In Wright's *Catal.*, p. 621, col. 1, he is called bishop of Bēth Remmān and Bēth ʿArbāyē (Bā-ʿarbāyā).

diocese of Taghrīth. He died A. Gr. 1214 = 903 A.D.[1], "aged about ninety years, of which he had been bishop for forty," and was buried in the convent of Mār Sergius. His works are numerous. He wrote commentaries on the whole Old and New Testaments[2], which are often cited by Bar-Hebræus in the *Auṣar Rāzē*. Of these that on the book of Genesis survives, though imperfect, in Brit. Mus. 17274[3], and there are extracts from them in Paris, Ancien fonds 35 (Zotenberg, *Catal.*, p. 156), and Bodl. Marsh. 101 (P. Smith, *Catal.*, p. 462). The Gospels and Pauline epistles (imperfect) are contained in Brit. Mus. Add. 17274 (Wright, *Catal.*, p. 620), the latter only in Bodl. Or. 703 (P. Smith, *Catal.*, p. 410) and Bodl. Marsh. 86 (*ibid.*, p. 418). His treatise on the *Hexaëmeron* in five books[4] is preserved to us in the Paris MS. Anc. fonds 120 (Zotenberg, *Catal.*, p. 197), and there are extracts from it in two other MSS. (*ibid.*, pp. 157, 159). The work *De Paradiso*, in three parts, dedicated to his friend Ignatius of ܡܪܘܢܐ (?)[5], is known to us only through the Latin translation of Andreas Masius, 1569[6]. The

[1] As correctly given in *B.O.*, ii. 218; Bar-Hebræus, *Chron. Eccles.*, ii. 217 (and by MS. C. also in i. 395).

[2] *B.O.*, ii. 130, note 3; 218, col. 2.

[3] Wright, *Catal.*, p. 620.

[4] *B.O.*, ii. 128, No. 1.

[5] *Ibid.*, ii. 218, col. 2.

[6] *Ibid.*, ii. 128, No. 2.

treatise on the soul[1] survives in Cod. Vat. cxlvii. (*Catal.*, iii. 273–274); it consists of 40 chapters, with a supplementary chapter to show that the dead are profited by offerings made on their behalf[2]. That on predestination and freewill, in four discourses, is extant in Brit. Mus. Add. 14731 (Wright, *Catal.*, p. 853). The *Disputations against Heresies*, spoken of by Moses's biographer in *B.O.*, ii. 218, col. 2, is probably identical with the work *On Sects* mentioned by Assemani at p. 131, No. 7. The *Festal Homilies* for the whole year[3] is extant in several MSS., *e.g.*, Brit. Mus. Add. 21210 (Wright, *Catal.*, p. 877) and 17188 (*ibid.*, p. 621), Paris, Anc. fonds 35 and 123 (Zotenberg, *Catal.*, pp. 156, 159)[4]. Besides these we have four funeral sermons[5], an admonitory discourse to the children of the holy orthodox church[6], and a discourse showing why the Messiah is called by various epithets and names[7]. Moses also wrote expositions of the sacraments of the church, such

[1] *B.O.*, ii. 131, No. 6.

[2] [It has been translated into German by O. Braun, *Moses bar Kepha und sein Buch von der Seele*, Freiburg i. B., 1891.]

[3] *B.O.*, ii. 131, No. 9.

[4] See also Cod. Vat. clix. (*Catal.*, iii. 316–317); on the Ascension, Cod. Vat. cxlvii. (*Catal.*, iii. 276).

[5] Brit. Mus. Add. 17188 (Wright, *Catal.*, p. 622).

[6] Brit. Mus. Add. 21210 (Wright, *Catal.*, p. 879).

[7] Brit. Mus. Add. 17188 (Wright, *Catal.*, p. 622).

as on the holy chrism, in 50 chapters, Cod. Vat. cxlvii. (*Catal.*, iii. 274) and Paris, Anc. fonds 123 (Zotenberg, *Catal.*, p. 159)[1], with which is connected the discourse on the consecration of the chrism in Brit. Mus. Add. 21210 (Wright, *Catal.*, p. 879); on baptism, addressed to his friend Ignatius, in 24 chapters, Cod. Vat. cxlvii. (*Catal.*, iii. 276), in connexion with which we may take the discourse on the mysteries of baptism in Brit. Mus. Add. 21210 (Wright, *loc. cit.*) and on baptism in Cod. Vat. xcvi. (*Catal.*, ii. 522)[2]; exposition of the liturgy, Brit. Mus. Add. 21210 (Wright, *Catal.*, p. 879) and Berlin, Sachau 62 (?); further, expositions of the mysteries in the various ordinations, Cod. Vat. li. (*Catal.*, ii. 320)[3]; on the ordination of bishops, priests, and deacons, Brit. Mus. Add. 21210 (Wright, *Catal.*, p. 879); on the tonsure of monks[4], Cod. Vat. li. (*Catal.*, ii. 322)[5]. He also compiled two anaphoræ[6], one of which has been translated by Renaudot, ii. 391. Lastly, Moses bar Kēphā was the author of a commentary on

[1] The Paris MS. Ancien fonds 35 contains another redaction in 36 chapters (Zotenberg, *Catal.*, p. 157).

[2] See also Cod. Vat. ccccxi., in Mai, *Scriptt. Vett. Nova Coll.*, v.

[3] See also Cod. Vat. ccciv., in Mai, *op. cit.*

[4] *B.O.*, ii. 131, No. 8.

[5] Compare Cod. Vat. cccv., in Mai, *op. cit.*

[6] *B.O.*, ii. 130, No. 4.

the dialectics of Aristotle, mentioned by Bar-Hebræus in *Chron. Eccles.*, ii. 215, and of a commentary on the works of Gregory Nazianzen, and an ecclesiastical history, mentioned by his biographer in *B.O.*, ii. 218, col. 2. The loss of this last book is to be regretted.

The contemporary Nestorian writers of mark are hardly more numerous.

In this century the foundations of Syriac lexicography were laid by the famous physician Abū Zaid Ḥonain ibn Isḥāḳ al-ʿIbādī of Ḥērtā (al-Ḥīrah)[1]. He applied himself to medicine at Baghdādh, under Yaḥyā, or Yuḥannā, ibn Māsawaihi (Māsūyah or Mesue); but an ill-feeling soon sprang up between teacher and pupil, and Ḥonain took his departure for the Grecian territory, where he spent a couple of years in acquainting himself with the Greek language and its scientific literature. He afterwards became physician to the caliph al-Mutawakkil. His downfall and excommunication were meanly brought about by a fellow-Christian of the same profession, Isrāʾīl ibn aṭ-Ṭaifūrī, and Ḥonain died soon after, 260 A.H. = 873 A.D.[2] Ḥonain composed most of

[1] Al-ʿIbādī was the *nisbah* of an Arab Christian of al-Ḥīrah. See Ibn Khallikān, ed. Wüstenfeld, No. 87. Latin writers generally call him Joannitius.

[2] See the *Fihrist*, pp. ٢٩٤ and 140; Ibn Abī Uṣaibiʿah,

his original works in Arabic, and likewise many of his translations from the Greek. 'Abhd-īshō' mentions but three books of his[1], viz., a book on the fear of God (which he wrote as a deacon of the church), a Syriac grammar, and a compendious Syriac lexicon. The lexicon has no doubt been in great part absorbed into the later works of Bar 'Alī and Bar Bahlūl[2]. The grammar seems to have been entitled *Kĕthābhā dhĕ-Nuḳzē*, or the "Book of (Diacritical) Points." It is cited by Bar-Hebræus in the *Auṣar Rāzē*[3] and by Elias of Ṭīrhān in his grammar[4]. Ḥonain also wrote a treatise *On Synonyms*, whether they be "voces æquilitteræ" (as *rĕghīz* and *raggīz*) or not (as *'āḳĕthā* and *karyūthā*). Extracts from this work have been preserved to us by a later compiler, who made use also of the canons of 'Ănān-īshō'

ed. Müller, i. 184; Ibn Khallikān, ed. Wüstenfeld, No. 208; al-Mas'ūdī, *Murūj adh-Dhahab*, ix. 173 *sq.*; Bar-Hebræus, *Chron. Syr.*, p. 170 (transl., p. 173; *B.O.*, ii. 270, note 3) [ed. Bedjan, p. 162]; *Chron. Eccles.*, ii. 197-199 (*B.O.*, ii. 438); *Hist. Dynast.*, p. 263 *sq.* (transl., p. 171 *sq.*); Wenrich, *De Auctt. Gr. Versionibus*, Index, p. xxxi; Wüstenfeld, *Gesch. d. arab. Aerzte*, No. 69.

1 *B.O.*, iii. 1, 165.

2 See Gesenius, *De Bar Alio et Bar Bahlulo Commentatio*, 1834, p. 7.

3 See Hoffmann, *Z.D.M.G.*, xxxii., 1878, p. 741.

4 Edit. Baethgen, p. 32; see Hoffmann, *Opusc. Nestor.*, p. xvii.

of Ḥĕdhaiyabh[1] (see above, p. 175). In Cod. Vat. ccxvii. (*Catal.*, iii. 504) there are excerpts from a medical treatise of Ḥonain, but no title is given[2]. Ḥonain, his son Isḥāḳ, and his nephew Ḥobaish ibn al-Ḥasan al-Aʿsam ("Stiff-wrist") were among the earliest and ablest of those Christians, chiefly Nestorians, who, during the 9th and 10th centuries, making Baghdādh their headquarters, supplied Muḥammadan scholars with nearly everything that they knew of Greek science, whether medicine, mathematics, or philosophy. As a rule, they translated the Greek first into Syriac and afterwards into Arabic; but their Syriac versions have unfortunately, as it would appear, perished, without exception[3].

[1] Hoffmann, *Opusc. Nest.*, pp. 2–49; see *B.O.*, ii. 308, col. 2, and Cod. Berlin, Sachau 72, No. 14. There is also a MS. in the collection of the S.P.C.K.

[2] Cod. Vat. cxcii. (*Catal.*, iii. 409), *Syntagma Medicum Syr. et Arab.*, is not likely to be his, but requires closer examination.

[3] This is a large subject, into which we cannot here enter, the more so as it pertains rather to a history of Arabic than of Syriac literature. We would refer the reader to Wüstenfeld, *Geschichte d. arab. Aerzte u. Naturforscher*, 1840; Flügel, *Dissert. de Arabicis Scriptorum Græcorum Interpretibus*, 1841; Wenrich, *De Auctorum Græcorum Versionibus et Commentariis*, 1842; Renan, *De Philosophia Peripatetica apud Syros*, 1852, sect. viii. p. 51; *Al-Farabi (Alpharabius) des Arab. Philosophen Leben u. Schriften*, by M. Steinschneider, 1869; A. Müller, *Die*

An elder contemporary of Ḥonain was Gabriel bar Bōkht-īshō', in Arabic Jabra'īl ibn Bakhtīshū' (or rather Bokhtīshū'), a member of a family of renowned physicians, beginning with George bar Bōkht-īshō' of Gundē-Shābhōr, whom we have mentioned above (p. 188). He was in practice at Baghdādh in 791, and attended on Ja'far ibn Yaḥyā al-Barmakī, became court physician to ar-Rashīd, and maintained this position, with various vicissitudes, till his death in 828[1]. 'Abhd-īshō' says that he was the author of a Syriac lexicon[2], which is our reason for giving him a

*Griechischen Philosophen in der arabischen Ueberlieferung*, 1873. Of Muḥammadan authorities two of the most important are the *Fihrist* of Abu 'l-Faraj Muḥammad ibn Isḥāḳ al-Warrāḳ al-Baghdādhī, commonly called Ibn Abī Ya'ḳūb an-Nadīm (died early in the 11th century), and the '*Uyūn al-Anbā fī Ṭabaḳāt al-Aṭibbā* of Muwaffaḳ ad-Dīn Abū 'l-'Abbās Aḥmad ibn al-Ḳāsim as-Sa'dī al-Khazrajī, generally known by the name of Ibn Abī Uṣaibi'ah (died in 1269). The former work has been edited by Flügel, J. Rödiger, and A. Müller, 1871–72, the latter by A. Müller, 1884. [The second volume of Berthelot's *La Chimie au Moyen Âge* is devoted to *L'Alchimie Syriaque*, and contains some interesting Syriac texts, which have been edited with the collaboration of M. Rubens Duval (Paris, 1893).]

[1] See Ibn Abī Uṣaibi'ah, ed. Müller, i. 127; Wüstenfeld, *Gesch. d. arab. Aerzte*, No. 28; Bar-Hebræus, *Chron. Syr.*, pp. 139–140, 170 (*B.O.*, ii. 271, note, col. 1) [ed. Bedjan, pp. 134, 162], and *Hist. Dynast.*, 235, 264.

[2] *B.O.*, iii. 1, 258. [But 'Abhd-Īshō''s words perhaps admit of a different interpretation.]

place here, but no such work is mentioned by the other authorities to whom we have referred[1].

Of Īshō' Marūzāyā, in Arabic 'Īsā al-Marwazī, from the city of Marū or Merv, little is known to us beyond the fact that he compiled a Syriac lexicon, which was one of the two principal authorities made use of by Bar 'Alī[2]. That he should be identical with the physician al-Marwazī, who lived about 567[3], seems wholly unlikely. We might rather venture to identify him with Abū Yaḥyā al-Marwazī, who was an eminent Syrian physician at Baghdādh, wrote in Syriac upon logic and other subjects, and was one of the teachers of Mattā ibn Yaunān or Yūnus (who died in 940)[4]. In any case, 'Īsā al-Marwazī seems to have flourished during the latter part of the 9th century, and therefore to have been a contemporary of Bar 'Alī[5].

Īshō', or 'Īsā, bar 'Alī is stated in Cod. Vat. ccxvii. (*Catal.*, iii. 504, No. xv.) to have been a pupil of Ḥonain. His father 'Alī and his uncle 'Īsā, the sons of Dā'ūd or David, were appointed

1 Compare Gesenius, *De BA et BB*, p. 7.

2 See Gesenius, *op. cit.*, p. 8; *B.O.*, iii. 1, 258.

3 *B.O.*, iii. 1, 437, 438, note 2.

4 See the *Fihrist*, p. 263; Ibn Abī Uṣaibi'ah, ed. Müller, i. 234–235.

5 [Bar Bahlūl speaks, in the preface to his lexicon, of the lexicon of *Zĕkharyā* Marūzāyā (Duval's edition, col. 3).]

by the catholicus Sabhr-īshō' II. (832–836) to the charge of the college founded by him in the convent of Mār Pethiōn at Baghdādh[1]. Bar 'Alī's lexicon is dedicated to a deacon named Abraham[2], who made certain additions to it after the death of the author[3].

Ishō' bar Nōn was a native of the village of Bēth-Gabbārē near Mosul. He was a pupil of Abraham bar Dāshandādh (see above, p. 186) at the same time with Abū Nūḥ al-Anbārī (see above, p. 191, note 3) and Timothy, his predecessor in the dignity of catholicus (see above, p. 191). He retired first to the convent of Mār Abraham on Mount Īzlā, where he devoted himself to study and to refuting the views and writings of his schoolfellow and subsequent diocesan Timothy, whom he spitefully called *Ṭūlēm-otheos* ("the wronger of God") instead of *Timotheos.* In consequence of a dispute with the monks he left Mount Īzlā and went for some months to Baghdādh, where he stayed at the house of George Māsawaihi (Māsūyah or Mesue) and taught his son Yaḥyā[4]. He then returned to Mosul, where he took up his residence in the convent of Mār

[1] *B.O.*, iii. 1, 257 ; Gesenius, *op. cit.*, cap. ii.

[2] Gesenius, *op. cit.*, p. 14.

[3] *Ibid.*, p. 21 ; see Hoffmann, *Syrisch-arabische Glossen*, 1874, and Payne Smith, *Thes. Syr.*, passim.

[4] See *B.O.*, iii. 1, 501 *sq.*

Elias, and lived there for thirty years, till the death of Timothy[1]. Through the influence of Gabriel bar Bōkht-īshōʿ (see above) and his son-in-law Michael bar Māsawaihi (Māsūyah or Mesue), the physician of the caliph al-Ma'mūn, he was appointed catholicus A. Gr. 1135 = 823–824 A.D.[2] He sat for only four years, and was buried, like his predecessor, in the convent of Kĕlīl-īshōʿ at Baghdādh. Of his ill-feeling towards Timothy I. we have already made mention; how he kept it up after Timothy's death, and what troubles he got into in consequence, may be read in the pages of Assemani (*B.O.*, iii. 1, 165). Bar-Hebræus has preserved some account of a disputation between him and a Monophysite priest named Pāpā[3]. 'Abhd-īshōʿ gives the following list of his works[4]—a treatise on theology, questions on the whole text of Scripture, in two volumes, a collection of ecclesiastical canons and decisions[5], consolatory discourses, epistles, a treatise on the division of the services, *turgāmē* or "interpreta-

[1] So Assemani, *B.O.*, ii. 435. Bar-Hebræus (*Chron. Eccles.*, ii. 181) says that he resided for thirty-eight years in the convent of Sa'īd near Mosul.

[2] Bar-Hebræus (*loc. cit.*) says 205 A.H. = 820–821 A.D.; see above, p. 193 *sq.*

[3] *Chron. Eccles.*, ii. 183–187.

[4] *B.O.*, iii. 1, 165–166. 'Amr ibn Mattā says that he wrote a commentary on Theologus, *i.e.*, Gregory Nazianzen, *B.O.*, iii. 1, 262, note 1.

[5] Compare *B.O.*, iii. 1, 279.

tions[1]," and a tract on the efficacy of hymns and anthems. Of the questions on Scripture there is a copy in the collection of the S.P.C.K., and of the consolatory discourses a mutilated MS. in the British Museum, Add. 17217 (Wright, *Catal.*, p. 613)[2]. The replies to the questions of Macarius the monk seem to belong to the treatise on the division of the services (*purrāsh teshmĕshāthā*), if one may judge by the first and only one quoted[3].

A disciple of Īshō' bar Nōn was Denḥā, or, as he is otherwise called in some MSS. of 'Abhd-īshō''s *Catalogue*, Īhībhā (or rather Hībhā, Ibas)[4]. Assemani places him under the catholicus Pethiōn (died in 740), but we prefer to follow the authority of John bar Zō'bī in his *Grammar*[5]. Denḥā was the author of sermons and tracts on points of ecclesiastical law, and of commentaries on the Psalms, on the works of Gregory Nazianzen (as

[1] See Badger, *The Nestorians*, ii. 19.

[2] The pious Monophysites of St Mary Deipara cut up this volume for binding, &c., as they did some other Nestorian books of value in their library.

[3] Cod. Vat. lxxxviii. 5 (*Catal.*, ii. 483); cl. 9 (*Catal.*, iii. 281); clxxxvii. 5 (*Catal.*, iii. 405). Assemani supposes that the next article in clxxxvii. does not belong to Theodore of Mopsuestia, but is taken from Īshō' bar Nōn's questions on Scripture.

[4] *B.O.*, iii. 1, 175.

[5] Wright, *Catal.*, p. 1176, col. 1.

contained in two vols. in the translation of the abbot Paul), and on the dialectics of Aristotle.

In 217 A.H. = 832 A.D., the same year in which Sabhr-īshō' II. succeeded to the patriarchate[1], a young man named Thomas, the son of one Jacob of Bēth Sherwānāyē, in the district of Salakh[2], entered the convent of Bēth 'Ābhē, which seems at this time to have fallen off sadly in respect of the learning of its inmates[3]. A few years afterwards (222 A.H. = 837 A.D.) we find him acting as secretary to the patriarch Abraham (also a monk of Bēth 'Ābhē, who sat from 837 to 850)[4]. By him he was promoted to be bishop of Margā, and afterwards metropolitan of Bēth Garmai, in which capacity he was present at the ordination of his own brother Theodosius (bishop of al-Anbār, afterwards metropolitan of Gundē-Shābhōr) as catholicus in 852[5]. Thomas of Margā (as he is commonly called), having been very fond from his youth of the legends and histories of holy men, more especially of those connected with his own convent of Bēth 'Ābhē, undertook to commit them to writing at the urgent request of the

[1] *B.O.*, ii. 435; iii. 1, 505 *sq.*

[2] *Ibid.*, iii. 1, 479; Hoffmann, *Auszüge*, pp. 244–245.

[3] *B.O.*, iii. 1, 488; comp. the ordinance of Sabhr-īshō', pp. 505–506.

[4] *B.O.*, iii. 1, 204, col. 1, 488, col. 2, 490, col. 2.

[5] *Ibid.*, iii. 1, 210, 510, col. 2.

monk ʿAbhd-īshōʿ, to whom he dedicates the *Monastic History*. Assemani has given a tolerably full analysis of this work, with a few extracts, in the *B.O.*, iii. 1, 464–501, throughout which volume it is one of his chief authorities. [It has now been published in a complete form by Budge, who has also supplied an introduction aud an English translation[1].] The MSS. available in Europe are—Cod. Vat. clxv. (*Catal.*, iii. 331), of which Codd. Vatt. ccclxxxi.–ii. are a copy (Mai, *Scriptt. Vett. Nova Coll.*, v.); Paris, No. 286 in Zotenberg's *Catal.*, p. 216 (also copied from Vat. clxv.); Brit. Mus. Orient. 2316 (ff. 182, 17th century, imperfect); Berlin, Sachau 179 (copied in 1882). Thomas also wrote a poem in twelve-syllable metre on the life and deeds of Māran-ʿammēh, metropolitan of Ḥĕdhaiyabh, which he introduced into his *History*, bk. iii. ch. 10; see *B.O.*, iii. 1, 485.

Īshōʿ-dādh of Marū or Merv, bishop of Ḥĕdhattā or al-Ḥadīthah, was a competitor with Theodosius for the patriarchate in 852[2]. According to ʿAbhd-īshōʿ, his principal work was a commentary on the New Testament, of which there are MSS. in Berlin, Sachau 311, and in the

[1] [*The Book of Governors: the Historia Monastica of Thomas Bishop of Marga*, A.D. 840, London, 1893.]

[2] *B.O.*, iii. 1, 210–212.

collection of the S.P.C.K. It extended, however, to the Old Testament as well, for in Cod. Vat. cccclvii. we find the portions relating to Genesis and Exodus[1].

In the *B.O.*, iii. 1, 213, ʿAbhd-īshōʿ names a certain Kendī as the author of a lengthy disputation on the faith[2]. Assemani places this "Candius" or "Ebn Canda" under the catholicus John IV., apparently on the authority of ʿAmr ibn Mattā. We suspect, however, that the person meant is ʿAbd al-Masīḥ (Yaʿḳūb) ibn Isḥāḳ al-Kindī, the author of a well known apology for the Christian religion, which has been published by the Society for Promoting Christian Knowledge[3]. The work dates from the time of the caliph al-Ma'mūn (813–833), and therefore synchronizes with the disputations of Theodore Abū Ḳorrah, bishop of Ḥarrān[4]. Being written in Arabic, it hardly belongs to this place, but is mentioned to avoid misapprehension.

[1] Mai, *Scriptt. Vett. Nova Coll.*, v. The name of the author is there given as Iesciuaad, doubtless a misprint for *dad*. We are therefore surprised to find Martin writing "Ichou-had évêque d'Hadeth," *Introd. à la Critique Textuelle du Nouveau Test.*, p. 99.

[2] The correct reading is *dhĕ-haimānūthā*.

[3] *The Apology of El-Kindi*, 1885. An English translation appeared in 1882, *The Apology of Al-Kindy*, &c., by Sir W. Muir.

[4] See Zotenberg, *Catal.*, No. 204, 1 and 8, and No. 205.

Theodore bar Khōnī is stated to have been promoted by his uncle John IV. to the bishopric of Lāshōm in 893[1]. He was the author of scholia (on the Scriptures), an ecclesiastical history, and some minor works.

To about this period probably belongs another historian, the loss of whose work we have to regret. This is a writer named Ahrōn or Aaron, who is mentioned by Elias bar Shīnāyā under 273 A.H. = 886–887 A.D.[2]

In the 10th century the tale of Jacobite authors dwindles away to almost nothing. Most of the dignitaries of the church composed their synodical epistles and other official writings in Arabic, and the same may be said of the men of science, such as Abū ʿAlī ʿĪsā ibn Isḥāḳ ibn Zurʿah (943–1008) and Abū Zakarīyā Yaḥyā ibn ʿAdī, who died in 974 at the age of eighty-one. About the middle of the century we may venture to place the deacon Simeon, whose *Chronicle* is cited by Elias bar Shīnāyā under 6 A.H. = 627–628 A.D. and 310 = 922–923[3]. The 11th century is somewhat more prolific.

A Persian Christian named Gīsā[4], leaving his

[1] *B.O.*, ii. 440; iii. 1, 198.

[2] See Baethgen, *Fragmente*, p. 3.

[3] *Ibid.*, p. 2; Bar-Hebræus, *Chron. Eccles.*, ii. 126, note 1.

[4] Others write Gaiyāsā.

native city of Ushnūkh or Ushnū in Adharbāigān, settled, after several removals, in the district of Gūbōs or Gūbās[1], one of the seven dioceses of the province of Melitēne (Malaṭiah), and built there a humble church, in which he deposited sundry relics of St Sergius and St Bacchus, and cells for himself and his three companions. This happened in 958[2]. As the place grew in importance, other monks gradually resorted to it, and among them "Mār(ī) Yōḥannān dĕ-Mārōn," or John (the son) of Mārōn[3], a man of learning in both sacred and profane literature, who had studied under Mār Mĕḳīm at Edessa. Gīsā, the founder of the convent, died at the end of twelve years, and was succeeded as abbot by his disciple Elias, who beautified the church. Meantime its fame increased as a seat of learning under the direction of John of Mārōn, and many scribes found employment there. The patriarch John VII., *da-sĕrīghtā*, "He of the Mat" (his only

[1] Bar-Hebræus, *Chron. Eccles.*, i. 401 *sq.*; *B.O.*, ii. 283, 350.

[2] *B.O.*, ii. 260. Gūbōs was on the right bank of the Euphrates, between the plain of Melitēne and Claudia.

[3] Abbeloos, in a note on Bar-Hebræus, *Chron. Eccles.*, i. 404, raises the question what connexion there may be between this historical personage and the somewhat shadowy "Joannes Maro," to whom Assemani has devoted a large space, *B.O.*, i. 496–520.

article of furniture)[1], was one of its visitors. Elias, on his retirement, nominated John of Mārōn as his successor, who, aided by the munificence of Emmanuel, a monk of Ḥarrān and a disciple of the maphriān Cyriacus[2], rebuilt the church on a larger and finer scale, whilst a constant supply of fresh water was provided at the cost of a Taghrītan merchant named Mārūthā. This was in 1001. About this time Elias bar Gāghai, a monk of Taghrīth, founded a monastery near Melitēne, but died before it was finished. His work was taken up by one Eutychus or Kulaib, who persuaded John of Mārōn to join him. Here again his teaching attracted numbers of pupils. At last, after the lapse of twelve years, when there were 120 priests in the convent, he suddenly withdrew by night from the scene of his labours and retired to the monastery of Mār Aaron near Edessa, where he died at the end of four years, about 1017. His commentary on the book of Wisdom is cited by Bar-Hebræus in the *Auṣar Rāzē*[3].

Mark bar Ḳīḳī was archdeacon of the Taghrītan church at Mosul, and was raised to the dignity of maphriān by the name of Ignatius in

[1] *B.O.*, ii. 132, 351.
[2] *Ibid.*, ii. 442.
[3] *Ibid.*, ii. 283; see also p. cl.

991[1]. After holding this office for twenty-five years, he became a Muḥammadan in 1016[2], but recanted before his death, which took place at an advanced age[3] in great poverty. He composed a poem on his own fall, misery, and subsequent repentance, of which Bar-Hebræus has preserved a few lines[4].

According to Assemani, *B.O.*, ii. 317 and cl., Bar-Hebræus mentions in his *Chronicle* that a monk named Joseph wrote three discourses on the cruel murder of Peter the deacon by the Turks at Melitēne in 1058. The anecdote may be found in the edition of Bruns and Kirsch, p. 252 (transl., p. 258) [ed. Bedjan, p. 238], but the discourses would seem rather to have dealt with the retribution that overtook the retiring Turks at the hands of the Armenians and the wintry weather.

Yēshū' bar Shūshan (or Susanna), syncellus of Theodore or John IX., was chosen patriarch by the eastern bishops, under the name of John X., in opposition to Ḥāyē or Athanasius VI., on whom the choice of their western brethren had fallen in

[1] Bar-Hebræus, *Chron. Eccles.*, ii. 257; *B.O.*, ii. 443.

[2] See Baethgen, *Fragmente*, pp. 105, 153; *B.O.*, iii. 289, note 1.

[3] According to Cardāḥī, *Liber Thesauri*, p. 140, in 1030 or 1040.

[4] *Chron. Eccles.*, ii. 289; *B.O.*, ii. 443, and also p. cl.

1058[1]. He soon abdicated, however, retired to a convent, and devoted himself to study. On the death of Athanasius he was reelected patriarch in 1064, and sat till 1073[2]. He carried on a controversy with the patriarch of Alexandria, Christodūlus, regarding the mixing of salt and oil with the Eucharistic bread according to the Syrian practice[3]. He compiled an anaphora, issued a collection of twenty-four canons[4], and wrote many epistles[5], chiefly controversial. Such are the letters in Arabic to Christodūlus on the oil and salt[6] and the letter to the catholicus of the Armenians[7]. The tract on the oil and salt is extant in Paris, Anc. fonds 54 (Zotenberg, *Catal.*, p. 71), and there is an extract from it in Suppl. 32 (Zotenberg, *Catal.*, p. 54). Bar-Shūshan also wrote four poems on the sack of Melitēne by the Turks in 1058[8], and collected and arranged the works of Ephraim and Isaac of Antioch, which he had

[1] Bar-Hebræus, *Chron. Eccles.*, i. 437 *sq.*; *B.O.*, ii. 141 (where there are errors, see Add., p. 475), 354.

[2] Bar-Hebræus, *Chron. Eccles.*, i. 445; *B.O.*, ii. 143 (where there are again many errors, see Add., p. 475), 355.

[3] *B.O.*, ii. 144, 356.

[4] Bar-Hebræus, *Chron. Eccles.*, i. 446; *B.O.*, ii. 355.

[5] Bar-Hebræus, *Chron. Eccles.*, i. 447; *B.O.*, ii. 355.

[6] *B.O.*, ii. 508, col. 2.

[7] *Ibid.*, ii. 211, 383; Berlin, Sachau 60, 1.

[8] Bar-Hebræus, *Chron. Syr.*, p. 252 (transl., p. 258) [ed. Bedjan, p. 238]; *B.O.*, ii. 317.

begun to write out with his own hand when he was interrupted by death[1].

Saʿīd bar Ṣābūnī lived during the latter part of the 11th century. He was versed in Greek as well as Syriac, and well known as a literary man[2], especially as a writer of hymns[3]. The patriarch Athanasius VII. Abu 'l-Faraj bar Khammārē (1091–1129) raised him to the office of bishop of Melitēne (Malaṭiah) in October 1094. His consecration took place at Ḳanḳĕrath, near Āmid, by the name of John, and he set out for Malaṭiah, which he entered on the very day that the gates were closed to keep out the Turks, who laid siege to it under Ḳilij Arslān (Dā'ūd ibn Sulaimān), sultān of Iconium. He was murdered during the course of the siege, in July 1095, by the Greek commandant Gabriel[4].

The Nestorian writers of these two centuries

[1] Bar-Hebræus, *Chron. Eccles.*, i. 447; *B.O.*, ii. 355.

[2] Bar-Hebræus, *Chron. Eccles.*, i. 463; *B.O.*, ii. 211–212.

[3] See one of these, an acrostic canon, used in the service of the assumption of the monastic garb, in Cod. Vat. li. (*Catal.*, ii. 321, No. 31), Brit. Mus. 17232 (Wright, *Catal.*, p. 372, No. 22), Paris, Suppl. 38 (Zotenberg, *Catal.*, p. 74, No. 34), Bodl. Hunt. 444 (P. Smith, *Catal.*, p. 243, No. 9).

[4] Bar-Hebræus, *Chron. Syr.*, pp. 278–279 (transl., pp. 284–285) [ed. Bedjan, p. 262].

are both more numerous and more important than the Jacobite.

We may place at the head of our list the name of Ḥĕnān-īshōʿ bar Sarōshwai, who must have lived quite early in the 10th century, as he is cited by Elias of Anbār, who wrote about 922[1]. He was bishop of Ḥērtā (al-Ḥīrah), and published questions on the text of Scripture and a vocabulary with glosses or explanations[2], which is constantly cited by his successor in this department of scholarship, Bar Bahlūl[3].

With Bar Sarōshwai we naturally connect Īshōʿ bar Bahlūl, in Arabic Abu 'l-Ḥasan 'Īsā ibn al-Bahlūl, the fullest and most valuable of Syriac lexicographers. His date is fixed by that of the election of the catholicus ʿAbhd-īshōʿ I., in which he bore a part, in 963[4].

ʿAbhd-īshōʿ in his *Catalogue*, *B.O.*, iii. 1, 261, mentions an author Abhzūdh, a teacher in some

[1] *B.O.*, iii. 1, 260, col. 2, at foot.

[2] *Ḥashḥāthā* are χρήσεις and λέξεις; see Hoffmann, *Opusc. Nestor.*, p. xiii.

[3] *B.O.*, iii. 1, 261; see Payne Smith, *Thes. Syr.*, passim.

[4] Bar-Hebræus, *Chron. Eccles.*, iii. 251; *B.O.*, ii. 442, iii. 1, 200, col. 2; Gesenius, *De BA et BB*, p. 26; see Payne Smith, *Thes. Syr.*, passim. An edition of his *Lexicon*, by M. R. Duval, is being printed in Paris at the expense of the French Government; [parts 1, 2, and 3 (extending to the end of ܣ) appeared in 1888, 1890, and 1892 respectively].

school or college (*eskōlāyā*), who composed a treatise containing demonstrations on various topics, alphabetically arranged and dedicated to his friend Ḳurtā[1]. In note 5 Assemani makes the very circumstantial statement, but without giving his authority, that Abhzūdh was head of the college founded at Baghdādh about 832 by Sabhr-īshō' II.[2], under Sergius (860–872). But, if this writer be identical, as seems probable, with the Bazūdh who was the author of a *Book of Definitions* described at some length by Hoffmann, *De Hermeneuticis apud Syros Aristoteleis*, pp. 151–153, we must place him nearly a century later, because he cites the "scholia" of Theodore bar Khōnī, who was appointed bishop of Lāshōm in 893[3]. The whole matter is, however, very obscure, and Hoffmann has subsequently (*Opusc. Nestor.*, p. xxii) sought to identify Bazūdh, who was also called Michael (*ibid.*, p. xxi), with the Michael who is mentioned as a commentator on the Scriptures by 'Abhd-īshō', *B.O.*, iii. 1, 147, and whom Assemani supposed to be the same as Michael bishop of al-Ahwāz (died in 852 or 854)[4]. All then that appears to be certain is that

[1] *B.O.*, iii. 1, 261. [2] *Ibid.*, ii. 435.

[3] See above, p. 222.

[4] *B.O.*, iii. 1, 210, note 2, col. 2. Michael's *Book of Questions* is quoted by Solomon of al-Baṣrah in *The Bee*, ed. Budge, p. 135.

the Persian Bazūdh also bore the Christian name of Michael, and that, besides the alphabetically arranged demonstrations and the *Book of Definitions,* he composed a tract on man as the microcosm[1].

Elias, bishop of Pērōz-Shābhōr or al-Anbār, flourished about 922, as appears from his disputes with the catholicus Abraham (905–937)[2], and his account of the miserable bishop Theodore of Bēth Garmai, who, after his deposition by John bar Ḥĕghīrē (900–905) and subsequent absolution by Abraham, became a Muḥammadan[3]. He was the author of a collection of metrical discourses in three volumes[4], an apology, epistles, and homilies[5].

George, metropolitan of Mosul and Arbēl, was promoted to this dignity by the catholicus Emmanuel about 945, and died after 987. He contested the patriarchate three times but in vain, viz.,—in 961, when Isrā'ēl was elected[6], in 963,

[1] Hoffmann, *op. cit.*, p. xxi.

[2] *B.O.*, iii. 1, 258, note 3; Baethgen, *Fragmente*, pp. 84, 141.

[3] *B.O.*, iii. 1, 234, col. 1, at foot.

[4] *B.O.*, iii. 1, 258–260; Cod. Vat. clxxxiii. (*Catal.*, iii. 383); Berlin, Sachau 132; collection of the S.P.C.K.; Cardāḥī, *Liber Thesauri*, pp. 72–76.

[5] In Cod. Vat. xci. (*Catal.*, ii. 491, No. 35) there is a homily ascribed to Elias of Anbār, but the Syriac text has Paul.

[6] *B.O.*, ii. 442.

when ʿAbhd-īshōʿ I. was the successful candidate[1], and in 987, when the choice of the synod fell on Mārī bar Ṭōbī[2]. His chief work was an exposition of the ecclesiastical offices for the whole year, in seven sections, of which Assemani has given a full analysis in *B.O.*, iii. 1, 518–540[3]. Some specimens of his *turgāmē* or hymns may be found in Codd. Vatt. xc. and xci. (*Catal.*, ii. 487, No. 27, and 490, No. 24), and Berlin, Sachau 167, 2.

The date of Emmanuel bar Shahhārē[4] is fixed by his presence at the consecration of ʿAbhd-īshōʿ I. in 963[5]. He was teacher in the school of Mār Gabriel in the convent called the Dairā ʿEllāitā at Mosul. Cardāḥī places his death in 980[6]. Besides some minor expository treatises, he wrote a huge work on the *Hexaëmeron* or six days of creation[7]. The Vatican MS.[8] contains twenty-eight discourses, of which the second is wanting, and a twenty-ninth

1 *B.O.*, ii. 442; iii. 1, 200, col. 2.

2 *Ibid.*, ii. 443.

3 See also Codd. Vatt. cxlviii., cxlix., and cliii., in *Catal.*, iii. 277 *sq.* In Cod. Vat. cl. (*Catal.*, iii. 280) there are questions regarding various services, baptism, and communion at Easter.

4 See *B.O.*, iii. 1, 540. In Arabic ash-Shahhār or, according to another reading, ash-Shaʿʿār (see end of this paragraph).

5 *B.O.*, iii. 1, 200, col. 2.

6 *Liber Thesauri*, p. 71.

7 *B.O.*, iii. 1, 277.

8 No. clxxxii., *Catal.*, iii. 380.

is added *On Baptism*. It is dated 1707. The MS. in the Brit. Mus., Orient. 1300, dated 1685, also contains twenty-eight discourses, of which the second is wanting[1]. Some of them are in seven-syllable, others in twelve-syllable metre[2]. Cardāḥī has published a specimen in his *Liber Thesauri*, pp. 68–71. Emmanuel's brother, ʽAbhd-īshōʽ bar Shahhārē, is mentioned by Assemani, *B.O.*, iii. 540, and by Cardāḥī. The latter has printed part of one of his poems, on Michael of Āmid, a companion of Mār Eugenius, in *Liber Thesauri*, pp. 136–137. It is taken from Cod. Vat. clxxxiv. (*Catal.*, iii. 395). But there the author is called Bar Shiʽārah, ܒܪܫܥܐܪܗ, and is said to have been a monk of the convent of Michael (at Mosul).

Somewhere about the end of this century we may venture to place a writer named Andrew, to whom ʽAbhd-īshōʽ has given a place in his *Catalogue*, and whom Assemani has chosen to identify with the well known Andrew, bishop of Samosāta, the opponent of Cyril of Alexandria[3]. The words

[1] There are two MSS. in Berlin, Sachau 169–170 and 309–310 (see Sachau, *Reise*, pp. 364–365), and one in the collection of the S.P.C.K.

[2] In the MS. Brit. Mus. it is said that this is only the fourth volume of the *Hexaëmeron*, ܡܘܒܠܬܐ ܪܒܝܥܝܬܐ ܣܗܪܒܬܐ ܕܫ̈ܬܐ ܝܘ̈ܡܬܐ.

[3] *B.O.* iii. 1, 202.

of ʿAbhd-īshōʿ, if we understand them rightly, mean that this Andrew wrote *turgāmē* (or hymns of a particular kind) and a work on *puḥḥām sĕyāmē*, the placing of the diacritical and vowel points and marks of interpunction[1]. He was therefore an inoffensive grammarian.

Elias, the first Nestorian catholicus of the name, was a native of Karkhā dhĕ-Gheddān[2], was trained in Baghdādh and al-Madāïn, and became bishop of Ṭīrhān, whence he was advanced to the primacy in 1028, and sat till 1049[3]. According to ʿAbhd-īshōʿ, he compiled canons and ecclesiastical decisions, and composed grammatical tracts[4]. According to Mārī ibn Sulaimān[5], he was the author of a work on the principles of religion in twenty-two chapters, which may be identical with the second of the above, and of a form of consecration of the altar (*ḳuddās al-madhbaḥ*). His *Grammar* was composed in his younger days, before he became bishop. It has been edited and

1 See Hoffmann, *Opusc. Nestor.*, pp. vii., viii. And so Abraham Ecchellensis rendered the words, *librum de ratione punctandi.*

2 In Arabic Karkh Juddān, in Bēth Garmai; see Hoffmann, *Auszüge*, pp. 254, 275.

3 *B.O.*, iii. 262-263; Bar-Hebræus, *Chron. Eccles.*, ii. 285-287.

4 *B.O.*, iii. 1, 265.

5 *Ibid.*, p. 263, col. 1.

translated from a MS. at Berlin[1] by Baethgen[2]. A tract of his on the diacritical points and marks of interpunction is cited and used by John bar Zō'bī[3].

Abū Sa'īd 'Abhd-īshō' bar Bahrīz was abbot of the convent of Elias or Sa'īd at Mosul, and a candidate for the patriarchate when Elias I. was elected in 1028. He was subsequently promoted to be metropolitan of Āthōr or Mosul[4]. He collected ecclesiastical canons and decisions[5], wrote on the law of inheritance[6], and an exposition of the offices of the church.

Assemani has assigned the same date to Daniel (the son) of Ṭūbhānīthā, bishop of Taḥal in Bēth Garmai, but without any sufficient reason[7]. If he be really identical with the Daniel to whom George, metropolitan of Mosul and Arbēl, dedi-

[1] Alter Bestand 36, 15, in *Kurzes Verzeichniss*, &c., p. 31.

[2] *Syrische Grammatik des Mar Elias von Tirhan*, 1880. [See Merx, *Hist. artis gramm. ap. Syros*, p. 154 *sq.*]

[3] See *B.O.*, iii. 1, 265, note 7; *Catal. Vat.*, iii. 411 (under No. ii.); Wright, *Catal.*, p. 1176, col. 2.

[4] *B.O.*, iii. 1, 263–264.

[5] *B.O.*, iii. 1, 279.

[6] *Ibid.*, p. 267, col. 2, lin. penult.

[7] That he follows 'Abhd-īshō' bar Bahrīz in the *Catalogue* of 'Abhd-īshō' is no evidence whatever as to his date; and the work mentioned in *B.O.*, iii. 1, 174, notes 3 and 4, is not by Bar Bahrīz, but by George of Mosul and Arbēl (see Cod. Vat. cliii.).

cated his exposition of the offices of the church, he must have lived about the middle of the previous century. He wrote funeral sermons, metrical homilies, answers to Scriptural questions and enigmas, and other stuff of the same sort. More important probably were his "Book of Flowers," *Kĕthābhā dhĕ-Habbābhē*, which may have been a poetical florilegium; his *Solution of the Questions in the Fifth Volume of Isaac of Nineveh's Works*; and his commentary on the *Heads of Knowledge* or maxims (of Evagrius)[1].

Conspicuous among the writers of this century is Elias bar Shīnāyā, who was born in 975[2], adopted the monastic life in the convent of Michael at Mosul under the abbot John the Lame[3], and was ordained priest by Nathaniel, bishop of Shennā (as-Sinn), who afterwards became catholicus under the name of John V. (1001–12)[4]. Elias was subsequently in the convent of Simeon on the Tigris opposite Shennā, and was made bishop of Bēth Nuhādhrē in 1002[5]. At the end of 1008 he was advanced to the dignity of metro-

1 *B.O.*, iii. 1, 174.

2 Rosen, *Catal.*, p. 89, col. 2.

3 *B.O.*, iii. 1, 266, note 3, 271, col. 1.

4 Baethgen, *Fragmente*, pp. 101, 151; 104, 153; compare Bar-Hebræus, *Chron. Eccles.*, ii. 261, 281; *B.O.*, ii. 444.

5 Baethgen, *Fragmente*, pp. 101, 152.

politan of Nisībis[1]. With the next patriarch, John VI. bar Nāzōl (1012–20)[2], previously bishop of Ḥērtā, he was on good terms; but he set his face against Īshō'-yabh bar Ezekiel (1020–25)[3]. Under Elias I. (1028–49) all seems to have been quiet again. That our author survived this patriarch is clear from his own words in *B.O.*, iii. 1, 268, col. 2, ll. 19, 20[4]. His greatest work is the *Annals* or *Chronicle*, of which unfortunately only one imperfect copy exists[5]. Baethgen has published extracts from it under the title of *Fragmente syr. u. arab. Historiker*, 1884, which have enabled scholars to recognize its real importance[6]. The exact date of the *Annals*, and probably of the writing of the unique copy, is fixed by the statement of the author, f. 15 b, that John, bishop of

[1] Baethgen, *Fragmente*, pp. 103, 152.

[2] *Ibid.*, pp. 104, 153; Bar-Hebræus, *Chron. Eccles.*, ii. 283; *B.O.*, ii. 446.

[3] *B.O.*, iii. 1, 272.

[4] Consequently the statement in *B.O.*, ii. 447, is inaccurate. Cardāḥī (*Liber Thesauri*, p. 84) names 1056.

[5] Brit. Mus. Add. 7197 (Rosen, *Catal.*, pp. 86–90; Wright, *Catal.*, p. 1206).

[6] Baethgen has overlooked Wright's *Catal.*, p. 1206, and the plate in the *Oriental Series of the Palæographical Society*, No. lxxvi. The Syriac text was evidently written by an amanuensis, whereas the older Arabic text was probably written by Elias himself. [Further extracts (from A.D. 133 to 622) in Lamy, *Élie de Nisibe, sa Chronologie*, Brussels, 1888 (*Bull. Ac. Roy. Belg.*).]

Ḥērtā, was ordained catholicus on Wednesday, 19th of the latter Teshrīn, A. Gr. 1324 (19th November 1012 A.D.), and that he still ruled the Nestorian Church "down to this year in which this work was composed, namely, A. Gr. 1330" (1018–19)[1]. After the *Annals* we may mention Elias's Syriac grammar, one of the best of the Nestorian writings on the subject[2], and his Arabic-Syriac vocabulary, *Kitāb at-Tarjumān fī ta'līm lughat as-Suryān* or "the Interpreter, to teach the Syriac Language." It has been edited by De Lagarde in his *Prætermissorum Libri Duo,* 1879, and was the storehouse from which Thomas a Novaria derived his *Thesaurus Arabico-Syro-Latinus,* 1636. Elias was also a composer of hymns, some of which occur in the Nestorian service-books[3], and of metrical homilies, apparently of an artificial character[4]. He

[1] There are some extracts from the *Annals* in Berlin, Sachau 108, 2.

[2] There are MSS. in the Brit. Mus. Add. 25876, Or. 2314 (frag.); Vat. Cod. cxciv. (*Catal.*, iii. 410), Codd. ccccx. ccccl. (Mai, *Scriptt. Vett. Nova Coll.*, v.); Palat. Medic. ccclxi. (*Catal.*, p. 419); Berlin, Sachau 5, 2, also 216, 1, and 306, 1; and in the collection of the S.P.C.K. The work has been edited by Dr R. Gottheil, Berlin, 1887; [and Merx has described it in his *Hist. artis gramm. ap. Syros*, chap. viii.].

[3] *E.g.*, Cod. Vat. xc. (*Catal.*, ii. 487), Nos. 13, 15, 17, 18; Cod. Vat. xci. (*Catal.*, ii. 491), Nos. 12, 14, 16, 17; Berlin, Sachau 64, 10.

[4] See Cod. Vat. clxxxiv. (*Catal.*, iii. 390), a poem on

edited four volumes of decisions in ecclesiastical law, which are often cited by ʿAbhd-īshōʿ of Nisībis in his *Collectio Canonum Synodicorum*[1]; indeed the third section, "On the Division of Inheritances," is entirely borrowed from the work of Elias[2]. Of his epistles that to the bishops and people of Baghdādh on the illegal ordination of Īshōʿ-yabh bar Ezekiel is preserved in Cod. Vat. cxxix. (*Catal.*, iii. 191)[3]. Six of his Arabic dissertations have been described by Assemani in the *B.O.*, iii. 1, 270–272. The most important of them appears to be No. 5, a disputation, in seven sessions or chapters, with the vizīr Abu 'l-Ḳāsim al-Ḥusain ibn ʿAlī al-Maghribī, preceded by a letter to the secretary Abu 'l-ʿAlā Ṣāʿid ibn Sahl. These meetings took place in 1026, and the work was committed to writing in 1027, after the death of the vizīr at Maiyāfāriḳīn in October, and published with the approbation of the celebrated commentator, philosopher, and lawyer Abu 'l-Faraj ʿAbdallāh ibn aṭ-Ṭaiyib[4], who was secretary to the

the love of learning, in which the letter Ālaph does not occur. It is printed by Cardāḥī in the *Liber Thesauri*, pp. 83–84.

[1] Mai, *Scriptt. Vett. Nova Coll.*, x.

[2] *B.O.*, iii. 1, 267–269; Mai, *op. cit.*, v. pp. 54, 220.

[3] *B.O.*, iii. 1, 272–273.

[4] He died in 1043; see *B.O.*, iii. 1, 544; Wüstenfeld, *Gesch. d. arab. Aerzte*, No. 132; Ibn Abī Uṣaibiʿah, ed.

patriarch Elias I. The anonymous work described in full by Assemani (*B.O.*, iii. 1, 303–306) under the title of *Kitābu 'l-Burhān 'alā ṣaḥīḥi* (or rather *fī taṣḥīḥi*) *'l-īmān*, "The Demonstration of the Truth of the Faith," is also by him[1].

Here we may pause in our enumeration to cast an eye upon some anonymous translations, which we are inclined to ascribe to the 10th and 11th centuries, and which are interesting as showing what the popular literature of the Syrians was, compared with that of their theologians and men of science.

We have already spoken of the older translation of *Ḳalīlagh wĕ-Damnagh*, made by the periodeutes Bōdh in the 6th century of our era (see above, p. 124). About the middle of the 8th century there appeared an independent Arabic translation from the Pahlavī by 'Abdallāh ibn al-Muḳaffa', which, under the name of *Kalīlah wa-Dimnah*, has been the parent of secondary versions in the Syriac, Persian, Greek, Hebrew, and Spanish languages[2]. The Syriac version was discovered

Müller, i. 239; Bar-Hebræus, *Hist. Dynast.*, p. 355 (transl., p. 233); *Chron. Syr.*, p. 239 (transl., p. 244) [ed. Bedjan, p. 226]; *Chron. Eccles.*, ii. 283.

[1] See the German translation by L. Horst, *Des Metropoliten Elias von Nisibis Buch vom Beweis der Wahrheit d. Glaubens*, Colmar, 1886.

[2] See Keith-Falconer, *Kalīlah and Dimnah or the Fables of Bidpai*, 1885, Introduction.

by the present writer in a unique MS. in the library of Trinity College, Dublin, and published by him in 1884[1]. It is evidently the work of a Christian priest, living at a time when the condition of the Syrian Church was one of great degradation, and the power of the caliphate on the wane, so that the state of society was that of complete disorder and licentiousness[2], a description which would very well apply to the 10th or 11th century. Indeed we could not place it much later, because part of the unique MS. goes back to the 13th century, and even its text is very corrupt, showing that it had passed through the hands of several generations of scribes. "The chief value of this later Syriac version is that it sheds light on the original text of the Arabic *K. w. D.* The Arabic text which the Syriac translator had before him must have been a better one than De Sacy's, because numbers of Guidi's extracts[3], which are not found at all in De Sacy's text, appear in their proper places in the later Syriac[4]."

To about the same period, judging by the similarity of style and language, we would assign

[1] Wright, *The Book of Kalīlah and Dimnah, translated from Arabic into Syriac.*

[2] See Wright's Preface, p. xi *sq.*

[3] See Guidi, *Studii sul Testo Arabo del Libro di Kalila e Dimna*, 1873.

[4] Keith-Falconer, *op. cit.*, p. lx.

the Syriac version of the book of *Sindibādh*. This work was translated, probably in the latter half of the 8th century, from Pahlavī into Arabic by Mūsā, a Muḥammadan Persian. It is, as Nöldeke has shown[1], the smaller of the two recensions known to the Arabs, the larger, entitled *Aslam* (?) *and Sindibādh*, being the work of al-Aṣbagh ibn 'Abd al-'Azīz as-Sijistānī. The smaller *Sindibādh* was in its turn done into Syriac, and thence into Greek by Michael Andreopūlus for Gabriel, prince of Melitēne (1086–1100), as discovered by Comparetti[2], under the name of Συντίπας (Sindipas), just as *Kalīlah wa-Dimnah* was translated by Symeon (the son of) Seth for the emperor Alexius Comnenus, who ascended the throne in 1081. The Syriac version, which bears the title of the *Story of Sindbān and the Philosophers who were with him*, has been edited by Baethgen, with a German translation and notes, from the unique MS. in the Royal Library at Berlin[3].

Somewhere between the 9th and 11th centuries we would place the Syriac translation of Esop's (Æsop's) *Fables*, which has been edited

[1] *Z.D.M.G.*, xxxiii. (1879), pp. 521–522.

[2] *Ricerche intorno al Libro di Sindibād*, 1869, p. 28 *sq.*; *The Folk-lore Society*, vol. ix. 1, p. 57 *sq.*

[3] Alt. Bestand 57, ff. 60–87. A small specimen had already been published by Rödiger, *Chrestom. Syr.*, 2d ed., pp. 100–101.

under a somewhat Jewish garb by Landsberger[1], who imagined himself to have found the Syriac original of the fables of Syntipas (Sindipas), whereas Geiger[2] clearly showed that we have here to do with a Syriac rendering of one of the forms of the fables of Esop. In fact, as Geiger pointed out, דסופוס is only a clerical error for דאסופוס. In Syriac MSS. of this collection the title is written ܕܝܘܣܦܘܣ, "of Josephus[3]." In some close relation to these stands the story of Josephus and king Nebuchadnezzar in the Berlin MS. Alt. Bestand 57, ff. 16–57, with which are interwoven a number of Esopic fables. They have been edited (with the exception of two) by Rödiger in his *Chrestom. Syr.*, 2d ed., pp. 97–100.

[In speaking of the works of Jacob of Edessa, mention was made (p. 147 *supra*) of the anonymous treatise *Causa omnium causarum*[4], which has been erroneously attributed to him[5]. Kayser[6] and

[1] מתליא דסופוס, *Die Fabeln des Sophos, Syrisches Original der Griechischen Fabeln des Syntipas*, 1859. Compare his earlier dissertation, *Fabulæ aliquot Aramææ*, 1846.

[2] *Z.D.M.G.*, xiv. (1860), p. 586 *sq.*

[3] *B.O.*, iii. 1, 7, with note 2. So, for example, MS. Trin. Coll. Dublin, B. 5, 32 (Wright, *Kalīlah and Dimnah*, pp. ix., x.).

[4] [It has the alternative title *Liber de cognitione veritatis.*

[5] As by Pohlmann, in *Z.D.M.G.*, xv. p. 648 *sq.*

[6] *Das Buch von der Erkenntniss der Wahrheit* (text) p. ii., note.

Nöldeke[1] have adduced reasons sufficient to prove that the book is from another hand, and at least not earlier than the 10th century. It gives an account of God, the worlds material and spiritual, and man, according to the views of the author's time. It claims to be "a common book for all peoples"; and the author, who was bishop of Edessa and therefore a Jacobite, shows a praiseworthy desire to avoid theological differences, and to treat such doctrines as the Trinity in a spirit of conciliation towards Jews and Mussulmans, as well as towards all fellow-Christians. The book exhibits in parts a somewhat mystical tone, akin to that of Stephen bar Ṣudhailē, but there is no evidence of direct dependence on him. The text was edited by Kayser in 1889 (Leipzig): his translation into German appeared posthumously in 1893 (Strassburg).]

In the 12th century we find that the number of Syrian writers, whether Jacobite or Nestorian, is small, but two of the former sect are men of real mark.

Abū Ghālib bar Ṣābūnī, the younger brother of Saʿīd bar Ṣābūnī (see above, p. 227), was almost as unfortunate as his brother. He was raised to the episcopate of Edessa after his brother's death

[1] *Literarisches Centralblatt* for 1889, col. 1003.]

by Athanasius VII., but speedily deposed on account of a quarrel, although many of the Edessenes, among them the king Baldwin, brother of Godfrey of Bouillon, took his part. He died of a fall from his horse, shortly after the death of the patriarch in 1129[1]. Though a good scholar and linguist, he does not appear to have written anything that has come down to our times. Assemani, it is true, ascribes to him three poems in twelve-syllable metre on the capture of Edessa by Zengī ibn Āḳ-sunḳur; but, as this took place in 1144[2], the writer must have been his successor, Basil bar Shumnā (1143–69)[3].

John[4], bishop of Ḥarrān and Mardē or Mārdīn, had charge of the Jacobite churches in the East, his diocese including Tell-Besmē, Kĕphar-tūthā, Dārā, Nisībis, Rās'ain, and the Khābhōrā or Khābūr. He was originally a monk of Edessa, was appointed bishop by Athanasius VII. in 1125, and was killed by a fall from his horse in 1165, at the age of seventy-eight[5]. He devoted

[1] See *B.O.*, ii. 212, 358–359; Bar-Hebræus, *Chron. Eccles.*, i. 467–479.

[2] *B.O.*, ii. cli. (comp. p. 317).

[3] See Bar-Hebræus, *Chron. Syr.*, p. 328 (transl., p. 335) [ed. Bedjan, p. 308]; *Chron. Eccles.*, i. 497, 547.

[4] His baptismal name was probably Jacob; see *B.O.*, ii. 230, col. 1, at the foot.

[5] *B.O.*, ii. 216, 226; Bar-Hebræus, *Chron. Eccles.*, i. 531.

himself chiefly to the restoration of the decayed churches and monasteries of his diocese, as may be seen from the autobiographical fragment in *B.O.*, ii. 217 *sq.* From the same document, pp. 224–225, it appears that he was fond of MSS., which he collected, repaired, and bound, and that he wrote with his own hand four small copies of the Gospels in gold and silver. He enjoyed a well earned reputation as a land-surveyor and practical engineer[1]. Bar-Hebræus notes his great liberality in redeeming the captive Edessenes who had been carried off by Zengī's troops[2]. The fall of Edessa (1144), however, was an event that got him into a great deal of trouble. He was ill-advised enough to write a treatise on the Providence of God, in which he maintained that chastisements of that kind were *not* sent upon men by God, and that, if the troops of the Franks (Crusaders) had been there, Edessa would not have been taken by Zengī. Such rank heresy of course brought down upon him the whole bench of bishops. He was attacked by the priest Ṣalībhā of Ḳarīgārah (?)[3], by John bishop of Kaisūm[4], John bar Andreas bishop of Mab-

[1] *B.O.*, ii. 226; Bar-Hebræus, *Chron. Eccles.*, i. 525–527.

[2] *Chron. Eccles.*, i. 501.

[3] Died in 1164, *B.O.*, ii. 362.

[4] *B.O.*, ii. 364; Bar-Hebræus, *Chron. Eccles.*, i. 501, 554, 559. Died in 1171.

bōgh[1], and Dionysius bar Ṣalībī[2]. He was also the compiler of an anaphora[3].

The star of this century among the Jacobites is undeniably Jacob bar Ṣalībī of Melitēne (Malaṭiah). He was created bishop of Mar'ash, under the name of Dionysius, by Athanasius VIII. (Yēshū' bar Ḳeṭrah, 1138–66) in 1145, and the diocese of Mabbōgh was also placed under his charge[4]. Michael I. (1166–99) transferred him to Amid, where he died in 1171[5]. The list of his works, as quoted by Assemani from a Syriac MS., is very considerable[6], and he has dealt with them at great length[7]. We may mention the following. (1) Commentary on the Old Testament, of which only one complete MS. exists in Europe[8]. The

[1] Afterwards of Ṭūr-'Abhdīn; Bar-Hebræus, *Chron. Eccles.*, i. 515. He composed both in Armenian and Syriac, *B.O.*, ii. 360, coll. 1, 2, 362, col. 1; Bar-Hebræus, *Chron. Eccles.*, i. 487. Died in 1156; *B.O.*, ii. 362; Bar-Hebræus, *Chron. Eccles.*, i. 517; see Brit. Mus. Orient. 1017 (Wright, *Catal.*, pp. 897–898).

[2] *B.O.*, ii. 207; Bar-Hebræus, *Chron. Eccles.*, i. 503.

[3] *B.O.*, ii. 230.

[4] *B.O.*, ii. 362; Bar-Hebræus, *Chron. Eccles.*, i. 513–515.

[5] *B.O.*, ii. 363, 365; Bar-Hebræus, *Chron. Eccles.*, i. 559.

[6] *B.O.*, ii. 210; comp. *Catal. Bibl. Laur. et Palat. Medic.*, p. 79.

[7] *B.O.*, ii. 157–208.

[8] At Paris, Suppl. 92, in Zotenberg's *Catal.*, No. 66. There are fragments in Anc. fonds 3 (Zotenberg, *Catal.*, No. 9); see also Cod. Vat. xcvi. 29, 42, 43 (Psalms), 30 (on the Prophets).

order of the books is—the Pentateuch, Job, Joshua, Judges, Samuel and Kings, Psalms, Proverbs, Ecclesiastes, the Song of Songs, Isaiah, Jeremiah and Lamentations, Ezekiel, Daniel, the twelve minor Prophets, and Ecclesiasticus. Each book has a material or literal and a spiritual or mystical commentary. Several of the books have two commentaries, one on the Pĕshīṭtā, the other on the Hexaplar text; Jeremiah has actually three, one on the Hexaplar, and two, a shorter and a longer, on the Pĕshīṭtā. (2) Commentary on the New Testament, from which Assemani has given many extracts[1]. The order of the books is—the four Gospels, the Revelation of St John, the Acts of the Apostles, the seven apostolic epistles, and the fourteen epistles of St Paul[2]. (3) A compend-

[1] *B.O.*, ii. 157–170.

[2] The Gospels are in Brit. Mus. Add. 7184; Cod. Vat. clv. 19–24, clvi., cclxxv.–ix.; Paris, Anc. fonds 33, 34 (Zotenberg, *Catal.*, Nos. 67–68); Bodl. Or. 703, 2. St Matthew, Bodl. Hunt. 247. Revelation, &c., Brit. Mus. Add. 7185; Bodl. Or. 560. Dudley Loftus was the first to make use of these commentaries in his two works, *The Exposition of Dionysius Syrus, written above* 900 *years since, on the Evangelist St Mark, translated by D.L.* (Dublin, 1672), and *A Clear and Learned Explication of the History of our Blessed Saviour J.C., . . . by Dionysius Syrus, . . . translated by D. L.* (Dublin, 1695); see Payne Smith, *Catal.*, p. 411, notes d and f. Loftus's manuscript translations are in the Bodleian Library, Fell 6 and 7. [Extracts from the Com. on the Apocalypse have

ium of theology, of which we do not seem to have any MS. in Europe; see *B.O.*, ii. 163, col. 1, ll. 13–15, and p. 170. (4) A copious treatise against heresies, dealing with the Muḥammadans, the Jews, the Nestorians, the Dyophysites or supporters of the council of Chalcedon, and the Armenians[1]. (5) A treatise on the Providence of God, against John, bishop of Mārdīn[2], apparently no longer extant. (6) Expositions of the Eucharistic service[3], of the Nicene creed[4], of the consecration of the chrism[5], of the services of consecration[6], and of the Jacobite confession of faith[7]. (7) Canons on confession and absolution[8].

been published, with notes and translation, by Dr J. Gwynn in *Hermathena* vi. 397 *sq.*, vii. 137 *sq.* (the latter containing a summary of Hippolytus's interpretation of Matt. xxiv. 15–22).]

1 *B.O.*, ii. 170, 211. The section against the Muḥammadans is contained in Cod. Vat. xcvi. 19, and that against the Nestorians in Paris, Anc. fonds 125 (Zotenberg, *Catal.*, No. 209, 2). There is an extract from the latter in Bodl. Or. 467 (P. Smith, *Catal.*, p. 561). From it is extracted the list of the Jacobite patriarchs in *B.O.*, ii. 323, note 1.

2 *B.O.*, ii. 207; see above.

3 *B.O.*, ii. 176–208; Cod. Vat. cii., ccclxi.; Brit. Mus. Or. 2307 (partly Arabic); Paris, Anc. fonds 35, 69, 125.

4 Cod. Vat. clix. 4; Bodl. Marsh. 101.

5 Cod. Vat. clix. 30 (in Arabic).

6 *B.O.*, ii. 171; comp. Cod. Vat. clv. 10, clix. 31.

7 Bodl. Marsh. 101, f. 31.

8 *B.O.*, ii. 171.

(8) Two anaphoræ or liturgies[1]. (9) Various prayers, prooemia, and sedrās[2]. (10) Homilies, *e.g.*, encomium on the patriarch Michael the Elder[3], on the Passion of our Lord[4], and on withholding the sacrament from those who abstain from communicating for a period of more than forty days[5]. (11) A commentary on the six *Centuries* of Evagrius[6]. (12) Two poems on the fall of Edessa (1144)[7], three on the fall of Marʽash (1156)[8], and two on another incident (1159)[9]. Among the works mentioned in the list in *B.O.*, ii. 210–211, we cannot find any traces of the *Commentarius in Scripta Doctorum*, the *Compendium Historiarum Patrum et Sanctorum et Martyrum*, and the *Compendium Canonum Apostolicorum*, nor of the commentaries on the books of *Dialectics*, *ibid.*, col. 1. Of the epistles two are extant in Arabic, Berlin, Sachau 61, 1, 2. From

[1] *B.O.*, ii. 175. [2] *Ibid.*, ii. 175.

[3] *Ibid.*, ii. 170. Read, with slight alterations, on the installation of a bishop or patriarch. Cod. Vat. li. 26, ccciv.; Paris, Suppl. 23.

[4] Cod. Palat. Medic. xl. (*Catal.*, p. 78).

[5] Cod. Palat. Medic. lxii. (*Catal.*, p. 107).

[6] Berlin, Alt. Bestand 37, 1.

[7] *B.O.*, ii. 317; Bar-Hebræus, *Chron. Syr.*, 328 (transl., p. 335) [ed. Bedjan, p. 308].

[8] *B.O.*, ii. 317; Bar-Hebræus, *Chron. Syr.*, 346–347 [ed. Bedjan, p. 324].

[9] *B.O.*, ii. 451–452; Bar-Hebræus, *Chron. Eccles.*, ii. 351.

a treatise *On the Structure of Man* there are two short extracts in Bodl. Marsh. 361, f. 39. Dionysius appears also to have revised the Jacobite order of baptism[1], and to have drawn up a volume of services for the days of the week[2].

Michael the Elder[3], the son of Elias, a priest of Melitēne, of the family of Kindasī[4], was abbot of the convent of Bar-ṣaumā, near Melitēne[5],

[1] Brit. Mus. Arund. Or. 11 (Rosen, *Catal.*, p. 62, col. 2).

[2] Cod. Vat. ccccxxv., in Mai, *Scriptt. Vett. Nova Coll.*, v.

[3] So called to distinguish him from his nephew Michael the Younger, Yēshū' Sephĕthānā or "Big-lips," who became patriarch at Melitēne (1199–1215), in opposition to Athanasius IX., Ṣalībhā Ḳĕrāḥā (the Bald), at Mārdīn (1199–1207), and John XIV., Yēshū' the scribe (1208–20).

[4] Bar-Hebræus, *Chron. Eccles.*, i. 537.

[5] Assemani expressly says "at Shennā" (read ܕܫܢܐ), *B.O.*, ii. 154, but the list of patriarchs at p. 323 does not give the word ܕܫܢܐ, though he repeats it in the translation (No. 100). In the *Dissert. de Monophysitis*, p. xcviii, he makes Michael belong to the convent near Melitēne, and merely mentions another convent of Bar-ṣaumā at "Sena" (see also the Index, p. 532). Langlois, in the preface to the *Chronique de Michel le Grand*, p. 3, thinks of a convent near Mārdīn, such as that restored by John, bishop of Mārdīn (*B.O.*, ii. 222, l. 19). We believe, however, that the convent near Melitēne is meant, as John of Mārdīn had acquired a certain reputation in what Abbeloos calls the "ars gromatica" (Bar-Hebræus, *Chron. Eccles.*, i. 526, note 1), wherefore it is said that Michael sent for him (*shaddar*

which we find him supplying with water, with the help of John, bishop of Mārdīn, in 1163[1]. He was elected patriarch in 1166, and held office till 1199[2]. He revised the Jacobite pontifical and ritual, arranging its contents under forty-six heads, as exhibited in Cod. Vat. li.[3], drew up an anaphora[4], wrote a tract setting forth the Jacobite confession of faith[5], a treatise against a Coptic schismatic, Mark the son of Ḳonbar, on the question of confession[6], and a poem on a case of persecution in 1159[7]. He also revised in 1185 the life of Abhḥai, bishop of Nicæa, having found most copies of it in a very disordered state[8]. His most

*bāthrēh*), and that John "returned to his diocese because the winter was at hand, meaning to come back in April" (p. 527).

1 Bar-Hebræus, *Chron. Eccles.*, i. 525.

2 *B.O.*, ii. 363–369; Bar-Hebræus, *Chron. Eccles.*, i. 535–605.

3 Assemani's *Catal.*, ii. 314 *sq.*; *B.O.*, ii. 155.

4 Cod. Vat. xxv. 8; Paris, Anc. fonds 68 (Zotenberg, *Catal.*, p. 49); Leyden, Cod. 1572 (*Catal.*, v. 73).

5 Bar-Hebræus, *Chron. Eccles.*, i. 549; Langlois, p. 331.

6 Bar-Hebræus, *Chron. Eccles.*, i. 573–575; *B.O.*, ii. 155, No. iii.

7 Bar-Hebræus, *Chron. Eccles.*, ii. 351.

8 See Brit. Mus. Add. 12174, No. 8 (Wright, *Catal.*, p. 1124); Cod. Vat. xxxvii. 12 (*Catal.*, ii. 247); *B.O.*, ii. 505, col. 2. But the account of the death of the emperor Constantius, and the lives of Jacob of Sĕrūgh and of Mār Aḥā, appear to be wrongly ascribed to him in *Catal. Vat.*, ii. 248–249.

important work was a *Chronicle*, from the creation to 1196 A.D., which was translated, with other works of his, into Armenian, and apparently exists in that language alone[1]. Some extracts from it were published by Dulaurier in the *Journal Asiatique* for 1848, p. 281 *sq.*, and 1849, p. 315 *sq.*, and the whole has been edited in a French translation by V. Langlois, *Chronique de Michel le Grand*, 1868. According to him the translator of the first part of the work was the vartabed David, and it was finished by the priest Isaac, who completed his task in 1248, continuing it down to his own day. A third person engaged in translating the works of Michael into Armenian was the vartabed Vartan[2]. Appended to the *Chronicle* is an extract from a treatise of his "On the Sacerdotal Order and its Origin," or "On the Origin of Sacerdotal Institutions," with a continuation by Isaac and Vartan[3], which is followed in the MSS. by the Jacobite "confession of faith[4]." Michael appears also to have written an ecclesiastical history, which is entirely lost to us. At

[1] The present writer has been recently informed that a copy of the original Syriac exists in the library of the convent of az-Za'farān near Mārdīn.

[2] Langlois, Préface, p. 10, and note 2.

[3] Langlois, p. 363 *sq.*

[4] Langlois, Préface, p. 8, at the top; Bar-Hebræus, *Chron. Eccles.*, i. 606, note 1, 6.

least Bar-Hebræus[1] speaks of his recording certain matters in his "Ekklēsiastikē," which do not appear in the *Chronicle*.

A thorn in the side of Michael was his disciple Theodore bar Wahbōn. He first appears on the stage in 1170[2], when the emperor Manuel sent Theorianus to the Armenian catholicus and the Jacobite patriarch with letters. Michael declined an interview, but sent John of Kaisūm to see Theorianus at Ḳalʿat ar-Rūm, and on his coming a second time to the same place selected Theodore bar Wahbōn as his representative[3]. Ten years afterwards, in 1180, when Michael was at Antioch, Ibn Wahbōn was made anti-patriarch at Āmid by certain malcontent bishops, under the name of

[1] *Chron. Eccles.*, i. 589.

[2] *Ibid.*, i. 549, 551, where 1172 is an error, as remarked by Abbeloos in note 1. John of Kaisūm, who was present on the occasion, died in 1171 (p. 559).

[3] The disputations held on these occasions were of course utterly fruitless. See Leunclavius, *Legatio Imp. Cæsaris Manuelis Comneni Aug. ad Armenios, sive Theoriani cum Catholico disputatio*, &c., 1578, and in Galanus, *Conciliationis Ecclesiæ Armenæ cum Romana* . . . pars i., 1690, p. 242 *sq.*; *Disp. Theoriani secunda*, in Mai, *Scriptt. Vett. Nova Coll.*, vi. pp. xxiii and 314 *sq.*, and in Migne, *Patrol. Gr.*, cxxxiii. 114 *sq.*; also Bar-Hebræus, *Chron. Eccles.*, i. 549–557; Langlois, *Chronique*, pp. 329–331; comp. Abbeloos's notes on Bar-Hebræus, pp. 550–552, and *B.O.*, ii. 364–365.

John[1]. Michael, however, at once took energetic measures[2], got hold of the anti-patriarch, formally deposed him, and shut him up in the convent of Bar-ṣaumā, whence he was afterwards allowed to make his escape by some of the monks. He fled to Damascus, where he tried in vain to bring his case before Ṣalāḥ ad-dīn, and thence to Jerusalem, after the fall of which city in 1187 he joined Gregorius Degha, the Armenian catholicus, at Ḳalʿat ar-Rūm and went with him to Cilicia, where the king, Leo, made him patriarch of the Jacobites in his territories. He died in 1193. According to Bar-Hebræus, Theodore bar Wahbōn was a good scholar, and could speak and write three foreign languages, Greek, Armenian, and Arabic[3]. He compiled an anaphora[4], wrote an exposition of the Eucharistic service[5], and a statement of his case against Michael in Arabic[6].

Of Nestorian writers there are scarcely any worth naming in this century, for the historian and controversialist Mārē bar Shĕlēmōn, otherwise

[1] Bar-Hebræus, *Chron. Eccles.*, i. 575 *sq.*; *B.O.*, ii. 213.

[2] Bar-Hebræus, *Chron. Eccles.*, i. 579; *B.O.*, ii. 214.

[3] *Chron. Eccles.*, i. 581.

[4] See Renaudot, ii. 409; *B.O.*, ii. 216; Payne Smith, *Catal.*, p. 241, note c.

[5] *B.O.*, ii. 216.

[6] Bar-Hebræus, *Chron. Eccles.*, i. 581, at the foot.

Mārī ibn Sulaimān, wrote in Arabic[1]; and Elias

[1] He flourished in the first half of this century (*B.O.*, iii. 1, 554–555, 582). His work is extant in the Vatican Library in 2 vols., cviii. and cix. (Mai, *Scriptt. Vett. Nova Coll.*, iv. 219–223), with the title *Kitāb al-Majdal* or "the Tower," wrongly ascribed to 'Amr ibn Mattā of Ṭīrhān. The first volume, transcribed in 1401, is theological and dogmatical; it comprises the first four sections. The second volume is theological and historical. The series of patriarchs ended with "71," 'Abhd-īshō' bar Mukl of Mosul (1138–47), but is continued down to Yabh-alāhā bar Ḳāyōmā of Mosul (1190), "qui nunc sedem tenet," *i.e.*, in 1214, when this volume was written. His epitomizer 'Amr ibn Mattā of Ṭīrhān lived in the first half of the 14th century (*B.O.*, iii. 1, 580, 586). To him is ascribed Cod. Vat. cx., which "autographus esse videtur" (Mai, *Scriptt. Vett. Nova Coll.*, iv. 224–227). It consists of five parts, of which the first is wanting in this MS., which has therefore no title. The series of catholics in pt. v., fundam. 2, is continued down to Yabh-alāhā (1281–1317). In pt. v., fundam. 3, sect. 6, we find the confession of faith of Michael, bishop of Āmid and Maiyāfāriḳīn (*B.O.*, iii. 1, 557), translated into Arabic by the priest Ṣalībā ibn Yoḥannā, whom G. E. Khayyath, archbishop of 'Amādia, asserts to be the real author of the whole work (see his *Syri Orientales seu Chaldæi Nestoriani et Romanorum Pontificum Primatus*, 1870, and comp. Hoffmann, *Auszüge*, p. 6). Cod. Vat. dclxxxvii. (Mai, *op. cit.*, v. 594) contains part of the same work as Cod. Vat. cx. (though the *Catalogue* calls it the *Majdal*, and ascribes it to Mārī), viz., pt. v., fundam. 1 and 2 ("usque ad Ebediesum Barsaumæ successorem, qui obiit die 25 novembris an. Christi 1147. Continuat eandem historiam Amrus Matthæi filius, a Jesuiabo baladensi, Ebediesu successore, usque ad Iaballahum III. Timothei secundi successorem,

III.[1], Abū Ḥalīm ibn al-Ḥadīthī, of Maiperḳaṭ, metropolitan of Nisībis and catholicus from 1175 to 1190, chiefly used the same language in his homilies and letters[2]. He is best remembered for having compiled and arranged the prayers in one of the service books, which is still called by his name, "the Abū Ḥalīm[3]."

Īshō'-yabh bar Malkōn was ordained bishop of Nisībis in 1190 by the catholicus Yabh-alāhā II. (1190–1222), was present at the consecration of

qui obiit die 31 ianuarii an. Christi 1222"!). Cod. Vat. dclxxxviii. is also said to contain "Historia Patriarcharum Chaldæorum sive Nestorianorum," from Addai and Mārī down to Yabh-alāhā bar Ḳāyōmā, by 'Amr ibn Mattā. "Hæc autem historia longe fusior est atque emendatior illa, quam Mares f. Salomonis conscripsit, de qua in præcedente codice"! And to add to the perplexity, Sachau describes his Cod. 12 (Arab.) as "Theil einer grossen Kirchengeschichte der Nestorianer. أَسْفَار الأَسْرار Bücher der Geheimnisse. Alte Papierhandschrift (14 Jh.). Es ist das كتاب المجدل von 'Amr b. Mattā aus Ṭīrhān." Possibly the MS. in the collection of the S.P.C.K. may give some light.

[1] *B.O.*, ii. 450, iii. 1, 287; Bar-Hebræus, *Chron. Eccles.*, ii. 367–369.

[2] *B.O.*, iii. 1, 290.

[3] Badger, *The Nestorians*, ii. 23: "The Aboo Haleem contains a collection of collects appointed to be read at the conclusion of the Nocturns of all the Sundays throughout the year, of the festivals, and the three days of the *Baootha d'Ninwâyê*, before the commencement of the Matins." See *B.O.*, iii. 1, 291–295.

his successor Sabhr-īshōʿ IV. (1222–25), and died under Sabhr-īshōʿ V. (1226–56), his follower at Nisībis being Makkīkhā, who was afterwards catholicus (1257–65)[1]. He wrote on questions of grammar, besides homilies, letters, and hymns, in which, however, he chiefly, if not exclusively, employed the Arabic language[2]. He is the same as Joseph bar Malkōn, bishop of Mārdīn, whose metrical tract on the points, entitled *Mĕṣīdhtā dhĕ-Nuḳzē*, or "the Net of the Points," is found in MSS., along with the grammatical writings of Elias bar Shīnāyā and John bar Zōʿbī[3]. This tract must therefore have been composed before 1190.

Simeon Shanḳĕlabhādhī or Shanḳĕlāwī, of Shanḳĕlābhādh or Shanḳĕlāwah[4], near Irbil, must have been a contemporary of Bar Malkōn, and perhaps somewhat senior to him. He was the teacher of John bar Zōʿbī, for whom he wrote a *Chronikon* or chronological treatise in the form of

[1] *B.O.*, iii. 1, 295, note 1.

[2] *Ibid.*, iii. 1, 295–306.

[3] *E.g.*, Cod. Vat. cxciv. (copied from a MS. written in 1246), and Brit. Mus. Add. 25876, f. 276 b (note the colophon, f. 290 b, Wright, *Catal.*, p. 1178); see *B.O.*, iii. 1, 308, col. 1, No. viii., and the Abbé Martin, *De la Métrique chez les Syriens*, 1879, p. 70 (at p. 68, l. 14, read ܕܢܨ̈ܝܒܐ, "the bishop of Nisībis"). [Compare Merx, *Hist. artis gramm. ap. Syros*, chap. viii.]

[4] See Hoffmann, *Auszüge*, p. 231, and note 1847.

questions and answers, explanatory of the various eras, the calendar, &c. There is a MS. in the British Museum, Add. 25875[1], and several at Berlin[2]. He was also the author of a moral poem in enigmatical language, of which ʿAbhd-īshōʿ thought it worth his while to write an explanation for his disciple Abraham[3]. To him is likewise ascribed "the questions of Simon Kēphā concerning the Eucharist and Baptism," which he appears to have introduced to the notice of his pupil John bar Zōʿbī[4].

John bar Zōʿbī flourished about the end of the 12th and the beginning of the 13th century. He was a monk of Bēth Ḳūḳā (or Ḳūḳē) in Ḥĕdhaiyabh, and numbered among his pupils Jacob bar Shakkō, or Severus, bishop of Mār Matthew (see below)[5]. He wrote metrical homilies, partly in seven-syllable, partly in twelve-syllable verse, on the chief points of the Nestorian faith[6]. One of

[1] Wright, *Catal.*, p. 1067.

[2] Sachau 108, 1, 121, and 153, 1, 3.

[3] Cod. Vat. clxxxvii. (*Catal.*, iii. 404); MS. Ind. Off. No. 9, "Tracts in Syriac," f. 204. It has been published by Cardāḥī, *Liber Thesauri*, p. 89. Cardāḥī calls the author *as-Sanḳalabarī*, blindly copying Assemani's *Sancalabarensis*, and places his death in 780 (see *B.O.*, iii. 1, 225, note 5, p. 226, note 7; and *Catal. Vat.*, iii. 405).

[4] *B.O.*, iii. 1, 562.

[5] Bar-Hebræus, *Chron. Eccles.*, ii. 409.

[6] Brit. Mus. Or. 2305; and apparently Berlin, Sachau 8.

these is mentioned by Assemani, *B.O.*, iii. 1, 309, note 1[1]; another, on the four problems of philosophy, is in Berlin, Sachau 72, 15. Bar Zōʿbī is, however, better known as a grammarian[2]. The larger of his two grammars is based on the works of previous writers, such as Severus Sēbōkht and Denḥā, commentators on Aristotle, and the grammarians Elias I., the catholicus, and Elias bar Shīnāyā, bishop of Nisībis[3]. The smaller grammar is an epitome in verse, accompanied by a metrical tract on the four chief marks of interpunction[4]. He seems also to have continued the treatise of Ḥonain *De Synonymis*[5], so that he may perhaps be Hoffmann's "analecta anonymus[6]."

As the lamp flares up before it expires, so the 13th century witnessed a faint revival of Syriac literature before its extinction.

David bar Paul is cited by Bar-Hebræus in

1 It has been translated by Badger, *The Nestorians*, ii. 151–153.

2 *B.O.*, iii. 1, 307; [Merx, *op. cit.*, chap. x.].

3 Part of this work, namely, the portion that deals with the marks of interpunction, has been edited and translated by Martin, *Traité sur l'Accentuation chez les Syriens Orientaux*, 1877.

4 MSS. of these grammars,—Cod. Vat. cxciv., ccccl.; Brit. Mus. Add. 25876; Or. 2314; Berlin, Alt. Best. 36, 16, and Sachau 216, 2, and 306, 2.

5 Berlin, Sachau 72, 14.

6 *Opusc. Nestor.*, p. iv.

the *Auṣar Rāzē*[1], and may therefore be supposed to have lived early in the 13th century. He was evidently a man of considerable culture, and a versifier. We have from his pen a poem on the letters of the Syriac alphabet[2], a note on the mutable letters[3], and a brief enumeration of the categories of Aristotle[4], a moral poem in twelve-syllable verse[5], another on repentance in an Arabic translation[6], and specimens of a third in Cardāḥī's *Liber Thesauri*, p. 138. Theological are a dialogue between a Malkite and a Jacobite on the hymn Trisagion[7] and a tract in Arabic on matters in dispute between the Jacobites and Malkites[8].

Jacob bar Shakkō (Shakkākō ?)[9], or 'Īsā, bar Mark, of Barṭellāi or Barṭullā, near Mosul, was a monk of the famous convent of Mār Matthew, of

[1] *B.O.*, ii. 243.

[2] Cod. Vat. ccxvii. (*Catal.*, iii. 505); Paris, Anc. fonds 118 (Zotenberg, *Catal.*, p. 166), 157 (*ibid.*, p. 147).

[3] Paris, Anc. fonds 164 (Zotenberg, *Catal.*, p. 213).

[4] Berlin, Alt. Best. 36, 13.

[5] Cod. Vat. xcvi. (*Catal.*, ii. 522).

[6] Cod. Vat. lviii. (*Catal.*, ii. 351).

[7] Cod. Vat. cxlvi. (*Catal.*, iii. 268), ccviii. (*Catal.*, iii. 498); Paris, Anc. fonds 134 A (Zotenberg, *Catal.*, p. 154), with an Arabic translation.

[8] Bodl. Hunt. 199 (P. Smith, *Catal.*, p. 449), Poc. 79 (*ib.*, p. 459).

[9] Written ܫܟܟܘ and ܫܟ݁ܟ݁ܘ.

which he afterwards became bishop by the name of Severus[1]. He was trained in grammar by John bar Zō'bī (see above) in the convent of Bēth Ḳūḳā (or Ḳūḳē) in Ḥĕdhaiyabh[2], and in dialectics and philosophy by Kamāl ad-Dīn Mūsā ibn Yūnus at Mosul[3]. He composed one of his works, the *Book of Treasures*, in 1231 and died in 1241[4], on his way to visit the aged patriarch Ignatius II. (maphriān 1215–22, patriarch 1222–53). He possessed a great many books, which were all conveyed to the *dēmosion*[5] of the ruler of Mosul.

[1] Bar-Hebræus, *Chron. Eccles.*, ii. 409 (a contemporary). In Cod. Vat. ccccxi. (Mai, *Scriptt. Vett. Nova Coll.*, v.) he bears the name of Jacob bar Talia, a corruption of Barṭellāyā. In MS. Berlin, Alt. Best. 38, 1 (if the *Catal.* be correct), he is called "metropolitan of the convent of St Matthew near Arbela," confusing Mār Matthew at Mosul with Bēth Ḳūḳā, where he was trained. Assemani and others have identified him with Jacob, bishop of Maiperḳaṭ (Mĕdhīnath Sāhdē). With Taghrīth he never had anything to do.

[2] Hoffmann, *Auszüge*, p. 215, note 1715.

[3] Born 1156, died 1224; Bar-Hebræus, *Chron. Eccles.*, ii. 411; Wüstenfeld, *Gesch. d. arab. Aerzte*, No. 229; Ibn Khallikān, ed. Wüstenfeld, No. 757; Ibn Abī Uṣaibi'ah, ed. Müller, i. 306.

[4] Assemani (*B.O.*, ii. 455) is mistaken; see also pp. 237 and 477.

[5] According to Abbeloos, Bar-Hebræus, *Chron. Eccles.*, ii. 412, "in ærarium publicum principis Mossulæ assumpti fuerunt." We suspect that the Christian bishop's library went to light the fires of the public bath.

His works are as follows. (1) The *Book of Treasures*, a theological treatise in four parts, viz., part i., of the three-one God; part ii., of the Incarnation of the Son of God; part iii., of the Divine Providence; part iv., of the creation of the universe, the angels, the different kinds of life, the soul of man, the resurrection, and the last judgement[1]. (2) The *Dialogues*, in two books. Book i., dial. 1, on grammar, followed by a discourse on the same in twelve-syllable metre; dial. 2, on rhetoric; dial. 3, on the art of poetry or metres; dial. 4, on the eloquence and copiousness of the Syriac language. Book ii., dial. 1, on logic and the syllogism; dial. 2, on philosophy, its kinds, divisions, and subdivisions, in five sections, viz., (*a*) on the definitions of philosophy, its divisions, &c.; (*b*) on the philosophic life and conduct; (*c*) on physics or physiology; (*d*) on the four disciplines, —arithmetic, music, geometry, and mathematics; (*e*) on metaphysics and theology[2]. Of his letters

[1] Cod. Vat. clix. (*Catal.*, iii. 307); Brit. Mus. Add. 7193 (Rosen, *Catal.*, p. 84); and in the collection of the S.P.C.K. An extract in Cod. Vat. ccccxi. (Mai, *Scriptt. Vett. Nova Coll.*, v.); see *B.O.*, ii. 237–240.

[2] Brit. Mus. Add. 21454 (Wright, *Catal.*, p. 1165); Göttingen, Cod. Orient. 18c; Bodl. Marsh. 528 (apparently imperfect, P. Smith, *Catal.*, p. 642). Excerpts in Berlin, Alt. Best. 38, 1. Book i., dial. 3, has been edited by Martin, "De la Métrique chez les Syriens," in *Abhand-*

two are extant, in verse, addressed to Fakhr ad-Daulah Mark bar Thomas and his brother Tāj ad-Daulah Abū Ṭāhir Ṣāʿid[1]. He also wrote a confession of faith regarding the Trinity and the Incarnation, which he himself cites in the *Book of Treasures*, part ii., chap. 14, and an exposition of the services and prayers of the church, which is referred to in the same work, part. ii., chap. 31 (on the addition of the words "who was crucified for us" to the Trisagion)[2]. Under the name of Jacob of Maiperḳaṭ we have an admonition addressed to persons seeking ordination as priests, which is found in many service books[3].

Aaron bar Maʿdanī (or Maʿdānī ?) had been recently appointed bishop of Mārdīn, under the name of John, when he was promoted by the patriarch Ignatius II. to the dignity of maphriān in 1232[4]. His bodily presence seems to have been

*lungen für d. Kunde d. Morgenlandes*, Bd. vii., No. 2, 1879; [and dial. 1 of the same book, with extracts from the metrical discourse that follows it, by Merx in the appendix to his *Hist. artis gramm. ap. Syros* (see also chap. xi.)].

[1] Brit. Mus. Add. 7193 (Rosen, *Catal.*, p. 84); see Bar-Hebræus, *Chron. Eccles.*, ii. 407, where the third brother Shams ad-Daulah is also mentioned.

[2] *B.O.*, ii. 240.

[3] *E.g.*, Cod. Vat. li. 9 (*Catal.*, i. 318); ccciv. (Mai, *Scriptt. Vett. Nova Coll.*, v.); Paris, Suppl. 22, 23, 38, 94 (the last in Arabic), see Zotenberg, *Catal.*, pp. 68, 72, 76; comp. *B.O.*, ii. 241.

[4] *B.O.*, ii. 454.

somewhat insignificant, and he was no orator, for which reasons he was unpopular[1]. In 1237 he went to Baghdādh, where in the following year he composed his panegyric on the holy Mār Aaron, and ingratiated himself with the three brothers Shams ad-Daulah, Fakhr ad-Daulah, and Tāj ad-Daulah, the sons of the archiater Thomas, who were in high favour at the court of al-Mustanṣir bi'llāh. He learned to speak and write Arabic thoroughly[2]. In 1244 he was recalled to Mosul and received with every mark of respect[3]. On the death of Ignatius in 1252, Dionysius (Aaron 'Angūr) was created patriarch[4], but a rival faction set up John bar Ma'danī[5]; and so the two ruled in a divided church till Dionysius was murdered in the convent of Bar-ṣaumā near Melitēne in 1261[6], after which time his rival sat alone till 1263[7]. John bar Ma'danī compiled an anaphora[8] and wrote a great many poems, of which Bodl. Hunt. 1 contains no less than 60[9]. Some of the more

[1] Bar-Hebræus, *Chron. Eccles.*, ii. 407.
[2] *Ibid.*, ii. 411. [3] *Ibid.*, ii. 413.
[4] *Ibid.*, i. 697, 701; *B.O.*, ii. 376.
[5] Bar-Hebræus, *Chron. Eccles.*, i. 707; *B.O.*, ii. 377.
[6] Bar-Hebræus, *Chron. Eccles.*, i. 737.
[7] *Ibid.*, i. 743.
[8] See Renaudot, ii. 512.
[9] See Payne Smith, *Catal.*, pp. 379–382, and MS. Berlin, Sachau 207, 3.

important of these are the poem on the soul, entitled "the Bird" (*Pūraḥĕthā*)[1], on the high origin of the soul and its degradation by sin[2], on the excellent path of the perfect[3], and on the capture of Edessa and other places by the Seljūḳ sultān ʿAlā'u 'd-dīn Kaiḳobādh in 1235[4]. Of his homilies Cod. Vat. xcvii. contains eighteen for various feasts in Arabic[5].

These writers are, however, all cast into the shade by the imposing figure of Bar-Hebræus, as we are accustomed to call him, one of the most learned and versatile men that Syria ever produced[6]. Abu 'l-Faraj Gregory[7] was the child of a physician at Melitēne (Malaṭiah) named Aaron, a convert from Judaism or of Jewish descent,

1 Bodl. Hunt. 1; Poc. 298 (P. Smith, *Catal.*, p. 641); Cod. Vat. cciv. (*Catal.*, iii. 489); Berlin, Sachau 61, 8.

2 Bodl. Hunt. 1; Cod. Vat. cciv.

3 Bodl. Hunt. 1; Poc. 298; Vat. cciv. Edited in part by Cardāḥī in the *Liber Thesauri*, pp. 66–68.

4 Hunt. 1. Palat. Medic. lxii. contains two poems on the love of God and the love of wisdom (*Catal.*, p. 108).

5 *Catal.*, ii. 523. There is one, also in Arabic, on repentance and death in Cod. Vat. ccxx. (*Catal.*, iii. 508).

6 *B.O.*, ii. 244 *sq.* See Gibbon's eulogy of him, *Decline and Fall of the Roman Empire*, ed. Smith, 1855, vol. vi., p. 55.

7 His baptismal name was John, as appears from the inscription on his tombstone; Badger, *The Nestorians*, i. 97. Gregory he probably adopted when he became a bishop.

whence his son got the name of Bar 'Ebhrāyā or Ibn al-'Ibrī, "the son of the Hebrew." He was born in 1226[1], and devoted himself from his boyhood to the acquisition of Greek and Arabic. A little later he applied himself also to theology and philosophy, besides practising medicine under his father and other distinguished physicians. His lot was cast, however, in evil days. In 1243 many of the inhabitants of Malaṭiah fled to Aleppo before the advancing hordes of Hulāgū and his Tatars, and his father would have been among the fugitives, had it not been for a lucky accident[2]. In the following year his father had actually to attend as physician upon one of the Tatar generals, whom he accompanied to Khartabirt, and on his return retired almost immediately from Malaṭiah to the safer city of Antioch[3]. Here Bar-Hebræus completed his studies and commenced his monastic life[4]. Thence he went to Tripolis, where he and Ṣalībhā bar Jacob Wagīh, of Edessa, were study-

[1] *B.O.*, ii. 263.

[2] *Ibid.*, ii. 244; Bar-Hebræus, *Hist. Dynast.*, p. 481 (transl., p. 315); *Chron. Syr.*, p. 503 (transl., p. 521), [ed. Bedjan, p. 477].

[3] *B.O.*, ii. 245; Bar-Hebræus, *Hist. Dynast.*, pp. 486–487 (transl., pp. 318–319); *Chron. Syr.*, 504–505 (transl., p. 522), [ed. Bedjan, p. 478].

[4] See the poem No. 29 in Cod. Vat. clxxiv. (*Catal.*, iii. 356).

ing medicine and rhetoric with a Nestorian teacher named Jacob, when they were summoned before the patriarch Ignatius II., on 14th September 1246, and ordained bishops, the former of Gūbōs (Gūbās) near Malatiah, the latter of ʻAkkō[1]. Bar-Hebræus was then just twenty years of age. In the following year he was transferred to Laḳabhīn, another diocese adjacent to Malaṭiah[2], by the patriarch Ignatius[3]. After the death of Ignatius, Bar-Hebræus took the part of Dionysius (Aaron ʻAngūr) against John bar Maʻdanī, and was transferred by him in 1253 to Aleppo[4], but quickly deposed by his old friend Ṣalībhā (who sided with John bar Maʻdanī)[5]; nor did he recover this see till 1258[6]. The next patriarch, Ignatius III. (Yēshūʻ), abbot of Gĕvīkāth near Mopsuestia[7], advanced him to the dignity of maphriān in 1264[8].

1 Bar-Hebræus, *Chron. Eccles.*, i. 667; *B.O.*, ii. 245, 374. From ʻAkkō Ṣalībhā was transferred to Aleppo, under the name of Basil (*B.O.*, ii. 375), and promoted in December 1252 by the patriarch John bar Maʻdanī to be maphriān, under the name of Ignatius (*B.O.*, ii. 377, 455). He died in 1258.

2 *B.O.*, ii. 260.

3 *Ibid.*, ii. 246; Bar-Hebræus, *Chron. Eccles.*, i. 685.

4 *B.O.*, ii. 246; Bar-Hebræus, *Chron. Eccles.*, i. 721.

5 *Ibid.*, i. 721. 6 *Ibid.*, i. 727.

7 He sat from 1264 to 1282.

8 *B.O.*, ii. 246; Bar-Hebræus, *Chron. Eccles.*, i. 749, ii. 433.

Henceforth his life was an active and busy one, and it seems almost marvellous that he should have studied and written so much, while in no way neglectful of the vast diocese committed to his charge. The story is told by himself in simple language in his *Ecclesiastical History*[1], with a continuation by his surviving brother Bar-ṣaumā Ṣafī, giving a nearly complete list of his works[2]. He died at Marāghah in Adhurbāigān on 30th July 1286, and the greatest respect was shown to his memory by Greeks, Armenians, and Nestorians alike, the shops being closed and no business transacted[3]. His body was conveyed to the convent of Mār Matthew at Mosul[4], where his grave was seen by Badger in October 1843[5]. Bar-Hebræus cultivated nearly every branch of science that was in vogue in his time, his object being on the one hand to reinvigorate and keep alive the Syriac language and literature, and on the other to make available to his co-religionists

[1] Bar-Hebræus, *Chron. Eccles.*, ii. 431–467; *B.O.*, ii. 248–263.

[2] Bar-Hebræus, *Chron. Eccles.*, ii. 467–485; *B.O.*, ii. 264–274. Two brothers died before him, Michael and Muwaffaḳ. See the poems Nos. 166 and 170 in Cod. Vat. clxxiv. (*Catal.*, iii. 358).

[3] *B.O.*, ii. 266; *Chron. Eccles.*, ii. 473.

[4] *B.O.*, ii. 460.

[5] *The Nestorians*, i. 97. For "1536" read 1537, and for "August" July.

the learning of the Muḥammadans in a suitable form. Hence his treatment of the Aristotelian philosophy, following in the footsteps of Ibn Sīnā (Avicenna) and other Arabian writers[1]. The *Kĕthābhā dhĕ-Bhābhāthā*, or "Book of the Pupils of the Eyes," is a compendium of the art of logic or dialectics, comprising an introduction on the utility of logic and seven chapters in which the author deals successively with the *Isagōgē* of Porphyry, the *Categories, De Interpretatione, Analytica Priora, Topica, Analytica Posteriora,* and *De Sophisticis Elenchis*[2]. In connexion with it we take the *Kĕthābhā dha-Sĕwādh Sophia* or "Book of the Speech of Wisdom," a compendium of dialectics, physics, and metaphysics or theology[3]. The large encyclopædia entitled *Ḥēwath Hekhmĕthā,* "Butyrum Sapientiæ," or less correctly *Ḥekhmath Ḥekhmāthā,* "Sapientia Sapientiarum," comprises the whole Aristotelian discipline. The first volume contains the *Logic,* viz., the *Isagōgē,*

[1] Compare Renan, *De Philos. Peripat. apud Syros* (1852), p. 65 *sq*.

[2] Brit. Mus. Or. 1017; Paris, Anc. fonds 138; Berlin, Alt. Best. 38, 2, 39; Sachau 140, 2, and 198, 8; Cambridge, collection of the S.P.C.K.

[3] Brit. Mus. Or. 1017; Paris, Anc. fonds 138 (Syr. and Arab.); Berlin, Alt. Best. 38, 4; Sachau 91 (Syr. and Arab.), also 140, 1, and 198, 9; Cambridge, coll. of the S.P.C.K.

*Categories*, *De Interpret.*, *Anal. Pri.* and *Poster.*, *Dialectica*, *De Sophist. Elenchis*, *Rhetoric*, and *Art of Poetry*. The second comprises the *Physics*, viz., *De Auscult. Physica*, *De Cœlo et Mundo*, *De Meteoris*, *De Generatione et Corruptione*, *De Fossilibus*, *De Plantis*, *De Animalibus* and *De Anima*. The third, in its first section, treats of the *Metaphysics*, viz., of the origin and writers of philosophy, and of theology; in its second section, of ethics, economics, and politics[1]. An abridgement of this large work is the *Tēgĕrath Tēgĕrāthā* or "Mercatura Mercaturarum," which goes over the same ground in briefer terms[2]. To this class too belongs a poem "On the Soul, according to the views of the Peripatetics," which is described as "mēmrā shīnāyā," *i.e.*, according to Assemani, riming in the letter *sh*[3]. Bar-Hebræus also translated into Syriac Ibn Sīnā's *Kitāb al-ishārāt wa 't-tanbīhāt*[4], under the title of *Kĕthābha dhĕ-Remzē wa-Mĕ-*

[1] Palat. Medic. clxxxvi.–vii., clxxvi.–ix. (=clxxxvi.; see Renan, *De Philos. Peripat. apud Syros*, p. 66); Bodl. Hunt. 1 (imperf.); compare also Palat. Medic. clxxxiii.–iv. and lxii. (p. 109).

[2] Palat. Medic. cc.; Berlin, Sachau 211; Cambridge, coll. of the S.P.C.K.

[3] *B.O.*, ii. 268, in the note, col. 2, No. 28.

[4] *Theoremata et Exercitationes*, a course of logic, physics, and metaphysics; see Wüstenfeld, *Geschichte d. arab. Aerzte*, p. 73, No. 61; *B.O.*, ii. 270, note 2.

*ʻīrānwāthā*[1], and another work of the same class, entitled *Zubdat al-Asrār* or "the Cream of Secrets," by his elder contemporary, Athīr ad-dīn Mufaḍḍal ibn ʻOmar al-Abharī (died in 1262)[2]. Nor did he neglect the study of mathematics and astronomy. In 1268 we find him lecturing on Euclid in the new convent at Marāghah, and again in 1272, at the same place, on the *Megistê* (Ἡ μεγάλη σύνταξις) of Ptolemy[3]. He drew up a *zīj*, *i.e.*, a set of astronomical tables or astronomical almanac, for the use of tiros[4]; but his principal work in this branch of science is the *Sullāḳā Haunānāyā* or "Ascent of the Mind," a complete treatise on astronomy and cosmography, which he composed in 1279[5]. His medical writings are more numerous, for Bar-Hebræus was famous as a physician[6] and had been in attendance as such on the Tatar

1 Cod. Vat. cxci.; Palat. Medic. clxxxv. (Arab. and Syr.); Paris, Anc. fonds 163.

2 See *Hist. Dynast.*, p. 485 (transl., p. 318).

3 *B.O.*, ii. 253; *Chron. Eccles.*, ii. 443.

4 *B.O.*, ii. 307; but the calendar there indicated is of later date.

5 Bodl. Hunt. 540; Paris, Anc. fonds 162. On the date see Payne Smith, *Catal.*, p. 584. [Chap. i. of the 2nd part, "a short treatise on Chartography and Geography," has been edited and translated into English by Gottheil in *Mittheilungen des Akademisch-Orientalischen Vereins zu Berlin*, No. 3 (1890).]

6 Wüstenfeld, *Gesch. d. arab. Aerzte*, No. 240.

"king of kings" in 1263[1]. He made, for example, a translation and an abridgement of Dioscorides's treatise Περὶ ὕλης ἰατρικῆς (De Medicamentis Simplicibus), under the title of *Kěthābhā dhě-Dhioskorīdhīs*[2], and wrote a commentary on the *Aphorisms* of Hippocrates in Arabic[3], and on the *Quæstiones Medicæ* of Ḥonain ibn Isḥāḳ in Syriac[4]. He also published the *Quæstiones* in an abridged Syriac translation[5]. Further, he is said to have written commentaries in Arabic on Galen's treatises *De Elementis* (Περὶ τῶν καθ' Ἱπποκράτην στοιχείων) and *De Temperamentis* (Περὶ κρασέων)[6]. He made an abridged version in Arabic of al-Ghāfiḳī's[7] "Book of Simples" (*al-adwiyah al-mufradah*)[8], and left an unfinished Syriac translation of the *Canon* (*al-Ḳānūn fi 'ṭ-Ṭibb*) of Ibn Sīnā[9]. A large medical treatise of his own com-

[1] *Chron. Eccles.*, i. 747.

[2] *B.O.*, ii. 268, in the note, col. 1, No. 13, and p. 270.

[3] *Ibid.*, ii. 268, col. 1, No. 15, and p. 270.

[4] Apparently unfinished, for Bar-ṣaumā is careful to add "as far as *Thīriaḳī*," *B.O.*, ii. 272, No. 28; see also p. 268, in the note, col. 2, No. 25.

[5] *B.O.*, ii. 270, No. 16.

[6] Wenrich, *De Auctorum Græc. Verss. et Commentt. Syriacis*, &c., 1842, pp. 242–243, 270; Wüstenfeld, *Gesch. d. arab. Aerzte*, No. 240.

[7] Wüstenfeld, *op. cit.*, No. 176; Ibn Abī Uṣaibi'ah, ed. Müller, ii. 52.

[8] *B.O.*, ii. 270, No. 14; 268, note, col. 1, No. 14.

[9] *Ibid.*, ii. 272, No. 24; 268, note, col. 2, No. 22.

position in Syriac is mentioned, but no special title is given[1]. As a grammarian Bar-Hebræus deserved well of his country, and his writings on this subject are now well known and appreciated by Orientalists. By making use of the work of previous grammarians, especially Jacob of Edessa, he has succeeded in giving a very full sketch of the language according to the Oriental system, with many valuable observations as to dialectic differences, &c. The larger grammar bears the title of *Kĕthābhā dhĕ-Ṣemhē*, "the Book of Lights" or "Rays[2]." It has been published, according to the Paris MS. Ancien fonds 166, by the Abbé Martin[3]. The smaller metrical grammar, *Kĕthābhā dhĕ-Ghrammatikī*[4], was edited so long ago as 1843 by Professor Bertheau of Göttingen, according to

[1] *B.O.*, ii. 272, No. 26.

[2] *Ibid.*, ii. 307.

[3] *Œuvres Grammaticales d'Abou 'l Faradj, dit Bar Hebreus*, vol. i., 1872. The chapter on the signs of interpunction, &c., was edited by Dr Phillips in 1869, in *A Letter by Mār Jacob, Bishop of Edessa, on Syriac Orthography.* [An exhaustive account of the book is given by Merx in his *Hist. artis gramm. ap. Syros*, chap. xii.] MSS. of this work are—Cod. Vat. ccccxvi., ccccxxii.; Bodl. Hunt. 1, Pocock 298; Paris, Anc. fonds 166; Brit. Mus. Add. 7201; Palat. Medic. cxxii.; Göttingen, Or. 18 b; Berlin, Alt. Best. 43, Sachau 307, 308; Cambridge, coll. of the S.P.C.K.

[4] *B.O.*, ii. 308.

the MS. Orient. 18 in the library of that university, but without the fifth section *De Vocibus Æquivocis*. Martin has republished it in his *Œuvres Grammaticales d'Abou 'l Faradj*, vol. ii., including the fifth section, according to the Paris MS. Ancien fonds 167[1]. A third, still smaller grammar, *Kĕthābhā dha-Bhĕlēṣūṣīthā* or "the Book of the Spark," was left unfinished by the author[2]. As a theologian, Bar-Hebræus's most useful work undeniably is the *Auṣar Rāzē* or "Storehouse of Secrets," the *Horreum Mysteriorum* as it is commonly called[3]. This is a critical and doctrinal commentary on the text of the Scriptures of the Old and New Testaments, based on the Pĕshīttā, but taking note of the various readings of the Hebrew text, the LXX. and other Greek versions, the later Syriac translations, and even the Armenian and Coptic, besides noting differences of reading between the Nestorians and Jacobites. The doctrinal portion is drawn from the Greek fathers and previous Syrian theologians, of course of the Monophysite school[4]. The *Mĕnārath Ḳudhshē*,

[1] Of this work there are many MSS. in Europe, differing from one another in the quantity of the scholia and the retention or omission of section 5.

[2] *B.O.*, ii. 272, No. 27.

[3] *Ibid.*, ii. 277.

[4] Portions of this work have been edited at various times, but a complete edition is still unachieved. Larsow made a very small beginning in 1858. See the list in

or "Lamp of the Sanctuary," is a treatise on the "bases" or first principles on which the church is established[1]. It deals in twelve "bases" with the following subjects:—(1) of knowledge in general, (2) of the nature of the universe, (3) of theology, (4) of the incarnation, (5) of the knowledge of celestial substances, *i.e.*, the angels, (6) of the earthly priesthood, (7) of the evil spirits, (8)

Nestle's *Brevis Linguæ Syr. Grammatica*, 1881, pp. 31–32. [There have since appeared editions of the notes on Proverbs, Ecclesiastes, Canticles and Wisdom, by Rahlfs (Leipzig, 1887); on Ruth, and the apocryphal additions to Daniel, by Heppner (Halle, 1888); on the Pauline epistles, by Loehr (Göttingen, 1889); on Daniel, by Freimann (Brünn, 1892); on Ecclesiasticus, by Kaatz (Frankfurt, 1892); and on Joshua and Judges, by Kraus (Kirchhain, 1894).] MSS. of this work—Cod. Vat. clxx., cclxxxii.; Palat. Medic. xxvi.; Bodl. Hunt. 1; Brit. Mus. Add. 7186, 21580, 23596; Berlin, Alt. Best. 11, Sachau 134; Göttingen, Orient. 18 a; Cambridge, coll. of the S.P.C.K.

[1] *B.O.*, ii. 284. MSS.—Cod. Vat. clxviii.; Paris, Anc. fonds 121; Cambridge, coll. of the S.P.C.K. This work has been translated into Arabic—Paris, Anc. fonds 128; Brit. Mus. 18296; Bodl. Hunt. 48; Berlin, Sachau 81; Cambridge, coll. of the S.P.C.K. Mr R. J. H. Gottheil has recently lithographed, "for private circulation only," a small portion of this work, viz., basis ii., ch. iii. sect. 3, paragr. *b*, on plants (26 pp. of text, 8 pp. of preface); the title is *A list of Plants and their Properties from the M*$^{e}$*nārat*$^{h}$ *Ḳud*$^{h}$*šē of Gregorius bar ʿEb*$^{h}$*râyâ edited by Richard J. H. Gottheil, B.A.* [Another extract, on geography, has been edited and translated by Gottheil in *Hebraica*, vol. vii., p. 39 *sq.*]

of the rational soul, (9) of free will and liberty, fate and destiny, (10) of the resurrection, (11) of the end of the world and the last judgement, (12) of paradise. The *Kĕthābhā dhĕ-Zalgē*, or "Book of Rays," is a compendium of theology, going over nearly the same ground as the previous work, in ten sections[1]. The *Kĕthābhā dh'Īthiḳōn*, or *Liber τῶν ἠθικῶν*, was composed at Marāghah in 1279. It has been fully analysed by Assemani in the *B.O.*, ii. 303 *sq.* Part i. treats of the exercises of the body and mind, such as prayer, manual work, study, vigils, fasting, &c.; part ii., of the regimen of the body; part iii., of the purifying of the soul from evil passions; part iv., of the adorning of the soul with virtues[2]. The *Kĕthābhā dhĕ-Yaunā*, or "Book of the Dove," is a similar work specially intended for the use of ascetics living in solitude as hermits. It is also divided into four parts, viz., (1) of the training of the body, *e.g.*, in alienation from the world, repentance,

[1] *B.O.*, ii. 297. MSS.—Cod. Vat. clxix.; Bodl. Or. 467, Hunt. 521; Paris, Anc. fonds 129, Suppl. 59; Brit. Mus. Or. 1017; Berlin, Sachau 85; Cambridge, coll. of the S.P.C.K. [A geographical extract has been edited and translated by Gottheil, *loc. cit.*]

[2] MSS.—Cod. Vat. clxxi.; Bodl. Marsh. 681, Hunt. 490; Brit. Mus. Add. 7194, 7195; Paris, Anc. fonds 122, Suppl. 75. There are two Arabic translations of this work; see Zotenberg, *Catal.*, p. 201, No. 247.

poverty, humility, patience, fraternal love, &c.; (2) of the training of the soul, *e.g.*, in quiet, religious exercises, prayer, watching, fasting, &c.; (3) of the spiritual rest of the perfect; and (4) an autobiographical sketch of his own spiritual life[1]. Bar-Hebræus also spent part of his time in excerpting, arranging, and commenting upon the *Book of Hierotheus concerning the hidden Mysteries of the House of God*[2]. In the commentary he chiefly follows that of Theodosius, patriarch of Antioch (see above, p. 206)[3]. He compiled an anaphora[4], published a confession of faith or creed[5], and approved the order of baptism of Severus, as translated by Jacob of Edessa[6]. More valuable than these is his *Kĕthābhā dhĕ-Huddāyē*, "the Book of Directions" or "Nomocanon," which is

[1] Bodl. Hunt. 1; Cambridge, coll. of the S.P.C.K. There is an Arabic translation, Paris, Anc. fonds 126, 145 (ff. 292–299).

[2] Probably a production of Stephen bar Ṣūdh-ailē; see Brit. Mus. Add. 7189, where we have the commentary of Theodosius, patriarch of Antioch, and compare Frothingham, *Stephen bar Sudaili*, p. 87 *sq.* See also above, p. 76 *sq.*

[3] Brit. Mus. Or. 1017. Other MSS.—Paris, Anc. fonds 138; Berlin, Sachau 206. The work seems to have been translated into Arabic (see Zotenberg, *Catal.*, p. 176).

[4] *B.O.*, ii. 275.

[5] *Ibid.*, ii. 276; Cod. Vat. clxxiii.

[6] See Cod. Vat. lii.; Paris, Anc. fonds 97; Medic. Palat. xliv.

for the Jacobite Church what the *Kunnāshā dhĕ-Ḳānōnē* of ʿAbhd-īshōʿ is for the Nestorian, both in ecclesiastical and secular matters[1]. To us Europeans the historical writings of Bar-Hebræus surpass in interest and value everything else that he has written. He planned and executed a *Universal History* in three parts[2]. Part i. contains the political *History of the World* from the creation down to his own times[3]. Part ii. is the history of the church from Aaron downwards, the treatment being exceedingly brief till we reach the post-apostolic period, when it becomes a history of the patriarchs of the church of Antioch, and finally, after the age of Severus, of the patriarchs of the Monophysite branch of that church down to the year 1285. The meagre continuation by a later hand reaches to 1495. Part iii. offers us the history of the Eastern division of the Syrian

[1] *B.O.*, ii. 299. Rendered into Latin by J. A. Assemani in Mai, *Scriptt. Vett. Nova Coll.*, x. MSS.—Cod. Vat. cxxxii., ccclvi.-vii., ccclviii.-ix.; Bodl. Hunt. 1; Paris, Anc. fonds 140; Berlin, Alt. Best. 40; Palat. Medic. lxi. It has been translated into Arabic.

[2] *B.O.*, ii. 311.

[3] This has been edited under the title of *Bar-Hebræi Chronicon Syriacum* by Bruns and Kirsch, with a Latin translation, in two volumes, 1789. Both text and translation are equally bad, and the work deserves a new edition. [There is now a better edition (by Bedjan), which appeared at Paris in 1890.]

Church from St Thomas the apostle onwards. From the time of Mārūthā (629) it becomes the history of the Monophysite maphriāns of Taghrīth, though a record is always carefully kept of the catholic patriarchs of the Nestorians. It closes with the year 1286, but there is a continuation by Bar-Hebræus's brother Bar-ṣaumā to 1288, and thence by another writer to 1496[1]. In the last years of his life, at the request of some Muslim friends in Marāghah, he undertook to make a recension in Arabic of the political history, which he all but finished within the space of one month before his last illness came on[2]. This edition is enriched with many references to Muḥammadan writers and literature which are want-

[1] Parts ii. and iii., which supplied Assemani with the greatest part of the materials for the second volume of his *Bibl. Orientalis*, have been edited by Abbeloos and Lamy in three volumes, viz., part ii. in two volumes, 1872–74, and part iii. in one volume, 1877, accompanied by a Latin translation and notes. It might be advantageously reprinted, if revised by a competent hand. MSS. of the entire history are—Cod. Vat. clxvi., ccclxxxiii.–viii.; Bodl. Hunt. 1; Palat. Medic. cxviii. Part i. is contained in Cod. Vat. clxvii. and Bodl. Hunt. 52; parts ii. and iii. in Brit. Mus. Add. 7198 and Cambridge Dd. 3, 8, 1, as also in the coll. of the S.P.C.K. Whether the Berlin MS., Sachau 210, contains the entire work or only a part of it we do not know; it is simply described as "Chronik des Bar Hebræus." There are excerpts in Cod. Vat. clxxiii.

[2] *B.O.*, ii. 264.

ing in the Syriac. It is entitled *al-Mukhtaṣar fi 'd-Duwal*, or "Compendious History of the Dynasties[1]." As a poet Bar-Hebræus is admired by his countrymen, and even Renan has thought the poem on the theme *Bona Lex sed Melior Philosophia* to be worthy of publication[2]. Some of the poems were badly edited and translated by Von Lengerke in 1836–38 according to the Paris MS. Ancien fonds 130; others have been published by the Maronite priest Augustinus Scebābi (الشّبابى) at Rome, 1877. The *Carmen de Divina Sapientia* was brought out so long ago as 1638 by Gabriel Sionita, and has been published at Rome in 1880 by Yoḥannā Noṭayn Darauni (يُوحَنَّا نُطَيْن الدَّرْعُونِى)[3]. In his youth Bar-Hebræus wrote a book on the interpretation of dreams, *pushshāḳ ḥelmē*[4]; and in his later years he made a collection of entertaining and humorous stories in Syriac, entitled *Kĕthābhā dhĕ-Thunnāyē Mĕghaḥḥĕkhānē*, with an Arabic

[1] Edited by Pocock, with a Latin translation, in 1663. MSS.—Cod. Vat. clxvii.; Brit. Mus. Add. 6944, 6952, 1, 23304-5; Bodl. Pocock 54, 162; Palat. Medic. cxvii.

[2] *De Philos. Peripat. ap. Syros*, p. 67.

[3] *B.O.*, ii. 308. MSS.—Cod. Vat. clxxiv.; Bodl. Hunt. 1, Marsh. 201; Paris, Anc. fonds 118, 130, 157; Palat. Medic. lxii. (*Catal.*, p. 110); see also Cod. Vat. ccccxxii.; Bodl. Poc. 298; Berlin, Alt. Best. 41, 2, 3, and Sachau 61, 4–6.

[4] *B.O.*, ii. 271, No. 20.

counterpart under the title of *Daf' al-Hamm* (دَفْع الهَمّ), "the Driving away of Care[1]." The contents of the *Tunnāyē* are, however, more varied than the title seems to promise, as may be seen from Assemani's enumeration of the chapters, *B.O.*, ii. 306[2].

Contemporary with Bar-Hebræus, though somewhat younger, we may place Daniel bar Khaṭṭāb, to whom Assemani has devoted two articles in the *B.O.*, ii., at pp. 244 and 463. Among the poems of Bar-Hebræus we find verses addressed to this Daniel by the Nestorian Khamīs bar Ḳardāḥē with his reply and another by Bar-Hebræus[3]. He composed abridgements in Arabic of several of Bar-Hebræus's works, *e.g.*, the *Nomocanon*[4], *Ethics*, *Auṣar Rāzē*, *Mĕnārath Ḳudhshē*, *Kĕthābhā*

[1] *B.O.*, ii. 268, note, col. 2, No. 31; p. 272, note 1.

[2] See a few short specimens in Kirsch and Bernstein's *Chrest. Syr.*, pp. 1–4, and in an article by L. Morales in the *Z.D.M.G.*, xl. p. 410 *sq.* MSS.—Cod. Vat. clxxiii.; Ind. Off. No. 9, "Tracts in Syriac," ff. 351–413. The *Daf' al-Hamm* is contained in Paris, Anc. fonds 160. The catalogue of Bar-Hebræus's works in *B.O.*, ii. 268, note, adds one Arabic book to this long list (col. 1, No. 19, at the foot) of which we know nothing but the title there given in Syriac, *Kĕthābhā dhĕ-Henyān Yuthrānē*, "On the Pleasure of Gain."

[3] Payne Smith, *Catal.*, p. 377; *Catal. Vat.*, iii. 358.

[4] *B.O.*, ii. 463; Cod. Vat. Arab. dcxxxvi. (Mai, *Scriptt. Vett. Nova Coll.*, iv. 573).

*dhĕ-Bhābhāthā*, and the larger grammar[1] An independent work of his, also in Arabic, treats of *The Bases, or First Principles, of the Faith and Consolation of the Hearts of Believers*[2].

With Daniel bar Khaṭṭāb we may close our list of Jacobite writers in the literature of Syria. The Nestorians kept the lamp burning for a little, though not much longer, as we shall presently see.

Shĕlēmōn, or Solomon, of Khilāṭ or Akhlāṭ, on the shores of Lake Van, was present as metropolitan of Pĕrath dĕ-Maishān or al-Baṣrah at the consecration of the catholicus Sabhr-īshō' in 1222[3]. Besides some prayers and short discourses (*mēmrōnē*), he wrote a treatise on the figure of the heavens and the earth[4], and compiled a volume of analecta, partly theological, partly historical, which he entitled *Kĕthābhā dhĕ-Dhebbōrīthā* or "the Bee." It is dedicated to his friend Narsai, bishop of Khōnī-Shābhōr or Bēth Wāzīk, called by the Arabs al-Bawāzīg or al-Bawāzīj[5], on the lesser Zāb. Of this work an

[1] *B.O.*, ii. 464.

[2] *Ibid.*, ii. 244; Cod. Vat. Arab. lxxiv. (Mai, *op. cit.*, iv. 153).

[3] *B.O.*, ii. 453, No. 75; Bar-Hebræus, *Chron. Eccles.*, ii. 371.

[4] *B.O.*, iii. 1, 310.

[5] See Hoffmann, *Auszüge*, pp. 189 and 296.

analysis has been given by Assemani in the *B.O.*, iii. 1, 309–324, and there is a German translation of it by Schönfelder, 1866. It has been recently edited by Mr E. A. W. Budge, of the British Museum, with an English translation, Oxford, 1886[1].

This was an age of song with the Nestorians, in which lived some of their favourite writers of hymns. (1) One of the most conspicuous of these is George Wardā (the Rose) of Arbēl or Irbil, whose poems have entered so largely into the use of the Nestorian Church that one of their service books is to this day called the *Wardā*[2]. His date may be gathered from certain of his hymns, which speak of the calamities of the years 1535–38 = 1224–27 A.D.[3] (2) About the same time flourished Masʿūd of the family Bēth Ḳashshā (in Arabic Ibn al-Ḳass), who was physician (*ḥakīm*) to the caliph al-Mustaʿṣim (1242–58), and outlived his

[1] MSS.—Cod. Vat. clxxvi., clxxvii.; Brit. Mus. Add. 25875; RAS. Add. 76; Munich, Cod. Syr. 7 (with an Arabic translation). Bodl. Pocock 79 and Paris, Anc. fonds 113, contain only an Arabic translation, different from that in the Munich MS.

[2] Badger, *The Nestorians*, ii. 25. A few specimens are given by Cardāḥī in the *Liber Thesauri*, p. 51. Badger has translated one, *op. cit.*, pp. 51–57.

[3] *Catal. Vat.*, iii. 391, at the top. Important MSS. of Wardā's hymns are Cod. Vat. clxxxiv.; Berlin, Alt. Best. 24, Sachau 188; Cambridge, coll. of the S.P.C.K.

patron[1]. One of his poems for the feast of the Epiphany occurs in Cod. Vat. clxxxiv. (*Catal.*, iii. p. 389)[2]. (3) Khamīs bar Ḳardāḥē of Arbēl was a younger contemporary of Bar-Hebræus, as appears from his correspondence with Daniel bar Khaṭṭāb (see above). He too has bequeathed his name to one of the Nestorian service books, which is still called the *Khamīs*[3]. (4) Gabriel Ḳamṣā (the Locust) was a monk of Bēth-Ḳūḳā. He became metropolitan of Mosul, and was present at the consecration of Yabh-alāhā III. in 1281[4]. There is a long poem of his in Cod. Vat. clxxx. (*Catal.*, iii. 376), treating of the creation, the incarnation, the life of our Saviour, the preaching of the apostles, and the praises of the fathers of the church, and concluding with an encomium on

[1] *B.O.*, iii. 1, 561; Bar-Hebræus, *Hist. Dynast.*, pp. 522–523 (transl., pp. 341–342).

[2] See Cardāḥī, *Liber Thesauri*, pp. 125–128.

[3] Badger, *The Nestorians*, ii. 24; see one of his poems translated, pp. 38–49. Cardāḥī gives some specimens in *Liber Thesauri*, pp. 59–62. Important MSS. of his poems are—Cod. Vat. clxxxv.-vi.-viii.; Brit. Mus. Add. 18716, f. 44 a, and Orient. 2304; Berlin, Sachau 178; see also Cod. Vat. lxxxix. and Brit. Mus. Or. 1300 at the end. Berlin, Sachau 229, contains a poem of Bar-Hebræus, amplified by Khamīs and later poets; compare *B.O.*, ii. 308, iii. 1, 566.

[4] *B.O.*, ii. 456. Cardāḥī has published a specimen, *Liber Thesauri*, pp. 107–113.

Sabhr-īshō', the founder of Bēth-Ḳūḳā. (5) John of Mosul was a monk of the convent of St Michael near that city[1]. His work entitled *Kĕthābhā dhĕ-Shappīr Dubbārē* was published at Rome in 1868 by E. J. Millos, archbishop of 'Aḳrā, as a school-book, under the title of *Directorium Spirituale.* It is, of course, impossible to say to what extent the original has been tampered with in such an edition, but there is a MS. in the Brit. Mus. Or. 2450[2]. The composition of the work is placed by Millos in 1245, and the death of the author by Cardāḥī (*Lib. Thes.*, p. 120) in 1270.

'Abhd-īshō' bar Bĕrīkhā holds nearly the same position in regard to the Nestorian Church that Bar-Hebræus does in relation to the Jacobite, though far inferior in talent and learning to "the Son of the Hebrew." He flourished under Yabhalāhā III., being firstly bishop of Shiggār (Sinjār) and Bēth-'Arbāyē about 1285[3], and afterwards, before 1291[4], metropolitan of Nisībis and Armenia. He died in 1318[5]. He has left us a list of his

[1] Cardāḥī (*Liber Thesauri*, p. 118) wrongly says "at Baghdādh."

[2] The most reverend editor inveighs in his preface against "the Prōṭāyē (Protestants), who believe in nothing at all"; see p. 14, l. 12.

[3] *B.O.*, i. 539.

[4] *Ibid.*, i. 538; iii. 1, 327, col. 2.

[5] *Ibid.*, i. 539; iii. 1, 3, notes 2, 3, 325, note 1.

own publications at the end of the *Catalogus Librorum*, in the *B.O.*, iii. 1, 325 *sq.* Several of these seem to be lost,—at least they do not appear in the catalogues of our collections,—such as the commentary on the Old and New Testaments[1], the *Kĕthābhā Ḳatholiḳos* on the marvellous dispensation or life of our Lord on earth[2], the *Kĕthābhā Skolastiḳos* against all the heresies[3], the book of the mysteries of the Greek philosophers[4], the twelve discourses comprising all the sciences[5], and the ecclesiastical decisions and canons[6], as also an Arabic work with the title *Shah-marwārīd* or "the King-pearl[7]." The *Margānīthā* or "Pearl" is a theological work in five sections, treating of God, the creation, the Christian dispensation, the sacraments of the church, and the things that prefigure the world to come. There is a careful analysis of its contents in *B.O.*, iii. 1, 352–360. It has been edited, with a Latin translation, in Mai, *Scriptt. Vett. Nova Coll.*, x., and done into English by Badger, *The Nestorians*, ii. 380 *sq.* The date of composition is 1298[8]. ʽAbhd-īshōʽ

[1] *B.O.*, iii. 1, 325.
[2] Id., *ibid.*
[3] Id., p. 360.
[4] Id., *ibid.*
[5] Id., *ibid.*
[6] Id., *ibid.*
[7] Perhaps only an Arabic recension or abridgement of the *Margānīthā*.
[8] MSS.—Cod. Vat. clxxv.–vi., ccccl vi.; RAS. Add. 76; Berlin, Sachau 4, 312; Cambridge, coll. of the S.P.C.K.

himself translated this work into Arabic in 1312, as we learn from 'Amr ibn Mattā in the *Majdal*, where large portions of it are quoted[1]. The *Collection of Synodical Canons* or *Nomocanon* is also fully analysed by Assemani, *B.O.*, iii. 1, 332–351. It has been edited, with a Latin translation, in Mai, *Scriptt. Vett. Nova Coll.*, x.[2] As a poet 'Abhd-īshō' does not shine according to our ideas, although his countrymen admire his verses greatly. Not only is he obscure in vocabulary and style, but he has adopted and even exaggerated all the worse faults of Arabic writers of rimed prose and scribblers of verse[3]. His principal effort in poetry is the *Paradise of Eden*, a collection of fifty poems on theological subjects, which has been analysed by Assemani, *B.O.*, iii. 1, 325–332[4]. This volume

[1] *B.O.*, iii. 1, 360, note 4; see Cod. Vat. lxv., cccvii., and Cod. Vat. Arab. cx. (Mai, *Scriptt. Vett. Nova Coll.*, iv.); compare *B.O.*, iii. 1, 589.

[2] MSS.—Cod. Vat. cxxviii., cxxix., ccclv.

[3] See Payne Smith's minute descriptions in his *Catal.*, p. 523 *sq.*

[4] MSS.—Cod. Vat. ccxlv., ccclxxix.; Paris, Anc. fonds 166; Berlin, Alt. Best. 41, 1, Sachau 1, 21, 80; Brit. Mus. Orient. 2302-3; Cambridge, coll. of the S.P.C.K. [The first part of the *Pardaisā* (25 poems) has been edited, with short notes in Arabic, by Gabriel Cardāhī (Beyrūt, Catholic Press, 1889). Specimens of the work, and of the scholia, with Latin translation, have also been published by H. Gismondi (*ibid.*, 1888). Cf. Nöldeke in *Z.D.M.G.*, xliii., 675 *sq.*]

was published by the author in 1291, and in 1316 he found that it was necessary to add an explanatory commentary[1]. Another collection of twenty-two poems, which may be regarded as parts of one composition, treating of the love of wisdom and knowledge, is found in Cod. Vat. clxxiv. (*Catal.*, iii. 359) and Bodl. Marsh. 201 (P. Smith, *Catal.*, p. 510); and a third, including the above and a selection from the *Paradise*, is contained in Bodl. Marsh. 361[2]. Of his minor works, enumerated in the *B.O.*, iii. 1, 361, the consolatory discourses, the letters, and the commentary on the epistle of Aristotle to Alexander concerning the great art (alchemy) seem to be lost. The *turgāmē* are collected in a MS. at Berlin, Alter Bestand 41, 4. His commentary on an enigmatical poem of Simeon Shanḳĕlāwī we have already mentioned (see above, p. 258). To us his most useful work decidedly is the *Catalogue of Books*, which forms the basis of vol. iii. part 1 of Assemani's *Bibl. Orient.* There is an older edition of it by Abraham Ecchellensis, Rome, 1653. It has been translated into English by

[1] *B.O.*, iii., 1, 327, col. 2.

[2] Payne Smith, *Catal.*, p. 523; see also p. 531, Nos. 30, 31. In Paris, Anc. fonds 104, there is a poem explanatory of the ecclesiastical calendar (Zotenberg, *Catal.*, p. 128).

Badger[1]. The *Catalogue* consists of four parts, viz., (1) the Scriptures of the Old Testament, with sundry apocrypha, *B.O.*, iii. 1, 5; (2) the Scriptures of the New Testament, p. 8; (3) the Greek fathers who were translated into Syriac, p. 13; (4) the Syriac fathers, chiefly, of course, of the Nestorian Church, pp. 65–362. It is to be regretted that ʻAbhd-īshōʻ contented himself merely with enumerating the titles of books, and never thought it worth his while to give the date of the writers, nor even to arrange his notices in any kind of chronological order[2].

[An interesting work of this period, which has only recently become known in Europe, is the biography of the catholicus Yabh-alāhā III. (1281–1317), from the pen of a contemporary. A copy of the only MS. known to exist was supplied to M. Bedjan, and by him published at Paris in 1888. It is a simple narrative, in charming style, of the life of Yabh-alāhā, who was a native of China and rose from a humble station to the headship of the Nestorian Church. It is especially valuable for the light it throws on the relations between the Mongolian princes of

1 *The Nestorians*, ii. 361. Badger ascribes the work to the year 1298, probably on the authority of his MS.

2 MSS.—Cod. Vat. clxxvi.; RAS. Add. 76 (imperfect); Rome, Bibl. Vitt. Eman. A. 1194, MSS. Sessor. 162; Cambridge, coll. of the S.P.C.K.

the period and their Christian subjects. A full account is given in Duval's article, *Journal Asiatique*, 1889, p. 313 *sq.*]

After 'Abhd-īshō' there are hardly any names among the Nestorians worthy of a place in the literary history of the Syrian nation. We may make an exception in favour of the catholicus Timothy II., who was elected in succession to Yabh-alāhā III. in 1318, having previously been metropolitan of Mosul and Irbil under the name of Joseph[1]. He wrote a work on the sacraments of the church, of which Assemani has given an analysis in *B.O.*, iii. 1, 572–580[2]. His death took place in 1328.

[1] *B.O.*, iii. 1, 567.

[2] Vat. cii.

# INDEX OF AUTHORS

## AND OF ANONYMOUS WORKS AND TRANSLATIONS.

N.B. *The more important references, viz. those to the paragraphs in which the respective authors or works are specially treated, are printed in darker type than the others.*


Aaron (Ahrōn) **222**

Aaron (or John) bar Ma'danī **263–265**, 267

*Abgar, Letters of* 26

Abhā **38**

Abhā bar Bĕrīkh-ṣebyanēh of Kashkar, *v.* Mār-abhā II.

'Abhd-īshō', *v.* Joseph of Ḥazzā

'Abhd-īshō' bar Bahrīz **234**

'Abhd-īshō' bar Bĕrīkhā of Nisībis 20, 30, 31, 32, 38, 42, 45, 50, 58, 59, 65, 90, 97, 100, 109, 110, 112, 114, 120, 124, 127, 128, 131, 132, 148, 168, 170, 173, 177, 180, 186, 187, 188, 189, 191, 194, 195, 212, 214, 217, 218, 220, 221, 228, 229, 232, 233, 238, 258, 278, **285–289**, 290

'Abhd-īshō' bar Shahhārē (Bar Shi'ārah ?) **232**

'Abhsamyā **41–42**

'Abhshotā **64**

Abhzūdh (Bazūdh ?) **228–230**

Abraham bar Dāshandādh **185–186**, 191, 216

Abraham of Kashkar (i) **118–119**, (ii) **119**, 131

Abraham of Nephtar (Nethpar) **111–112**, 178

Abraham of Nisībis **114**, 119, 129, 168

Abraham the Mede **63**

Abū Ghālib bar Ṣābūnī **243–244**

Abū Ḥalīm **255–256**

Acacius of Āmid **51**, 59

Acacius of Seleucia **59–60**, 63

*Acts of the Apostles, Apocryphal* 26

*Adam, Testament of* 25

*Addai, Doctrine of* 9, 43

*Æsop's Fables* **241–242**

Aḥā **46**
Ahrōn, *v.* Aaron
Aḥū-dh'emmēh **97–98**
Alāhā-zĕkhā **181–182**
*Alexander, Pseudo-Callisthenes's Life of* **139–140**, 201
'Ănān-īshō' of Ḥĕdhaiyabh **174–176**, 212
Andrew **232–233**
Antonius the Rhetorician **203–204**
Aphraates 4, 5, 9, 10, **32–33**, 143, 159
*Apocrypha* **5–6, 25–27**
Ara **61**
Athanasius II. of Balad, **154–156**

Bābhai bar Neṣībhnāyē 167, **184–185**
Bābhai the archimandrite 126, 128, 130, 131, **167–169**, 177
Balai **39–40**
Bar 'Alī 212, **215–216**
Bar Bahlūl 212, **228**
Bardesānes (Bar Daisān) **28–30**, 61
Bar-Hebræus 2, 20, 22 n., 23, 32, 39, 41, 42, 58, 70, 77, 97, 100, 102, 116, 121, 122, 123, 133, 139, 142, 144, 148, 149, 158, 163, 164, 166, 172, 181, 187, 194, 195, 203, 204, 205, 206 n., 208, 211, 212, 217, 224, 225, 245, 253, 254, 259, **265–281**, 284, 285
Bar-'idtā **131–132**
Bar Sāhdē **185**
*Bar-samyā, Martyrdom of* 43
Bar Sarōshwai, *v.* Ḥĕnan-īshō'
Bar-ṣaumā of Nisībis, **57–58**, 81
Bar-ṣaumā the archimandrite **65–66**
Bar Shi'ārah, *v.* 'Abhd-īshō' bar Shahhārē
Bazūdh (or Michael), *v.* Abhzūdh
*Beth Sĕlōkh, History of* 44
Bōdh **123–124**, 239

Candius, *v.* Kendī
*Causa Causarum* 147, **242–243**
*Chronicon Edessenum* 41, **101–102**, 201
*Clement's Recognitions* 61
Constantine of Ḥarrān **160–161**, 162
*Constitutiones Apostolorum* 27
Cosmas **56**
*Curetonian Gospels* **7–13**
Cyprian of Nisībis **189–191**, 205
Cyriacus **165–166**, 196, 197
Cyrillōnā **40–42**

Dādhā **54–55**
Dādh-īshō' (i) **56**, (ii) **131**, 167
Daniel bar Khaṭṭāb **281–282**, 284
Daniel bar Maryam **180**
Daniel bar Moses **163**
Daniel of Ṣalaḥ **159–160**
Daniel of Tūbhānīthā **234–235**
David bar Paul **259–260**
David of Bēth Rabban **183–184**
*De Fato* **30**

Dĕnaḥ-īshō', *v.* Īshō'-dĕnaḥ
Denḥā (or Īhībhā) **218–219**, 259
*Didascalia Apostolorum* 27
Dionysius (or Jacob) bar Ṣalībī 17, 144, **246–250**
Dionysius of Tell-Maḥrē 2, 41, 52, 78, 80, 84, 105, **196–203**, 204
*Doctrina Apostolorum* 27

*Edessene Chronicle*, *v. Chronicon Edessenum*
Elias bar Shīnāyā of Nisībis 32, 132, 148, 158, 163, 182, 183, 194, 195, 222, **235–239**, 257, 259
Elias of al-Anbar 228, **230**
Elias (of Dārā ?) **82**
Elias of Merv **179–180**
Elias I. of Ṭīrhān 212, **233-234**, 236, 259
Elias the patriarch **161–162**
Elisha (or Hosea) of Nisībis **60**
Emmanuel bar Shahhārē **231–232**
Ephraim Syrus 9, 10, 11, 29, **33–37**, 38, 39, 41, 52, 53, 72, 122, 162, 226
*Eusebius—Theophania, History of confessors in Palestine, and Ecclesiastical History*, 61

Gabriel bar Bōkht-īshō' **214–215**, 217
Gabriel Ḳamṣā **284–285**
Gabriel of Hormizdshēr **120–121**
Gabriel Taurĕthā **180–181**
George, bishop of Sĕrūgh 67, 151, 154
George, bishop of the Arab tribes 32, 70, 144, **156–159**
George of Bĕ'elthān **164–165**, 194
George of Kaphrā **178–179**
George of Martyropolis **160**, 162
George of Mosul and Arbēl 180, **230–231**, 234
George Wardā **283**
Gregory the abbot **42–43**

*Ḥabbībh, Martyrdom of* 43
Ḥannānā of Ḥĕdhaiyabh **124–127**, 167
Harmonius **29**
Ḥĕnān-īshō' I. **181–182**, 183, 184
Ḥĕnān-īshō' bar Sarōshwai **228**
*Herod and Pilate, Letters of* 26
Ḥonain ibn Isḥāḳ 10, 176, **211-213**, 214, 215, 259, 272
Hosea of Nisībis, *v.* Elisha

Ibas (Īhībhā) (i) 48, **49–51**, 59, 64, 65, 72, (ii) *v.* Denḥā
Isaac of Antioch 39, **51–54**, 72, 226
Isaac of Nineveh **110–111**, 235
Īshō' bar 'Alī, *v.* Bar 'Alī
Īshō' bar Bahlūl, *v.* Bar Bahlūl
Īshō' bar Nōn 186, **216–218**
Īshō' Marūzāyā **215**
Īshō'-dādh of Merv **220–221**
Īshō'-dĕnaḥ of al-Baṣrah **195**

Īshō'-yabh (or Joseph) bar Malkōn **256–257**
Īshō'-yabh I. of Arzōn 125, **129–130**
Īshō'-yabh II. of Gĕdhālā 168, **169–170**, 172
Īshō'-yabh III. of Ḥĕdhaiyabh **171–174**, 175, 178, 179, 180, 183

Jacob bar Ṣalībī, *v.* Dionysius
Jacob (or Severus) bar Shakkō 164, 258, **260–263**
Jacob Burdĕ'ānā **85–88**, 97
Jacob of Edessa 4, 17, 24, 67, 74, 84, 90, 91 n., 93, **141–154**, 156, 158, 175, 273, 277
Jacob of Maiperḳaṭ **263**
Jacob of Nisībis **31–32**, 33, 122
Jacob of Sĕrūgh 39, **67–72**, 76, 77, 78, 79, 110, 150 n., 162
*Jacob of Serugh, Lives of* 67
Januarius Candidatus **156**
John bar Aphtōnyā **83–85**
*John bar Aphtōnyā, Life of* 84
John bar Cursus of Tellā 73, **81–83**, 86
John bar Ma'danī, *v.* Aaron
John (or Yēshū') bar Shūshan 53, **225–227**
John bar Zō'bī 218, 234, 257, **258–259**, 261
John I. of Antioch **139**
John of Asia or Ephesus, 2, 80, 85, 87, 89, **102–107**, 108, 200, 202
John of Bēth Garmai (i) **63**, (ii) **176–177**
John of Dārā 200, **204–205**
John of Ḥarrān and Mārdīn **244–246**, 248, 251
John of Mārōn **223–224**
John of Mosul **285**
John of Nisībis **114–115**
John Sābhā **109–110**
*Joseph, Poem on the history of* 37, 40
*Joseph and Āsyath, History of* 25, **113**
Joseph bar Malkōn, *v.* Īshō'-yabh .
Joseph Hūzāyā **115–116**, 124, 150, 175
Joseph of Ḥazzā (Ḥazzāyā) **127–129**, 167, 168
Joseph of Melitene **225**
Joseph of Seleucia **121–122**
Joshua the Stylite 68, **77–78**, 101, 202
*Jubilees, Book of* 25, 98
*Julian, Romances of*, **99–101**

*Kalīlah and Dimnah* (*Ḳalīlagh wĕ-Damnagh*) **124**, **239–240**, 241
*Karkaphensian tradition* **20–25**, 175
Kendī (Candius) **221**
*Kĕthābhā dha-Khĕyānāyāthā*, *v. Liber Naturalium*
*Kĕthābhā dhĕ-Nāmōsē dh'Athrawāthā*, *v. De Fato*
Khamīs bar Ḳardāḥē 281, **284**
Kūmī **65**

*Laws of the Emperors* **95–97**

Lazarus bar Sābhĕthā 199, **204**
Lazarus of Bēth Ḳandasā **162–163**
Leo **160–161**
*Liber Naturalium* **132–133**

*Malkite Version* **17–19**
Ma'nā **62–63**, 64, 94
Mārā III. of Āmid 73, **83**, 108
Mārabhā I. 19–20, **116–118**, 119, 120, 121, 122
Mārabhā II. **186–187**
*Mārī, Acts of* 44
Mārī the Persian 48, 49, 51, **59**
Mark bar Ḳīḳī **224–225**
*Martyrologies* **43–46**
Mārūthā of Maiperḳaṭ **44–46**, 137
Mārūthā of Taghrīth 46, **136–137**, 279
*Massoretic MSS.*, 4, **20–25**, **150–151**
Mas'ūd **283–284**
*Mĕ'ārath Gazzē* 25 n., **98–99**, 201
Mĕshīḥā-zĕkhā **130–131**
Michael I. (the Elder) 246, 249, **250–253**, 254
Mīkhā (i) **60**, 63 (ii) **183**
Millēs **30–31**
Moses (or Severus) bar Kēphā **207–211**
Moses of Aggēl 13, 25, 108, **112–113**

Narsai **58–59**, 63, 114, 115, 116, 150
*Nestorian Chronicle*, **183**
Nonnus of Nisībis **205–206**

*Old Syriac Gospels* 8, 10, 13

Paul bar Ḳaḳai **63**
Paul of Callinīcus **94–95**
Paul of Tellā **14–16**, 25, 134
Paul the abbot 95 n., **135–136**, 149, 219
Paul the Persian **122–123**
Paulonas or Paulinus **38**
*Περὶ εἱμαρμένης*, *v. De Fato*
*Pĕshīṭtā* **3–13**
Peter of Calliuīcus **113–114**
Pethiōn **195**
Philip **30**
Philoxenus of Mabbōgh **13–14**, 16, **72–76**, 77, 112
Phocas bar Sergius of Edessa **93**
Probus **64–65**, 89, 94
*Protevangelium Jacobi* 26
*Psalm* CLI. 25
*Psalms, Apocryphal* 25 n.

Rabbūlā 9, 11, 39, **47–49**, 62, 112
Romanus the physician (Theodosius of Antioch) 77, **206–207**, 277

Sabhr-īshō' the catholicus 125, **133–134**
Sabhr-īshō' Rusṭam **177–178**
Sāhdōnā of Halamūn **170–171**, 180
Sa'īd bar Ṣābūnī **227**, 243
*St John Baptist, Prayers of* 26

*St Paul, Apocalypse of* 26
*St Peter, Doctrine of* 26
Samuel **66**
*Sanḥērīb, History of* 25
Sergius of Rās-'ain **88–93**, 94, 97, 119, 120
*Service-books* **27–28**
Severus bar Shakkō, *v.* Jacob
Severus Sēbōkht **137–139**, 141, 154, 259
*Sharbēl, Hypomnemata of* 43
Simeon Barḳāyā **132**
Simeon bar Ṣabbā'ē **30–31**
Simeon bar Ṭabbākhē of Kashkar **188**
Simeon Ḳūḳāyā **79**
Simeon of Bēth Arshām 57, 58, 62, **79–81**, 108, 202
Simeon of Beth Garmai **134**
Simeon Shanḳēlāwī **257–258**, 288
Simeon the deacon **222**
Simeon the Stylite **55–56**
*Simeon the Stylite, Life of* 56, 66
*Sindbān (Sindibādh), Story of* **240–241**
Solomon of al-Baṣrah **282–283**
Stephen bar Sūdhailē 69, **76–77**, 243
Sūrēn or Sūrīn **189–190**

*Tatian's Diatessaron* **7–10**, 35
Theodore bar Khōnī **222**, 229
Theodore bar Wahbōn **253–254**
Theodore bar Zarūdī **93**
Theodore of Merv 90, **119–120**
Theodosius of Antioch, *v.* Romanus
Theodosius of Edessa **203**
Theophilus of Edessa 152 n., **163–164**
*Thomas, Gospel of* 26
Thomas of Ḥarḳel or Heraclea **16**, 84, 134, 151 n.
Thomas of Margā 131, 183, 184, 205, **219–220**
Timothy I. 186, **191–194**, 216
Timothy II. **290**
*Titus of Bostra's Discourses* 61
*Transitus beatae Virginis* 26

*Versions of the Bible* **3–20**

Wardā, *v.* George
*Women, Book of* 5

*Yabh-alāhā III., Life of* **289–290**
Yazīdādh **61**, 63
Yēshū' bar Shūshan, *v.* John

Zacharias Rhetor 83, 88, 89, **107–108**, 113
Zenobius **38–39**, 41, 52

www.ingramcontent.com/pod-product-compliance
Lightning Source LLC
Chambersburg PA
CBHW050337230426
43663CB00010B/1897
* 9 7 8 1 6 0 6 0 8 2 6 0 7 *